A
Psychological
Approach to
Theology

LIVING ISSUES
IN RELIGION

Edited by
MILES H. KRUMBINE, D.D.

By the same author

THEISM AND THE MODERN MOOD

THE PHILOSOPHY OF THE ABBÉ BAUTAIN

A Psychological Approach to Theology

WALTER MARSHALL HORTON

Oberlin College ·

19   31

HARPER & BROTHERS
PUBLISHERS — NEW YORK and LONDON

A Psychological
Approach to Theology

To

George A. Coe

Whose teaching provided the initial stimulus
to which this book is a belated response

Preface

THIS book has a double object—to make an intellectual experiment, and to work out a constructive statement of my religious credo.

The intellectual experiment consists in the attempt to approach all the cardinal problems of religious thought from a consistently psychological point of view. For reasons set forth in Chapter I, I believe this is a valuable and necessary experiment to make just at the present time; and to this primary aim I have subordinated my secondary aim whenever the conditions of the experiment seemed to require me to do so. My personal credo, as it appears in this book, is thus somewhat foreshortened and truncated; for there are many important areas of religious interest and religious faith which are invisible from the psychological angle. Frankly, I have more religious convictions than are expressed in these pages. I am profoundly convinced, for example, of the importance of the *sociological* approach to theology, to which Walter Rauschenbusch gave himself with such enthusiasm; but the reader of this book will get only occasional glimpses of the vast territory which he surveyed in his *Theology for the Social Gospel*—not because I am unaware of its existence, or doubt its importance, but because my approach is different.

Yet I confess that the adoption of this specific point of view foreshortens my credo much less than might be expected, for the psychological approach to theology is one which I have found peculiarly congenial to my way of thinking, and my religious convictions express themselves naturally in that style. Ever since Professor G. A. Coe introduced me to the psychology of religion, I have been convinced that its bearing upon theology is of the most crucial importance, and that the psychological approach to theology is the most direct of all possible approaches, for the central religious problem, as I see it (perhaps because of my evangelical religious training!) is the psychological problem—how may personality be unified, energized, and directed to worthful ends? From that time on, all my most serious efforts to deal with theological questions have tended, almost in spite of myself, to take a psychological form; and it is therefore possible for me to combine my intellectual experiment with my credo without serious distortion to the latter.

Both the experiment and the credo occupy the whole volume; but roughly speaking, the first four chapters stick closer to the theme anounced in the title, while readers of my *Theism and the Modern Mood* will find its sequel in Chapters V to VIII. Otherwise stated, the whole argument of the present book, with its division into three parts, may be seen as a constructive expansion of the argument which was briefly sketched in Chapters III and IV of my earlier book.

I am indebted to Professor Gardner Murphy, Dr. Irene Gates, and Mr. James Croswell Perkins for criticizing parts of the manuscript; to my editors, Miles Krumbine and Eugene Exman, for going over the whole with great care; to my wife, for invaluable clerical assistance; to Professors G. A. Coe and A. C. McGiffert, Jr., for criticising the initial plan of the book; to Professor George Herbert Palmer for permission to quote from his unpublished lectures on "Redemption"; to the editors of the *Journal of Religion* and the *Student World* for permission to reprint material originally appearing in their pages; and to the following publishing houses for permission to quote copyrighted material: The Macmillan Company; Harcourt, Brace and Company; Henry Holt & Company, Inc.; Charles Scribner's Sons; Robert McBride & Company; D. Appleton and Company; The New Republic, Inc.; The Modern Library, Inc.; *Mental Hygiene Magazine*; The Century Co.; Dodd, Mead and Company; Longmans, Green and Co.; W. W. Norton and Company, Inc.; Columbia University Press; Yale University Press; Jonathan Cape & Harrison Smith, Inc.

W. M. H.

Oberlin, Ohio, March 31, 1931

Contents

Introduction

Part I. Religion and Personal Development

Part II. Christianity and Personal Development

Introduction

In which theology and psychology are summoned to a disarmament conference, and invited to sign a pact of mutual amity and respect, to the end that they may jointly promote the cause of the development of human personality.

The most important intellectual circumstance with which theology has to reckon in our generation is the rapid progress and phenomenal popularity of the infant science of psychology.

Certainly if one had to characterize this post-war period in a phrase, one could hardly do better than to call it an age of psychology. In place of the social idealism of the decade before the war, in place of the eager interest in great public issues which rose to its climax in the willing sacrifices of the war itself, and the sanguine hopes of the period between the Armistice and the fiasco of Versailles, we have reverted to an intense interest in the workings of our own minds. Disappointed in our hopes for a social millennium, we are thrown back upon ourselves, and the age-old quest of individual salvation (or "self-realization," as the preferred phraseology now goes) has once more been taken up. Some are seeking their happiness in riotous self-expression; and with them, Freudian psychology (with its enticing sex appeal and its apparent[1] justification for throwing off all social restraints) has enjoyed a veritable *succès de scandale*. Some are making a god of commercial success; and with them, the psychology of advertising and aggressive salesmanship has become the basis of the only devotional exercises they practice. Some

---

[1] The word "apparent" should be underscored. It would be most unfair to make Freud responsible for all the excesses that have been committed in his name. His recent writings, especially his book called *Beyond the Pleasure Principle*, make it quite clear that he does not regard vulgar hedonism as the ethical consequence of his psychology.

I

have been left mentally crippled by the war; and scientific psychiatry is their only hope. All of us have been more or less infected with the restlessness and mental maladjustment of our cynical, jaded, confused and overstimulated times; and mental hygiene, with its promise of self-knowledge, and guidance in the quest of happiness, answers to our yearnings most directly. It is not surprising, under the circumstances, that psychological games should hold the place of honor among our parlor amusements; that psychiatry and psychoanalysis should become substitutes for religious confession and counsel; and that conversation should be interlarded and overloaded with terms like "repression," "reaction," "inferiority complex," "integration," "adjustment," and "sublimation."

It is not likely that the popular vogue of psychology will last forever. The very intensity of the craze is the measure of its brevity. Psychology is being done to death by the fervor of its devotees; and psychological catchwords are being worn out, before their time, by too insistent repetition. Already there are signs that the age of psychology has passed its climax; and new interests are beginning to compete in the bidding for popular attention. The unemployment crisis and the business depression, the simultaneous outbreak of political revolution in widely separated parts of the world, the growing fear of a new world conflict, all are forcing once more upon our attention those great social issues which we have been trying to dodge; while Einstein and Whitehead, Shapley and Millikan, Eddington and Jeans are tempting us to forget our complexes and our political worries alike, in the presence of the wonders and mysteries of the uncharted cosmic deeps. The "social emphasis," so insistent in pre-war theology,[1] will perhaps return upon us with redoubled

---

[1] Represented by such books as Henry Churchill King's *Theology and the Social Consciousness*, Wm. DeWitt Hyde's *Outlines of Social Theology*,

force before long; while already, glimmering in the less immediate future, one can foresee the advent of an age of cosmology, when the religious implications of the new mathematics, and the new astronomy, and the new physics will be eagerly debated.

But now is the precise moment—now, at the close of the age of psychology, when the assured results of the new science begin to stand forth, and the distorting influence of popular overemphasis begins to diminish, while popular interest still remains at a high pitch—now is the time for theology to attempt to consolidate the gains and discount the losses of the age of psychology, by digesting and assimilating all that is valid in this whole movement of thought, and putting it in its rightful place in the general body of human wisdom. For theology is the custodian of the general body of human wisdom; and every advance in human knowledge must result in a theological readjustment.

This conception of theology, as "custodian of the general body of human wisdom," will doubtless seem strange to some. In many minds, the word "theology" is synonymous with something so unalterably fixed and static, something so remote from the affairs of this present world, that its only relation to contemporary thought is a negative one: it tends to resist, stubbornly, any new idea that is inconsistent with its own preconceived dogmas. Firm in the conviction that it possesses the whole substance of divine truth, theology ignores the achievements of human thought as long as possible, and makes alterations in its traditional thought-forms only under pressure of the gravest necessity. So the common conception runs; and it is not without its justification. Ultimately, every important advance in human knowledge affects theology; but

Gerald Birney Smith's *Social Idealism and The Changing Theology*, and above all, by Walter Rauschenbusch's *Theology for the Social Gospel.*

"ultimately," in this connection, means literally "last of all"! First on the scene is the pure scientist, quick to discover the truth because impelled by pure disinterested curiosity. After him hastens the applied scientist, eager to assimilate truth as soon as it is discovered, and put it promptly to work. Next, at a more leisurely pace, comes the philosopher, open-minded as a rule, but so much concerned with maintaining a balanced view of the whole system of things that he views radical innovations with a cautious and critical eye. Last of all, with halting step and troubled mien, comes the theologian, anxious to know what this new thing may be, but already prepared to dispute it!

Now theology has good reason to refrain from a too hasty and precipitate acceptance of new ideas. There is a certain tidal ebb and flow in human opinions, as there is in feminine styles; and it is only near the close of such a cycle of thought that one can properly discriminate between the fads and fancies of the moment and the new truth which must be assimilated because it is destined to endure. If theologians had meekly swallowed the whole Freudian system in the first days of its extreme popularity, they would now have a good deal to disgorge! But it must be admitted that, during the last few centuries at least, theology has often exhibited a kind of stubborn refractoriness, a kind of incapacity to accept and digest new truth, which has resulted in an almost total loss of the immense prestige which she formerly enjoyed. Once she was called "Queen of the Sciences"—*deservedly*, for she had mastered all the learning of the age, and harmonized it with the wisdom of the ages. In the great theological system of St. Thomas Aquinas—still the crowning achievement of Western thought, so far as symmetry and proportion are concerned—all known truths and all tested values, whatever their origin might be, were gladly made welcome. As the four cardinal virtues of the Greeks were made the basis upon which the structure of Christian ethics was erected, so the secular science of Aristotle and Ptolemy was made to furnish solid walls and buttresses for the high vaults and pinnacles of Platonic mysticism and Christian faith. Even the Jewish and Moslem philosophers, his chief antagonists, were treated with courtesy and respect by the open-minded Thomas; and he made it his practice to sift each error carefully, to conserve the measure of truth it was sure to contain. We build no such cathedrals of thought today. Some time in that period of slow ossification and decay that lies between the thirteenth and sixteenth centuries, theology suffered a "failure of nerve"; and the rise of modern science found her in a timorous and suspicious mood. Twice in the last four centuries, she has been caught *in flagrante delictu*, fighting against the truth, and has been publicly disgraced: once in the case of the nascent physical sciences, which she tried to strangle in the cradle in the days of Copernicus and Galileo; once again in the case of the biological sciences, against whose conclusions she set herself with frantic vehemence in the days of Darwin and Huxley. Today, the former queen of the sciences has become in the eyes of the multitude a scolding, addle-pated old crone, fair game at all times for teasing and merriment.

There are some of us who find it impossible to join in the merriment, or to chime in with that general disparagement of theology which seems to be stylish today—even amongst theologians. We are not sorry that theology has been worsted in the warfare with science, and reduced to a mood of proper humility; but we are sorry to see the queen's throne vacant, and we see no promising aspirants for the position. We recognize that it was a good and necessary thing for science, art, philosophy, morals, and politics to cut themselves loose from the leading-strings of theology; but we fear that unless this declaration of independence can be followed up—and that very soon—by some sort of articles of confederation, our civilization may dissolve into fragments. And how else can science, art, philosophy, morals, and politics come into fruitful federal relations again, except by the mediation of some generally acceptable theory of the ultimate meaning of life; that is, a theology? Philosophy, you say, might take its place. Yes; but it would have to be a philosophy of *life*, like that of the Stoics, furnishing motives and sanctions as well as ideals and beliefs; and then it would be to all intents and purposes a theology, however radical its conclusions might be. Mental hygiene, it has been suggested,[1] might fill the vacancy, for it represents an attempt to coördinate all the sciences in the interest of human welfare. The suggestion is a brilliant one, and points in the right direction; but as yet there is no prospect that the hard-worked technicians who comprise the personnel of the Mental Hygiene Movement are ready to furnish us with a comprehensive theory of life. So we dare to hope that our generation may see theology experiencing a real rejuvenescence—theology in the grand style and the hospitable mood of St. Thomas Aquinas, but without his dogmatic presuppositions; theology no longer shrinking from new truth, but eager to peer through Galileo's telescope, and sail with Darwin on the *Beagle*, and participate in every new adventure of thought which the advance of science makes possible.

It is not only the theologians who feel the need of a revival of theology. The layman feels it, too; and not a few indignant appeals are being addressed to the theologians, demanding that they cease dabbling in irrelevant matters and apologizing for their own existence, and get

---

[1] By Professor Harry Elmer Barnes, in his paper on "Medical Science Versus Religion as a Guide to Life." *New York Times*, Dec. 30, 1928.

back once more to their proper task of discovering some central meaning in the riddle of existence. The late Dr. Slosson, in his *Sermons of a Chemist*, presented a particularly telling challenge to theology in the following words:

In the intellectual crisis of the present, which comes from the sudden influx of novel and unassimilated facts and theories from scientific research, we are not getting the help that we have a right to expect from those who now occupy our pulpits, and I fear that we shall get still less from their successors. For, either from lack of taste or from defect of training, the graduates from our best theological seminaries do not seem to be concerned with such questions. . . . They seem to be smartly up to date and keenly alive on all topics but one, and that is theology. Most of them do not seem to have any, or any interest in any. By theology I do not mean a particular system of dogmatic doctrine, but rather the habit of thinking about the fundamentals of faith and reason, about the metaphysics that lie at the base of physics, the psychology that controls character and motivation, the personal philosophy that is the compass of conduct. It is the schools of science, not the schools of theology, that are turning out the thinkers in such fields.

We are in the midst of the greatest revolution of thought that the world has ever seen, the Einstein theory of relativity, the Planck theory of quanta, the chromosome theory of heredity, the hormone theory of temperament, the new knowledge of the constitution of the universe and of the workings of the human mind. These ideas will influence the philosophy, theology, religion, and morals of the future as much as the Copernican theory influenced those of the sixteenth century and the Darwinian theory of the nineteenth. Such questions would have aroused the keenest interest in the minds of men like Edwards, Berkeley, Calvin, Wesley, Aquinas, Augustine, or Paul. . . . A student of engineering or biology will sit up half the night discussing these theories and their application to life, but your modern theological graduate is bored by them. He has learned how to give the glad hand to the strangers at the church door and can teach Boy Scouts how they should salute the flag—

things that a pumphandle or drill-sergeant could do as well—but he is not qualified to lead his people through the mazes of modern thought. Since sermons have become sociological instead of philosophical, serious-minded people are going elsewhere to get their metaphysics and often getting a poor brand of it from unqualified dispensers. When a young preacher does touch upon such topics—which fortunately is seldom—he is apt to reveal a materialistic conception of matter that sounds amusingly antiquated to his scientific hearers. . . .

Unless the preacher gets accustomed to deep diving while he is young, he is apt to swim shallower and shallower as he gets on in life. Unless he has once thought things through for himself he will be at the mercy of every passing fad that blows. Theological schools ought to teach theology.

Eloquence of tongue and charm of manner will not compensate for want of thought. In time any congregation will tire of a diet exclusively of boneless sermons stewed in cream.[1]

Such a theology as Dr. Slosson demands has now been in the making for well over a century. When eighteenth-century Rationalism and Kantian Idealism upset the intellectual equilibrium of Europe, there were theologians like Schleiermacher who rode the whirlwind, and endeavored to restate Christian truth in terms of the new philosophy. When Darwinian evolution exploded like a bomb beneath the very corner-stone of traditional theology, there were religious thinkers like Henry Drummond who refused to be stampeded into panic-stricken denunciation of the new theory, and endeavored to reconcile it with the fundamentals of the inherited faith. Since that time—taught by the humiliating outcome of the Darwinian controversy—theologians have been increasingly wary about premature condemnation of new scientific views; and the disposition has increasingly developed to make loyalty to truth, wherever found, a cardinal virtue. When the

---

[1] E. E. Slosson, *Sermons of a Chemist*, pp. 39-41. N. Y., Harcourt, Brace and Company, 1925. Quoted by permission.

"Higher Criticism" of the Bible became a matter of controversy in the latter part of the nineteenth century, there were many theologians who joined in the popular hue and cry against it; but there were many others who consecrated their lives to the pursuit of the unbiased truth about the matter; and within a generation, theologians like Ritschl in Germany, Sabatier in France, and William Newton Clarke in America had solidly built the new Biblical learning into the very foundations of their systems of thought. Today, it has become almost customary for theologians of the more liberal sort to go through a kind of periodical stock-taking: to reckon up, after each new movement of thought and each new development in scientific theory, the changes in theology which the new knowledge necessitates. Accepting frankly the assumption that human knowledge is still in its infancy, and that in religion as in science we have still much to learn, theologians of this sort regard every such change in theology (provided it be truly necessitated by the facts) as an advance and not as a retreat; and they watch all new scientific developments with the utmost interest, eager to assimilate them at the earliest possible moment; that is, as soon as the smoke of scientific combat and criticism begins to clear away, and the truth that is to endure begins to tower above the surmises and theories that cling to it like temporary scaffolding. Theology so conceived is the friend and not the enemy of the sciences. In this democratic age, she is not likely to be restored to her ancient position as queen of the sciences; but, after a sufficient period of good behavior, she might be elected to preside over their deliberations and arbitrate their disputes.

It is in this spirit and with this intent that this book is written. It is an attempt to take stock of the assured results of the new psychology, and, quite without dogmatic presuppositions, to see to what theological conclusions they lead, and what theological readjustments they require. It is high time that this was done; for psychology has now been a science for well over a generation, and its teachings have been the object of almost frenzied popular enthusiasm for over a decade. Though the "assured results" of psychology are still obscured by popular misinterpretations and by the warfare of the schools—Freudians, Behaviorists and "Gestalters" so busily engaged in berating one another that no common word seems to issue from their midst!—nevertheless, the extreme importance of the *alleged* results of psychology, and their very direct bearing upon the problem of human destiny, fairly shout at the theologian to come down into the arena and take a hand in the discussion. Much pioneer work has already been done. The practical bearings of the new psychology upon religious education and pastoral guidance have been discussed in a multitude of books. The theoretical difficulties which psychology raises for religion have been discussed in many others—sometimes polemically, sometimes philosophically.[1] The psychology of religion has been cultivated with enthusiasm for a quarter of a century and more.[2] Several books have appeared in which the theological implications of psychology have been more systematically explored. So far as I know, however, this book is

---

[1] Out of a wealth of literature, the following especially significant titles may be cited: Hadfield, *Psychology and Morals*; Mackenzie, *Souls in the Making*; Weatherhead, *Psychology in the Service of the Soul*; Hocking, *Human Nature and Its Remaking*; Elliott (H. S.), *The Bearing of Psychology on Religion*; Coe, *The Motives of Men*; Grant, "Religious Values in Mental Hygiene: the Moral and Religious Life of the Individual in the Light of the New Psychology" in *Mental Hygiene*, Vol. XII, No. 3, July, 1928.

[2] To name only a few classical works, in the order of their appearance: Starbuck, *Psychology of Religion* (1899); James, *Varieties of Religious Experience* (1902); Ames, *The Psychology of Religious Experience* (1910); Leuba, *A Psychological Study of Religion* (1912); Coe, *Psychology of Religion* (1916); Pratt, *The Religious Consciousness* (1920).

among the first to approach the whole problem of building a theology from the psychological point of view. It
will not be the last; for many minds are already at work
along these lines.[1]

The purpose of this introductory chapter is to discuss
the general problem of the proper relation between theology and psychology, against the background of the long-
standing controversy between science and theology, now
rapidly moving toward a peaceful conclusion. When the
general bearing of psychology upon theology has thus
been determined, and the nature of our "psychological
approach" thus defined, we can then proceed, in the main
body of the book, to map out afresh the whole field of
theology, as it looks from the psychological angle.

I. THE LATEST PHASE OF THE CONFLICT BETWEEN
SCIENCE AND THEOLOGY

A first glance at the present state of the conflict between
science and theology would seem to cast doubt upon the
statement that it is "moving toward a peaceful conclusion." Just as the last echoes of the evolution controversy
are beginning to die away, and even Roman Catholic theologians are beginning to affirm that, rightly interpreted,
evolution is not inconsistent with Christian faith,[2] the new

---

[1] Two German theologians, Faber (*Wesen der Religionspsychologie und
Ihre Bedeutung für die Dogmatik*) and Wobbermin (*Systematische Theolo-
gie nach Religionspsychologische Methode*, still incomplete) may perhaps
rightly claim to be the pioneers in the psychological approach to theology.
Their interest is, however, almost exclusively in the theological bearings
of the psychology *of religion*; and the recent prodigious development of
applied psychology and mental hygiene has left no mark upon their
thought. A noteworthy recent book, which shows the influence of the latest
psychological tendencies, is Clifford E. Barbour's *Sin and the New Psychology*.

[2] For example, a Roman Catholic theologian has recently written a
warmly appreciative discussion of General Smuts' book on *Holism and*

psychology comes upon the scene; and, in certain quarters, it is greeted with an outburst of theological hostility which seems to presage the reopening of the controversy. Particularly since psychology has entered upon its behavioristic phase, one seems to note a marked heightening of the emotional tension. Take, for example, Mr. Harvey Wickham's book, *The Misbehaviorists*, which I have heard publicly and enthusiastically recommended by a Methodist bishop, and which seems to be having quite a run in theological circles. Wherein does Mr. Wickham's book, with its tone of contemptuous ridicule, differ from the books which were written to prove that the Darwinian theory was a tissue of absurdities, and could safely be ignored? *Mutatis mutandis*, it might have been written early in the seventeenth century, and designed to warn good Christian men against the heresies of Copernicus and Galileo. I hold no brief for the infallibility of psychologists, and I suspect they need to listen occasionally to the friendly ridicule of such witty observers as Mr. Lee Wilson Dodd, whose book, *The Golden Complex*, should tickle the risibility of Dr. Adler himself.[1] But Mr. Wickham's temper differs altogether from Mr. Dodd's, and one need only read his prefatory remarks to discover that his jousting is in deadly earnest. He feels that Christian faith is seriously menaced by this impudent young science, and he proceeds to mock, castigate and spit upon the leaders of every prominent school of psychology, with all the pious fury of a veritable *auto-da-fé*.

Evolution. Others have found in Lloyd Morgan's *Emergent Evolution* a form of the doctrine which, with various reservations, they can accept.

[1] Less polemical in tone, and more discriminating in its attack, is the symposium entitled *Behaviorism: a Battle-Line* (Cokesbury Press, Nashville). This, in spite of its alarmist title, and a certain note of contemptuous sarcasm which runs through some of the contributions, represents a serious and much-needed attempt at a philosophical criticism of the fundamental assumptions of one important school of psychology. It is a pity that no avowed behaviorist was invited to contribute to the symposium.

Unless we learn wisdom from past mistakes, the conflict between science and theology may easily break out again in our generation, over the issue of psychology; and it may assume a highly aggravated form; for psychology is that science which most nearly affects our deepest religious interests. A man may remain relatively indifferent when science remolds his picture of the inanimate world, or even his picture of the place of mankind among the animal species; but when science thrusts her dissecting-knife in among his vitals, and proposes to deal with all his inmost motives, hopes, and aspirations as coolly as she deals with frogs and worms in the zoölogical laboratory, then it takes a tough mind to remain unmoved, and a level head to remain impartial. Already there are signs of panic in the theological camp. The reverend president of a denominational college recently expressed himself substantially as follows on the subject of behaviorism: "My object is to have this college produce healthy, upright, clean-minded young people, who may be expected to lead happy married lives." This was his major premise. His minor premise (that behaviorists are unfortunate in their marital relations?) was unstated. His conclusion, however, had no ambiguity about it: he was not going to have any behaviorists on his faculty, to corrupt the morals of his students. Is it fanciful to recognize in this utterance the same spirit which sent Giordano Bruno to the stake, and threatened Galileo with torture? Not that our psychologists are likely to lose their lives or even their jobs in many instances in this somewhat more enlightened age; but if fear and hostility could kill . . . After all, it may be found that *odium theologicum* has not yet lost much of its intensity!

Yet there is reason to hope that psychology, in spite of the crucial problems which it raises, may not become the occasion of any such acrimonious disputes as those which marked the coming of age of the physical and biological sciences; for there are signs that both science and theology are beginning to see through the fallacies which underlay their former misunderstandings—and when once these fallacies are thoroughly exposed, it will become harder and harder to repeat them.

On the one hand, students of the logic of the sciences are coming more and more clearly to recognize that science never tells the whole truth about anything—although it very properly aims to have something to say about everything. The "limitations of science" have yet to be precisely defined. Eddington, speaking from the standpoint of the exact or physical sciences, restricts the domain of science to the realm of the precisely measurable, and excludes from it all aspects of reality which cannot be registered in some "pointer-reading" upon a dial.[1] Ellwood, speaking from the standpoint of the social sciences, protests against this narrowing of the definition of science, and identifies science broadly with all "tested knowledge that comes from experience, by using any and all methods which will reduce to a minimum errors of judgment";[2] but he, too, recognizes that the domain of science has its limitations. It is safe to say that no careful philosophical survey of the domain of science could ever identify the scientific "world of description," composed of publicly verifiable facts and laws, with the whole real world, the "world of appreciation," the world of meanings, purposes, and values in which our most familiar and important experiences take place.[3] The world of science

---

[1] *The Nature of the Physical World*, Chap. XII.

[2] *Man's Social Destiny*. Pp. 92, 93, etc. Published by The Cokesbury Press, Nashville.

[3] Cf. Royce, *The Spirit of Modern Philosophy*, Lecture on "The World of Description and the World of Appreciation."

floats in the world of immediate experience like an island in the sea. A scientific explanation is therefore always a *partial* explanation; and a scientific account of a phenomenon is always an *abstract* account, which is to the concrete phenomenon itself as a blue-print is to a cathedral, or a medical manikin is to the living human body. Hence it is always fallacious to assert—as scientists have been prone to assert—that the phenomenon is "nothing but" what science reveals it to be; or that aspects of experience which science tacitly assumes to be negligible or nil (because irrelevant from its specialized point of view) are thereby "proved" to be "unreal."

Theologians, on their part, are coming likewise to sense the fallacy involved in their former position; the fallacy, namely, of attempting to segregate certain sacred regions of reality from all intrusions of profane curiosity, and trying to prevent scientific analysis from penetrating these barriers in its onward march—as if scientific explanation of a phenomenon destroyed its religious significance; as if the Divine could live only in darkness and inexplicability, and could be chased off the scene by the advancing light of knowledge! As the realm of scientific law has steadily and irresistibly widened its domains, some theologians have continued to contest its progress at every step; but others have begun to perceive that, disastrous as the advance of science may be to certain outworn scientific notions which have been accidentally incorporated in sacred books and theological systems, it is powerless to disturb the central convictions on which the religious life depends. The dignity of man, considered in his possibilities; the unworthiness of man's actual condition; the existence of saving and hallowing influences which are capable of lifting him from his actual to his ideal estate; the ultimately spiritual character of the universe, guaranteeing the final triumph of life over matter, and man's higher over his lower nature: these are the basic religious convictions; and although new scientific knowledge is constantly requiring their restatement, it can never overturn them, as it could never have created them. Such convictions spring from an attitude of man toward his world which is the precise opposite of the scientific attitude, but which is equally legitimate and equally necessary: an attitude which involves an integral reaction of the whole man to the whole of his environment, whereas the scientific attitude involves a very partial and specific reaction to certain abstract cross-sections of the environment.[1] If, as Professor Hocking maintains, these two attitudes of "effortless attention" to the whole of things, and "effortful attention" to the details of things, must alternate rhythmically, like rest and work, in every normal life,[2] then not only are religion and science equally legitimate human activities, but the types of experience to which they lead must be equally represented in any comprehensive philosophy of life. There can be no ultimate conflict between science and theology.

Some contemporary thinkers are content to drop the whole subject of the relations between science and theology at this point. "Enough of a painful subject!" they seem to say. "Let it be confessed on both sides that there has been tyrannical encroachment, in the past, of science upon the sphere of theology, and of theology upon the sphere of science. Henceforth, let boundaries be kept inviolate, lest this hard-won truce be broken. Let science keep strictly to the realm of facts, eschewing high-flown theories; let theology keep strictly to the task of inter-

---

[1] See Rahn, *Science and the Religious Life*, for a discrimination between the scientific and religious attitudes in terms of physiological psychology. See also, Woodburne, *The Religious Attitude*.

[2] See the chapter on "The Principle of Alternation" in Hocking's *Meaning of God in Human Experience*.

preting religious experience and religious faith; thus there will be no future conflicts between them, since they will be moving on different planes, and can never meet."

But is a legal separation the best that can be hoped for in the future relations of this quarrelsome pair? They did not get on well with each other; but are we sure they can get along without each other? Is it possible for science to eschew theology, or for theology to confine itself to grandiose generalizations? In such a case, would there not be an added sting in the popular jest, according to which the scientist is to be defined as "a man who knows more and more about less and less, until he knows everything about nothing," while the philosopher (or theologian) is to be defined as "a man who knows less and less about more and more, until he knows nothing about everything"? Science, without a dash of religious faith and hope to lead it on, and a dash of speculative daring in the organization of its data, would become a dreary and chaotic collection of meaningless and unrelated facts. Theology, without the facts of science to ballast its conclusions and keep its feet on the ground, would float up into cloudland and dissolve into pure moonshine. Philosophy and common sense are mediators between science and theology; and unless, through their mediation, there is a constant interchange of ideas between the two former antagonists, neither of them can flourish; and the hope of continued peace between them will prove fatuous. The only way for theologians to escape this *impasse* is for them to accept resolutely (with a full realization of the difficulties of their position!) the rôle of custodians of the whole body of human wisdom, and interpreters of the meaning of all the sciences. Once more, theology must become queen of all the sciences!

This statement of the relation between theology and the sciences needs careful qualification. I do not mean to imply that religion as such is totally blind and ignorant, so that theology must needs rely for guidance upon wholly secular sources of enlightenment. This view is, of course, widely held. Professor T. N. Carver, of Harvard, used to tell his classes that the function of religion in society is like that of a brass band in a regiment of soldiers: it inspires, but should not presume to lead. Professor Harry Elmer Barnes, in a recent number of the *Scientific Monthly*,[1] described the theologians of the future seeking God, "if at all, by means of the test-tube, the compound microscope, the interferometer, the radium tube and Einstein's equations," and in general acting as "ringside spectators of the observatory and the laboratory, doing their best in the way of an amateurish appreciation of what is going on therein"—with a view, apparently, to passing on this second-hand information to religion, which in itself contained no light at all.

Such a conception of the respective rôles of religion, theology, and science underestimates the power of insight which religion possesses, and overestimates the ability of science to furnish guidance to life. Science never speaks in the imperative, but only in the future conditional. "*If* you wish to do so and so," she says, "you must fulfill precisely the following conditions: and the results will be thus and thus." That helps to guide us; it keeps us from running blindly and heedlessly into paths that do not lead to the desired results. But science cannot tell us what results are desirable; in all matters of value she remains coolly neutral. Good and evil, beauty and ugliness, are all the same to her. Professor Barnes apparently does not see this; and he accordingly fails to distinguish between wisdom and science—which leads him to assume an absurdly patronizing attitude toward the seers and the sages of an-

[1] May, 1929, p. 441.

tiquity.[1] He finds it impossible to understand how well-informed moderns like Dr. Fosdick and Sherwood Eddy, who have traveled widely and thought deeply upon the problems of our age, can sincerely look up to an illiterate ancient like Jesus of Nazareth, "who lived a restrained and provincial existence in a very backward economy." Still less can he see how they can find anything to conserve in the God whom Jesus worshiped, Jahveh, whose anthropomorphic figure was "slowly and painfully evolved" by a horde of half-starved Semitic nomads, lamentably ignorant of modern astrophysics. Now let it be granted that these gentlemen are *better informed* than Jesus of Nazareth: does it therefore follow that they are *wiser* than he? Granted that the modern schoolboy knows more about the earth and the stars than did the ancient Hebrew prophets; does it follow that he is better able than they to solve the eternal problem of religion: How had we best think of and deal with the Determiner of Destiny in order to live the best possible life in this actual world? May it not be that the thoughts which they so "slowly and painfully evolved" out of bitter experience and ardent hope have at least as much to contribute to modern theology as any suggestions we may get from astrophysics? To look down upon Jesus and the prophets from the heights of our modern scientific learning is much like looking down upon the masters of music from the heights of our modern knowledge of acoustics. Every modern conservatory graduate knows more of the physics of sound and probably more of harmony and counterpoint than the unlettered Franz Schubert; but let him not feel too superior on that account! Is our age with all its technical skill so conspicuous for its wisdom of life, that it is entitled to look down upon the age of Socrates and the age of Jesus?

---

[1] Same article. Much of this material was reprinted, in somewhat altered form, in *The Twilight of Christianity*.

Theology's primary source of insight, then, is not scientific but religious; and theology's primary responsibility is not to bring religion scientifically up to date, but to interpret to our age the ancient wisdom enshrined in religious experience. Theology works under a commission from mankind, not on a permit issued by the scientists. Long before science dawned upon the horizon, mankind had begun exploring the cosmic mystery through religious experience, and formulating its findings in theological propositions. The quest has not been wholly in vain, however often it has gone astray. The findings of religious seers cannot claim exactitude, and must be continually corrected in the light of new knowledge; but they are the most precious heritage that man possesses. The great and primary source of wisdom upon which theology must draw is the literature in which these religious findings have been expressed. It is to be found in the sacred books of the ancient East, of which the greatest is the Bible; in the *Confessions* of St. Augustine, the Franciscan *Fioretti*, the *Imitation of Christ*, and other classics of medieval piety; in modern religious biographies such as those from which William James compiled his classic book on *The Varieties of Religious Experience*. In this treasury of the wisdom of life there is much dross which science helps the theologian to detect; but science cannot of itself replace it with gold, for science does not profess to give insight into life's meanings and ideal possibilities. As the interpreter of religious experience, theology is obliged to seek an answer to the question which the religious yearnings of man perpetually thrust upon her: How, in the present imperfect state of human knowledge, should man think about ultimate reality, and how should he guide his steps, in order to escape life's pitfalls, and attain the utmost fullness of life of which humanity is capable? Some answer to this question man must have. He cannot get it from all the sciences put together. Theology must answer, in all humility yet in all boldness, speaking in the name of the saints and sages of antiquity, testing and correcting their intuitive wisdom in the light of science, philosophy, and common sense.[1]

Granting that theology's primary responsibility is to interpret and test the unconscious wisdom which resides in religious experience, we must nevertheless go on to insist that this process of interpretation and testing is a two-sided affair, in which science has as much the duty to point out the vagaries and fanaticisms of religion as religion has the duty to point out the limitations of science. Religious experience tastes of life more deeply and more fully than scientific investigation; it has magnificent intuitions of life's meaning, purpose, and ultimate destiny, of which science can know nothing; but if religion's dreams are to be translated into sober actuality, science must aid. Science is supreme in the realm of ways and means, as religion is supreme in the realm of ends and meanings.

Religion has seldom been recreant to her task of seeing life steadily and seeing it whole—seeing life in its ideal significance, as it might be, with all lesser ends subordinated to the supreme end of man's full realization of his potentialities—but for lack of a scientific technique, religion has perpetrated the most egregious blunders in the endeavor to realize this ideal. She has relied upon magical incantations, sacrificial offerings, and miraculous divine interventions to bring about results which can be accomplished only by the patient study of the orderly processes

---

[1] It is possible, of course, to stretch the definition of science to include philosophy, common sense and religious wisdom, and justify it by pointing to certain analogies between successful truth-seeking in all three fields, as Professor Wieman does in his articles in the *Christian Century*, January 29 and February 12, 1930. I fully grant Professor Wieman's contention, but think his terminology is confusing.

of nature, and the patient fitting of means to ends. Disappointed in her dream of a better life here and now, achievable in part through human effort, she has conceived lurid apocalyptic dreams of a world that is utterly different and wholly separate from this, with which one may communicate and into which one may be translated only by weird and unearthly channels. Thus she has incurred the suspicion that her dreams are essentially unrealizable and fantastic.

The suspicion is unjust. At its best, religious experience gives insight into life as it really might be, and some day will be, if the right conditions are met; and science may aid enormously in making religion's dreams come true, by defining the conditions which must be met if they are to be realized. All the sciences, in their *practical* bearing, are unequivocally to be regarded as friends of religion and theology, whatever may be true of their *theoretical* bearing. Physics and biology in their theoretical aspect have committed many metaphysical fallacies, appearing to give us a barren, mechanistic world in which religion was almost suffocated; but in their practical aspect, as *engineering* and *medicine*, they have done more to give reason for faith in the supremacy of Spirit over all material obstacles than all the miracles of the Old and New Testaments. What the same careful methods, applied by psychology to the study of the heights and depths of human experience, may accomplish for the release and development of personality is a thought which modern theology cannot contemplate without a sense of awe and tremulous expectation.

2. HOW THEOLOGY AND PSYCHOLOGY MIGHT COME TO TERMS

Supposing, then, that it has been decided to treat psychology as the friend and not the enemy of theology, how are its services to be enlisted in the task of theological re-construction? What, precisely, is the bearing of psychology upon theology? What would it mean to adopt a "psychological approach to theology"? What are the terms on which theology and psychology might agree, as a basis of coöperation?

In the light of our general proposals for perpetuating peace and fraternity between science and theology, certain stipulations must at once be laid down. Theology, on the one hand, must not deny the right of psychology to investigate according to its own methods and to explain according to its own presuppositions everything that lies within its proper field, even though this may seem to expose the most sacred recesses of the religious life to the profaning glance of inquisitive and cold-blooded scientists. Theology must, moreover, agree without reservations to alter, amend, or cancel altogether whatsoever there may be in the dogmas of the past that is flatly and decisively contradicted by any new facts that psychology may reveal. Herewith, theology must irrevocably abandon all pretension to possess, in the Bible, in the creeds of the Church, in the teachings of Jesus, or anywhere else, truth that can be called "infallible" or "final," and is not subject to revision. Psychology, on the other hand, must agree to recognize the limitations that are inherent in any specialized scientific point of view, and therefore grant the possibility that other points of view, and other explanations of the same phenomena, are possible and legitimate. Psychology may demand instant and respectful obedience when speaking in the name of the Facts; but theology cannot be expected to accept without criticism the philosophical theories and unconscious assumptions with which the facts of psychology are entangled. In general, psychology must admit that (like all the sciences) it is more competent from the practical than from the theoretical point of view; and must grant theology's right, when seeking to build a general theory of life upon the findings of psychology, to view these findings through corrective lenses, designed to compensate for the specific type of myopic squint from which psychology suffers.

When these principles are applied to the burning issue of behaviorism—over which, as we saw, there is danger of a fresh outbreak of the conflict between science and theology—it promptly resolves itself into a "tempest in a teapot." Behaviorism as a method of scientific exploration —approaching the study of the mind through the objective study of the adaptive responses of the organism to its environment—is surely "as innocent as it is useful."[1] It has solved many psychological riddles which failed to yield to the introspective method of approach; and its findings must therefore be viewed, by all candid minds, as an important segment of the truth about human personality. It is only when Professor Watson, and the over-enthusiastic adherents of the school, put in their claim to have discovered the *whole truth* about man, and deny the very existence of anything that is not visible through the behavioristic microscope, that serious problems are raised for theology; and these problems, when examined for a moment in clear daylight, are all seen to be unreal.

But can theology stand calmly by, while behaviorism announces that thought and consciousness, will and purpose, freedom and immortality, are all pure myths? Well, if there were any scientific justification for these announcements, there would indeed be reason for excitement— reason for insanity and suicide, in fact!—but there is none. No scientist has the right to announce, as part of his discoveries, anything which he had already assumed before his investigations began. Now behaviorism rests upon the assumption that consciousness and free-will can safely be

---

[1] Cf. Patrick, "Should Religion Stand in Fear of the Behavioristic Psychology?" *Christian Century*, September 18, 1929.

ignored in the study of psychology, just as modern physics rests upon the assumption that meanings, purposes, values, and Aristotelian "final causes" can safely be ignored in the study of inanimate Nature. For behaviorism to deny the existence of that which it deliberately ignores, and to claim scientific authority for this pronouncement, is to commit what might be called "the fallacy of the forgotten assumption"—a fallacy whereby many a clever debater dazzles his opponents, triumphantly pulling out of his hat, as a conclusion, what he had surreptitiously smuggled in at the beginning, as an axiom.

The reality of mind and consciousness cannot be impugned by mere logical legerdemain. The certainty of their existence is prior to all other certainties. Eddington has clearly shown that the concepts of physics constitute a circular chain of mutually supporting definitions, which are totally meaningless apart from some ultimate reference to conscious human experience.[1] If physics cannot do without some ultimate reference to human consciousness, how much less psychology! The behaviorist and the physicist can ignore the reality of the world of thought only so long as they remain in their laboratories, looking at the world intensively, with a one-eyed squint; the moment they step out upon the street, they become conscious of themselves as free and purposeful.

There will be no further discussion of behaviorism in this book. The factual findings of behaviorism will be gladly accepted and used, along with the findings of other schools of psychology; and the attempt will be made to combine them with the insights of common sense and the insights of religion, so as to tell the truth about man's nature and destiny as fully and comprehensively as our limited knowledge permits. The Freudian psychology will

---

[1] *Op. cit.*, pp. 260-272.

be regarded as another abstract cross-section of the truth about human nature, less scientifically precise than behaviorism, and somewhat tainted with mythology and charlatanry, but nearer to common sense, and immensely serviceable in certain fields where behaviorism is inadequate. "Gestalt" psychology will occasionally be used as a corrective of both. The bizarre and ill-informed opinions which Dr. Freud has expressed upon the subject of religion will not be taken more seriously than they deserve; but this will not dissuade us from listening attentively to his findings in the field of abnormal psychology; nor will the equally ill-founded opinions of Professor Watson incline us to disparage all the truly scientific findings of the behavioristic school.[1] So far as possible, we shall be non-sectarian in our psychology, presenting an account of human nature which would be equally acceptable to moderate behaviorists like Dr. Burnham, or moderate Freudians like Dr. Hadfield; but where the doctors disagree, we shall have to use the layman's privilege and rely on our own common sense.

But what, more precisely, is the bearing of psychology upon theology; and how should one construct a theology in order to make psychology's contribution stand forth in bold relief? A suggestive answer to this question was made some years ago by Professor Leuba in his *Psychological Study of Religion*;[2] and we can hardly do better than to begin our discussion by quoting his challenging words:

---

[1] I believe that Barbour is quite unjustified in rejecting behavioristic psychology *in toto* on account of its philosophical inadequacy, and basing his discussion of *Sin and the New Psychology* exclusively upon Freudian psychology. Both behaviorism and Freudianism have committed philosophical blunders, but they both have great value *as science*; while "Gestalt" psychology, whose philosophical point of view is much sounder than either, has so far proved scientifically barren.

[2] From *A Psychological Study of Religion*, by James H. Leuba, Preface, pp. viii, ix; pp. 260, 261. (1912.) By permission of the Macmillan Company, publishers.

Religion . . . needs as much as any other practical activity the kind of purification and guidance that science provides. It needs in particular the insight into the dynamics of conscious life which can be contributed, not by studies in comparative religion nor by criticism of sacred texts, but only by psychology.

Every once in a while theologians, finding their skein hopelessly tangled, raise a cry for a return to origins, by which they mean a return to the Church Fathers and to the sacred writings. The cry of the psychologist is not for a return to the teachings of any man or group of men, but to human nature. He does not inquire, for instance, what any particular person or group of persons taught concerning saving practices and beliefs; but he tries to discover the psychological processes involved in the experience called salvation, and he knows that success will mean the great initial step toward a scientific control of the factors entering into that experience. The great task of the psychologist in the field of religious life is to return, through the distortions and worthless accretions resulting from centuries of groping, to what is fundamental and essential in human nature. . . .

What has Christian Theology done in the course of two thousand years to increase our knowledge of "sin," its central problem? . . . The eradication of moral evil is a problem demanding for its solution a knowledge far more difficult of attainment than that which has already enabled us to master many bodily diseases; nothing will suffice short of an exhaustive knowledge of general psychology, individual and social; in particular a knowledge of psychology in its relation to physiology.

The indifference of those who are supposed to be the custodians of religious knowledge to the only ways by which knowledge on the cardinal problems of practical religion can be increased, excusable a hundred years ago, has become a scandal and a public danger—a scandal and a danger which will continue as long as the Christian Church seeks its information on sin and the means to righteousness only in its own sacred Scriptures and in unanalyzed experience.

I believe that Professor Leuba has singled out, clearly and convincingly, the point at which psychology impinges upon the field of theology—the point from which, accordingly, our psychological approach to theology must set out. It is, as he suggests, upon the general theory of "Man, Sin and Salvation," *the practical, moralistic side of theology*, that psychology's bearing is most direct. This part of theology might be characterized, in less traditional and technical terms, as the part which deals with the question, "What must I do to release my personality from all that impedes its full development?" or more positively, "What must I do to secure the fullest and most harmonious realization of my ideal possibilities?" This, translated into terms of the contemporary cult of self-realization, is the precise equivalent of the ancient question, "What must I do to be saved?"—the central question of practical theology. Like the central question of practical medicine—"What must I do to get well?"—this is a thoroughly empirical question, to which a scientific answer should be given. It is, in fact, the same question raised from the physiological to the personal plane; and as the physician's answer depends upon the development of biological science, the clergyman's answer *ought* to be brought into close relation with psychological science.

But if Professor Leuba suggests very clearly the point at which psychology bears most directly upon theology, he also illustrates the dangers and limitations involved in a purely psychological point of view. In his enthusiasm for psychology, he attempts to maintain that it may not only *contribute to* theology, but may actually *replace* it! Theology, he says, bears a relation to psychology "similar to that of alchemy to chemistry"; and he ventures to predict that when theology becomes fully scientific, it will become, literally, "a branch of psychological science."[1] The

---

[1] *Op. cit.*, pp. 250, 276. The whole chapter on "Theology and Psychology" leads up to this somewhat bizarre conclusion.

logical corollary of this point of view appears in Professor Leuba's contention (in Chapter I) that all divine beings, from primitive ghosts and gods up to the Christian God, are simply creations of the human mind, having no existence except a "purely subjective existence" in the mind of the believer.

This, I say, illustrates the "dangers" of the purely psychological point of view—by which I mean, not that it imperils traditional belief, but that it imperils the truth. It imperils the truth precisely as does every specialized scientific point of view: by seeing things out of focus, and refusing to admit the existence of anything beyond its own limited field of vision. One need not be a naïve believer in the existence of Apollo, or Jahveh, or Allah to protest against this reduction of all the gods to the status of subjective delusions. Any candid atheist ought to be able to perceive the fact that all the great gods represent, at the very least, aspects of nature, or phases of the character of events, which have evoked a characteristic emotional response in the worshiper. They may not exist precisely as conceived; but in almost every case, the idea of a god may be said to correspond to *something objectively real*. To refuse to admit this is to commit what has been called "the fallacy of psychologism." Logically, Professor Leuba should not stop at this point! He should go on to deny the existence of the external world, and the existence of other human beings; since one can give a psychological and "purely subjective" account of the process by which we come to believe in them!

There are those who would claim that any psychological approach to theology must inevitably fall victim to the "fallacy of psychologism," and end in pure subjectivism, or, at least, in a purely humanistic creed, whose limited horizon would shut out God, prayer, immortality, and all that lies above and beyond the immediate here and now.[1] It must be frankly admitted that the psychological approach tends to throw the "human" side of theology (Man, Sin, Salvation) into the foreground, while it throws the "divine" side of theology (God, Christ, the Spirit, the Church, the Future Life) into the background. But does it *eliminate* or *minimize* the divine side of theology? Not if we go about the task with our eyes open, and there is anything divine to discover! For consider: the psychological approach to theology must of course include the findings of the psychology *of religion*, as the most important part of its data; and the psychology of religion, broadly interpreted, involves not only a description of what goes on in the mind of the religious man, but a description of the objective conditions—social, natural, and ultimately metaphysical—which elicit the religious response and nourish the religious life.

A glance at the history of the psychology of religion in the last quarter-century will reveal a distinct trend away from individualistic subjectivism, toward a more objective and cosmic emphasis in the interpretation of religion. In its first period (that is, until about 1910) the psychology of religion was concerned almost exclusively with the problem of the function of religion in the life of the individual; and the verdict was that religion unifies and energizes personality, and gives an emotional tang to life. In the second period (approximately from 1910 to 1920) the function of religion in the life of the *race* became the leading problem; and the verdict was substantially as follows: *Just as religion unifies and stabilizes the individual by organizing the elements of his character around some ideal focus of attention, so it unifies and stabilizes society by organizing its ideal aspirations around certain values socially recognized as supreme.* In the third or

---

[1] This is the main thesis of F. Ménégoz's remarkable book, *Le Problème de la Prière*.

most recent period (since 1920) the psychology of religion has extended its outlook from the social to the cosmic sphere; and religion is now commonly defined as *a dangerous venture into the field of ultimate metaphysics, in quest of cosmic alliance and support*—a venture which at the worst leads man to retreat into a dreamland of fantasy, as an escape-reaction against uncertainty, but which at the best leads him into an imperfect but life-sustaining adjustment to what is deepest in reality.[1]

The psychological approach to theology must necessarily take its start from the individual quest of personal development—a point of view which at once sets it in sympathy with the spirit of this restless age—but it will inevitably be led out of the individual sphere into the social and cosmic spheres, in the endeavor to define the conditions that control and the resources which aid man in this quest. If the secret of personal development lay

---

[1] *First period, 1899-1910.* Chief problem, psychology of conversion. Chief method, the questionnaire. Greatest book, James's *Varieties of Religious Experience.* Definition of religion: "feelings, acts, and experiences of individual men in their solitude, so far as they apprehend themselves to stand in relation to whatever they may consider the divine" (p. 31).

Second period, 1910-1920. Chief problem, religion and social morality. Chief method, "folk psychology." Greatest book, Ames's *Psychology of Religious Experience.* Definition of religion: "Consciousness of the highest social values" (p. 168).

Third period, 1920-. Chief problem, religion and ultimate reality. Methods varied and complex. Greatest book, Pratt's *Religious Consciousness.* Definition of religion: "the serious and social attitude of individuals or communities toward the power or powers which they conceive as having ultimate control over their interests and destinies" (p. 2). Recent presentations of this point of view: Woodburne, *The Religious Attitude*; Flower, *An Approach to the Psychology of Religion*; Wieman, *The Wrestle of Religion with Truth.*

If it be asked what conception of the relation of *theology* to *religion* has emerged from the investigations of religious psychologists, the answer might be given, epigrammatically, as follows: *Theology is the endeavor to organize the whole of human knowledge in the service of religion's endeavor to bring man into right organic relations with the whole of Reality. It unifies knowledge in order to help religion to unify life.*

wholly within the control of the individual, or wholly in the use of secular agencies, there would be no need of pushing on in quest of further resources—and there would be no theology in the proper sense of the word. But since the conditions which govern the growth and health of personality extend out into the social and cosmic spheres, we shall find that, before we have finished with our quest of the good life, all the major topics of theology will pass in review before us: in Part I, Man, Sin, and Salvation; in Part II, Christ and the Church; in Part III, God and Immortality.

The three stages of the quest of the good life define for us, then, the three divisions of theology. In Part I, the individual will be at the focus of attention; and the problem will be to determine the psychological conditions of personal development, noting the place which religion holds among the various ways and means of self-realization. In Part II, our horizon widens to include the whole field of human society and history; and the problem will be to define the place of Christ and Christianity among the various religious movements and forces which promote the "abundant life." In Part III, our horizon again widens—enormously, this time, to include the cosmic and metaphysical realms—and the quest of the good life closes with an inquiry into the ultimate Source and Ground of personal development (God) and the ultimate goal to which it leads.

If this order of topics has the disadvantage of putting man first and God last, it has at least the merit of proceeding logically from the known to the unknown, from the empirical to the metaphysical. In the first part, where the whole point of view is practical and empirical, psychology will be taken at its full face value—for it will be in its own proper field—and the whole effort will be to give science its full rights in the field of theology. In the last two parts, where the argument mounts continually higher toward the metaphysical plane, the psychological approach will be less direct. *No doctrine will be formulated until its meaning for religious experience has first been described and analyzed, psychologically*; but it will be necessary to postpone final statement of the doctrine until the psychological analysis of it has been corrected for faulty perspective, and the danger of subjectivism or "psychologism" thus eliminated.

A word as to the assumptions and mental reservations which the author may be suspected of carrying with him into this investigation. It is impossible, of course, for anyone to wipe the slate of his mind clean of all preconceptions, and disburden himself of all cherished convictions; and I do not pretend to have done so. I believe that there is great wisdom in the insights of religious genius; and I also believe that we here in the Western world possess a great treasure-house of religious insight in the Christian tradition. I shall therefore assume that, however far Christian theologians may have strayed from the truth, the basic concepts of Christian thought are not meaningless concepts, and deserve at least the courtesy of a respectful investigation. In the background of all my thought, I suppose, there stands the traditional outline of Christian theology, and it is upon that screen that the findings of psychology are to be projected. From time to time, traditional theological views will be mentioned; and even when they are not mentioned, their presence may be felt. Yet it is my sincere intention to make this book a genuine intellectual experiment; and if I bring with me a particular background of belief, I mean to hold it hypothetically, subject to verification or correction. May the reader consent to believe in my sincerity, and meet me halfway!

If there is one Christian principle to which I am disposed to cling with special pertinacity, it is perhaps the principle expressed in the well-known words of Jesus: "Whosoever shall seek to save his life shall lose it; and whosoever shall lose his life shall preserve it." I am convinced that the contemporary quest of self-realization can succeed only if the individual learns anew to forget himself in loyal devotion to great social ends; and I am convinced that the human race, like the human individual, can find peace and fullness of life only as it discovers some object of devotion above and beyond itself. This conviction, I confess, is implicit in the whole plan and structure of the book; but I believe that the findings of psychology will abundantly sustain it, as we proceed. The newest science and the most ancient wisdom will be found to unite their testimony and support one another, upon this point at least.

3. DIFFICULTIES OF THE UNDERTAKING

The modern theologian is in a dilemma. Caught between the pull of traditional wisdom on the one hand and the pull of experimental science on the other, he is apt to steer a somewhat devious course. If he could believe in the infallible authority of Church or Scripture, he might ignore science. If he could believe in the all-sufficiency of science as a guide to life, he might ignore the garnered wisdom of the past. As it is, he can choose neither horn of the dilemma, and appears to halt indecisively between two contrary points of view. From both sides, he is exposed to attack. Naturalistic thinkers will characterize him scornfully as a "wabbly modernist," only half released from the shackles of supernaturalism, and a victim of "wishful thinking." Conservative religionists, on the other hand, will regard him as a traitor to religious tradition, already past the halfway mark on the road to atheism. He himself will often wonder if he is not trying to carry water on both shoulders, and his arguments will sometimes seem to start out for one objective and arrive at the reverse. Perpetually losing his intellectual balance in the effort to reach out for larger comprehension, and perpetually regaining it by hasty qualifications and recantations, he is not always a dignified figure. Yet unless he keeps at his task, weaving threads of understanding across the chasm that has opened between our religious traditions and our scientific achievements, our civilization will split in two.

It is not an easy task. If the critics of theology would fairly envisage the colossal sweep of the undertaking which it involves, they might perhaps adopt a more sympathetic tone. Once admit the principle that the findings of science have a bearing upon theology, and you are deluged with facts and theories clamoring for attention. Biological evolution seems so important that you gird up your loins for a serious study of it—and just then chaos breaks loose in the realm of physics! Dazzled by the brilliant metaphysical implications of the new physics, you plunge into relativity and quantum theory, trying desperately to keep up with Einstein on the strength of high-school mathematics—when, just as you are deciding to take a course in the infinitesimal calculus, the mental hygiene movement begins to get under way, and some earnest person announces that it is destined to shelve theology altogether! Fascinated by the implications of mental hygiene, you turn to the study of general and applied psychology—only to discover that there apparently exists no *general* psychology to apply, but only a series of warring schools of psychology, each speaking a jargon of its own and casting aspersions upon all the rest!

The theologian who for the first time "takes a flier" in contemporary science may well emerge from his little venture in a somewhat chastened mood; and as he sits down to think it over, he may perhaps decide thenceforth to stick to his own last, and content himself with expounding God, Man, Sin, and Salvation in traditional terms, modifying or reinterpreting them only when absolutely driven to it by facts too patent to be overlooked. He can find many weighty considerations to confirm him in his conservative attitude. If he is acquainted with the history of Christian doctrine, he can point out that theology has more often erred on the side of excessive intellectual hospitality than on the opposite side. Under the influence of Clement, Origen, and the other Platonizing Fathers of the ancient Catholic Church, theology became so heavily weighted down with Greek metaphysics that she has been staggering under the load ever since; and one of the chief problems of modern theology has been to distinguish between the abiding elements in Christian experience and the obsolete Greek terminology in which they were expressed. Under the influence of Abelard and Aquinas, medieval theology trustfully accepted Aristotelian science *en bloc* and built it into the structure of Christian thought —so successfully, that when modern science demolished Aristotelian science, the whole structure that had been built upon it tumbled down with it. It would seem as though any alliance between theology and secular learning tended to become an entangling alliance; and conservative religion is not without reason when she warns unwary young theologians against yielding to such allurements:

"See, my children," she says, "how fast and furious is the flux of worldly thought! How quickly do scientific and philosophic theories succeed one another! Here is a theory which but yesterday I was indignantly required to accept, on penalty of being dubbed 'medieval'; today it is rejected, and another proclaimed in its stead. I have outlived many such changes, and shall outlive many more. The wisdom of the ages is more reliable than the vagaries of the moment; venture not forth into the current of contemporary thought, lest you be swept from your eternal moorings. What shall it profit you to gain the whole world of secular learning, and lose that sensitiveness to spiritual things which is your very soul, and the secret of your power?"

These are powerful considerations,[1] and it is impossible for theology wholly to escape the pull of them. Certainly it is a mistake for her to permit secular learning to engulf and devitalize the religious tradition which is her peculiar heritage and her chief reason for existing; and whenever she permits it, a violent reaction in religious thought is sure to occur. Such a reaction is now under way in Germany under the leadership of Karl Barth, who proposes to upset and bring to naught the whole liberal movement in theology inaugurated by Schleiermacher, as a punishment for its fatal concessions to secular culture and the modern temper. Yet as one looks at the achievements of modern theology in the past century, is it possible to say that it has all been a great mistake? Can one regret that John Fiske and Henry Drummond espoused the doctrine of Evolution and made it the basis of their theism, just when most of their fellow Christians were denouncing it as atheistic? that, more recently, the influence of scientific Biblical criticism and the "new social conscience" permeated the thought of a whole generation of theologians? that the appeal to dogmatic authority has come to be generally replaced by the appeal to experience? One sees, to be sure, that many damaging concessions to secular thought have been made, which time has proven to have

---

[1] For an effective statement of these considerations, with specific application to psychology, see John Baillie, *The Interpretation of Religion*, p. 405: "That which is 'up-to-the-moment' only lasts a moment. . . . Those of our contemporaries who are so eager to express their Christianity in terms of the 'scientific' thought of their own decade—psycho-analysis, auto-suggestion, instinct, psychology, behaviorism, spiritism, relativity, an undisciplined evolutionism, and the like—are running the risk of appearing to their successors of a future age ten times more antiquated . . . than the authors of the *De Civitate Dei*, the *Summa Theologiæ*, and the *Institutio Christianæ Religionis*." Published by Charles Scribner's Sons, New York. (1928.)

been unnecessary; but the type of theology which risks such concessions is at least *alive*, and intelligible to the man on the street.

There will never be a dearth of people who make it their main business to guard the "deposit of faith," and raise the alarm whenever they feel it is endangered. The theologian, if he is wise, will always keep one ear open to their warnings—not because he fears to be denounced as a heretic, but because conservatism stands for truths and values he is in danger of forgetting. But with the other ear he must listen to the babble of sounds that arises from the contemporary scientific arena, and try to sense its significance. In a word, he must be a philosopher—less interested in pure speculation, less given to abstruse terminology than most philosophers, and more conscious of his responsibility as a practical guide, but equally open-minded and equally willing to follow "whithersoever the argument leadeth." He cannot be an expert in all the sciences, but he may well choose some one science, such as psychology, and use it as a means of keeping his feet upon the ground. If this method and attitude came to be adopted generally by theologians, theology would regain her ancient prestige among the sciences on a new basis of fellowship and *camaraderie*. Her relation to the sciences would no longer be that of a queen to her handmaidens; but it would be something better. It would be more like the relation between the initiator and the collaborators in a great coöperative adventure, like Byrd's Antarctic expedition, or Noguchi's investigation into the causes of yellow fever in Africa. Only in this case, the object of the quest, to which theology would invite all comers to contribute, would be nothing less than the discovery of the conditions under which man might enjoy complete liberation from all hampering ills, and the fullest possible realization of all his hidden possibilities.

Part I
Religion and Personal Development

In which the psychological conditions of mental health and moral power are studied; and religion is found to occupy a central place among the agencies making for personal development.

> "See, I have set before thee this day life and good, and death and evil . . . therefore choose life, that both thou and thy seed may live.
>
> (*Deuteronomy* 30:15, 19.)

Theology has always had much to say about human nature —mostly by way of disparagement. That human nature, since Adam's fall, has become a "mass of perdition," a "running sore," incessantly bringing forth acts of iniquity "as a blazing furnace incessantly casts forth flame and sparks"; such, in its more emphatic expression, is the theological estimate of unregenerate human nature. This estimate must not, of course, be taken without qualification. It is much softened by the fact that, buried beneath the wrack and ruin of the Fall, vestiges of a previous "state of integrity" were believed to be discernible—just enough to remind man of his divine origin and former high estate, and to explain why, under certain conditions, he was able to respond to the solicitations of divine grace. Nevertheless the proposition holds good that, ever since St. Augustine (one might almost say, St. Paul), a pessimistic view of human nature has been the corner-stone upon which most systems of Christian theology have been erected.

In our psychological reconstruction of theology, the first task that confronts us is the laying of a new corner-stone. Since the fateful year 1859, the old one has been crumbling, under the assaults of Darwinian biology. Instead of a fallen creature, we now see in man a slowly rising creature. Instead of tracing his origin to Adam and Eve and the Garden of Eden, we now begin with Amœba, Paramecium, and the primeval slime! This sounds revolutionary enough, to be sure; and yet the doctrine of Evolution alone would not necessarily alter our theory of human nature in any very drastic sense. Adam, after all, was only a convenient peg upon which to hang observations concerning human nature; and if these observations still held good, it would not greatly matter whether we looked upon man as a fallen creature stumbling to his feet again, or as a rising creature just learning to walk for the first time. Pascal's acute observations on human nature are not wholly vitiated by his pre-Darwinian point of view. The really crucial question is, not whether we inherited these human traits of ours from Adam or from *Pithecanthropus Erectus*, but whether traditional theology was correct in its disparaging description of these inherited traits, and precise in its pessimistic estimate of our present human possibilities. Psychology is now engaged in amassing great stores of information bearing directly upon this question; and it will be our task in this and the succeeding chapter to weigh the significance of its testimony. In this, its own field, psychology's testimony may well outweigh the combined testimony of the Fathers, and settle disputes which have been fruitlessly agitated ever since St. Augustine locked horns with Pelagius.

Following an ancient theological convention which appears to have its uses, let us consider man first in his "state of integrity" and then in his "state of corruption"; or, to translate the old distinction into modern terminology, let us first consider the original nature and ideal possibilities of normal human beings, deferring to our next chapter the problem of the abnormal ills and perversities with which our race is beset.

I. ORIGINAL HUMAN NATURE

For some years after Darwin announced his epoch-making discoveries there was, naturally enough, a tendency to exaggerate the dominating significance of man's biological heritage, and to attribute to the new-born infant a formidable array of fixed and inflexible instincts acquired by his ancestors in their struggle for existence. A popular theory expressive of this tendency is the theory of "recapitulation," according to which the instincts ripen one after another in the individual in an order roughly corresponding to the order of their appearance in the race; and each individual thus is fated to rehearse in his own experience the whole story of biological evolution. From this point of view, man's life appears to flow inevitably along certain well-marked hereditary grooves, and the possibility of improving it by education, or social reform, or religious regeneration looks like a rather forlorn hope. "You can't change human nature," is the verdict which must be passed upon every idealistic project. The only promising way of improving our human lot would seem to be to breed a better race, with better instincts—hence the Eugenics movement.

In recent years, the notion of instinct has been subjected to severe scrutiny by the psychologists; and many tendencies which used to be traced to heredity are now commonly regarded as nothing but habits acquired at an early age. Some indeed claim that there are no human instincts at all; while there is a general disposition to simplify the elaborate tables of instincts that were popular a dozen years ago. Even those instincts which remain on the approved list are described as highly flexible *aptitudes to learn*, rather than precise and stereotyped *patterns of conduct*. Without becoming involved in purely verbal disputes, and allowing for a certain amount of exaggeration in the statement of new points of view, we are perhaps fairly safe in summarizing the assured results of psychological investigation, to date, in the following four propositions concerning original human nature:

1. *We inherit from our human and animal ancestors a complex physical organism, equipped from the very start*

with protective devices, whose use does not have to be learned. To enter into the use of our muscles, our sense-organs, our circulatory, digestive, and respiratory systems, etc., we need only to await their full physiological development—which is reached in some cases even before birth. The *coördination* of these organic activities must for the most part be learned; but we are equipped at birth with a variety of useful *reflexes* which represent the native beginnings of the coördinating process. These include sneezing, sucking, grasping, kicking, turning the head at a touch on the cheek, and many other elementary reactions.

2. *Not ready-made equipment, but learning capacity, is the major element in our biological heritage.* We could not, of course, get started in life without a certain amount of ready-made physiological equipment; but our superiority to other animals consists precisely in the remarkable flexibility and adaptability of our native equipment. On the family tree which connects all existing forms of life with their common ancestry in the primeval slime, there are two great branches, which diverge from the main trunk at an early period: the Vertebrates, who wear their skeleton on the inside, and the Arthropods, who wear theirs on the outside. Along each of these two lines, Nature has risen to great heights, but by diverse methods. In the Arthropod division she has relied mainly upon instinct; and her masterpieces in that line are to be seen in the rigid but marvelously complicated societies of the ants and the bees, in which individual initiative and intelligence count but little. Even here, it is probable that the working of instinct is not so inflexible as was formerly supposed; but there can be little doubt that, relatively speaking, the Arthropods are more governed by instinct than the Vertebrates. The superiority of man, the highest of the Vertebrates, over all the Arthropods and the rest of the Vertebrates, consists in the superior adaptability of

his native equipment. This superiority does not appear immediately at birth; on the contrary, the human infant is grotesquely clumsy and helpless as compared with other young animals; but the device of nature known as the *prolongation of infancy*, whereby man and other mammals are subjected to a long period of parental care and education, makes him eventually able to fend for himself better than any instinct-guided creature can do.

3. *Many of the well-marked tendencies which are called instincts when they appear in other animals appear in us, too, in a more flexible form, as powerful impulsive drives, connected with characteristic emotions.* Professor Allport in his *Social Psychology*[1] refers to these impulsive reactions as "prepotent reflexes," and describes them as "imperative in their action, protective or adaptive in their effect, and prepotent in their ascendance over other stimuli in controlling the common path." They fall into two main classes: "avoiding reactions," destined to rescue the organism from danger or discomfort, and accompanied by "contractive" emotions of fear or anger; and "approaching responses," destined to bring the organism into touch with sources of nourishment or satisfaction, and accompanied by "expansive" emotions of love or joy—when the source of satisfaction is within reach. The impulse to avoid heat and cold (to say nothing of hard work and responsibility) belongs in the first class; hunger and sex belong conspicuously in the second.

The handling of these blind, imperative urges constitutes a large part of the problem of right living. Theology has looked upon them with a baneful eye, and insisted that until they are thoroughly "mortified," we are still under the dominion of the "old Adam." Freudian psychology, on the other hand, warns us against the

---

[1] Page 49. Published by Houghton Mifflin Company, Boston.

danger involved in the effort to repress them. There can be no doubt that they constitute a grave menace to the higher moral life, since they are fundamentally individualistic—even the craving to love, or to be loved, is thoroughly individualistic at the physical level—yet when rightly "conditioned" they may become the solid basis of strong character. To eradicate them in part, by a policy of Puritan repression, may dampen a man's fire and energy; to eradicate them altogether would mean death.[1]

4. *Besides these rather specific impulsive drives, we are equipped with many general traits or aptitudes, characteristic of all men as men, but existing in various degrees in different individuals.* Among these general human traits we might name, in addition to the general adaptability already mentioned, such things as curiosity, play, constructiveness, language, sociability, morality, religion, and most general of all, the urge toward completeness or wholeness of life.[2] Intelligence testing and comparative

---

[1] Cf. Dewey, *Human Nature and Conduct*, pp. 156, 157: "In the career of any impulse activity there are speaking generally three possibilities. It may find a surging, explosive discharge—blind, unintelligent. It may be sublimated—that is, become a factor coördinated intelligently with others in a continuing course of action. . . . Or again a released impulse activity may be neither immediately expressed in isolated spasmodic action, nor indirectly employed in an enduring interest. It may be 'suppressed' . . . An isolated or spasmodic manifestation is a sign of immaturity, savagery; a suppressed activity is the cause of all kinds of intellectual and moral pathology." In seeking to avoid the first of these alternatives, many over-conscientious religious enthusiasts fall victim to the last. Published by Henry Holt & Company, Inc., New York. (1922.)

[2] Cf. Hadfield, *Psychology and Morals*, pp. 61, 66. "Every organism is impelled to move toward its own completeness. . . . So persistent and strong is this law that no organism can rest until it has satisfied its hunger by achieving its complete self. . . . If you cut off the limb of a newt, so strong is this impulse that the organism sets to work until it has grown a new limb and restored the newt to wholeness. If we inflict a wound on our body, immediately every part of the bodily organism sets to work to restore the injured part . . . The self, like every organism, moves towards its own completeness." Published by Robert M. McBride & Company, New York. (1925.)

psychology have amassed a great deal of evidence indicating that general ability to learn or to adapt is a native capacity more highly potent in man than in any other animal, and more highly potent in some men than in others. We may pretty safely assume, then, that the same is true of other human traits, in spite of the fact that their generality and high flexibility make it more difficult for psychologists to agree about them than about such specific tendencies as hunger and fear.

A specific physiological basis for many of these general traits can be found. For example, curiosity can be viewed as a natural outgrowth of certain simple reflexes—turning the eye toward a bright moving object, cocking the ears at a sudden sound, manipulating things with the fingers and putting them in the mouth—all of which can be seen in very young infants. Or again, æsthetic appreciation may be traced in part to the rhythmic character of bodily processes. Yet it is probable that the true basis of such general tendencies as these is to be found in nothing less than *the whole structure of the organism, interrelated with the whole of its environment.*[1]

---

[1] That the real unit of behavior is not the simple, unrelated reflex, but the response of the whole organism to the total situation, is being strongly urged by the advocates of the "Gestalt Psychology." The idea is not a new one; biology has long granted its truth. For analytic purposes it is desirable to resolve the unity of the organism-plus-environment into smaller units; but to get a proper perspective upon the nature of the general human traits now under consideration, we must look at them from the wider point of view. "Breathing," says John Dewey, "is an affair of the air as truly as of the lungs; digesting an affair of food as truly as of tissues of the stomach. . . . They are things done by the environment by means of organic structures or acquired dispositions." (*Human Nature and Conduct*, p. 14. Published by Henry Holt & Company, Inc.) If this is true of breathing and digesting, how much more is it true of language and morality.

It is from this point of view that Professor Hocking refers to curiosity, play, etc., as "necessary interests." (*Human Nature and Its Remaking*, Chap. X.) They are necessary, that is to say, not in the sense that they are motivated by particular organic urges which, like hunger, imperatively

Theology has been much concerned over the question of the basis of morality and religion in original human nature. Morality has been regarded by some as the outcome of a sort of sixth sense known as conscience, an innate ability to discern between good and evil. By others, it has been described as a product of the altruistic sympathy which springs from the "parental instinct." Now it would be foolish to deny that there are aspects of our instinctive heritage that are especially significant for morality; yet it is probably better to describe it as a general human capacity or necessary human interest, rooted in the objective fact that the individual cannot effectually accomplish his destiny apart from harmonious and well-regulated social relations. Religion is best regarded from a similar point of view. It has been seriously urged that there is such a thing as a specific religious "instinct"; but the attempt to isolate it has always broken down. It has been pointed out that man's aptitude for religion depends upon his ability to use language and frame abstract concepts, or upon his possession of a "surplusage of responses"[1] which makes the problem of integration and adjustment peculiarly acute for him. These are important observations; but it should be noted that man's aptitude for philosophy and for play depends upon these same conditions. Religion is the most general and most inclusive of human activities, and nothing less than *the whole of human nature, in its relation to the whole universe,* will

demand satisfaction, but in the sense that the whole structure of the human organism, plus that of human society and the universe, makes it necessary to develop these interests if man is to achieve real health of personality. The forms in which they express themselves are as protean as the forms of human society; but while social institutions come and go, these general traits and tendencies of human nature remain relatively more stable—resembling in this respect the structure of the solar system rather than the customs and conventions of society.

[1] The reference is to Leuba, *Psychological Study of Religion,* Chap. III, and Wieman, *The Wrestle of Religion with Truth,* p. 109.

serve as its basis. Religion is man's need of adjusting the various elements of his nature to one another, and of adjusting his whole nature to the whole environment on which he must depend if he is to fulfill that urge toward personal completeness which is the most general and pervasive of all human traits.

If life's fire and driving energy are derived largely from those blind impulsive drives which link us with the other animals, its meaning and destiny are rather to be discerned in those general traits and tendencies which distinguish us from other animals. There is nothing to compel us to follow this higher path; nothing to prove that it is better. If satisfaction of desire be the test of the good life, it must be admitted that a happy, harmonious life can be achieved upon the animal plane of existence. There is a kind of animal contentment—graphically described by Walter Pitkin in his portrait of "The blessed vegetable"—whose perfect state of "adjustment," based on the satisfaction of all the immediate biological cravings, seems to put to shame the uneasy, ever-aspiring, ever-dissatisfied life of the statesman, the artist, and the saint.[1] Yet there are present in most of us vague longings for a more-than-animal existence—longings which do not point to a definite object of desire, nor clearly indicate how they are to be satisfied, but which persistently becloud our happiness so long as we fail to follow their leading. It is possible to lay these yearnings to rest by persistently ignoring them and retreating to the animal plane; but most of us

---

[1] See Walter B. Pitkin's *Psychology of Happiness*. Defining happiness in terms of adjustment between one's desires and one's native equipment, Mr. Pitkin numbers his human vegetable among the "blessed," while he reckons Woodrow Wilson among the "damned." This should be enough to warn one against interpreting the good life as simply the "well-adjusted" life. A man may be adjusted at various levels; and it may be better to be somewhat maladjusted at a high level than to be perfectly adjusted at a low one.

would tacitly agree with the judgment of John Stuart Mill: that it is "better to be a man dissatisfied than a pig satisfied." Once committed to this principle, we are obliged to hold our impulsive nature in check from time to time, while we listen for the still small voice of our higher nature. It is very still and very small; it does not spur us to immediate action with any such imperative urge as that which springs from our specific biological cravings. We cannot long defer action when we crave food and drink; we can and usually do defer action when it is knowledge, or beauty, or wholeness of life that we crave. Many human beings live so close to the verge of starvation and exhaustion that their higher potentialities have little opportunity to unfold; others, living a leisurely and prosperous existence, fail to follow the leading of their higher cravings because, as we say, "They don't know what's the matter with them." They know they are uneasy, and dissatisfied, but they need some one to tell them what it is that they want, and how it is to be found. So indefinite, so hard to read, is the lure of our higher destiny!

St. Augustine provided the perfect formula for all our higher human potentialities when he said: "Thou madest us for Thyself, and our heart is restless until it repose in Thee." We are made for a life of eager intellectual inquiry, a life of creative work and recreative play, a life of æsthetic appreciation and of loyal devotion to great social institutions. We are made for morality and religion, since we are so made that we can find full satisfaction only in harmonious relations with one another in worshipful dependence upon the Determiner of Destiny. Yet we are not *driven* to any of these things with imperative directness; we are simply *restless*, afflicted with a sense of emptiness in our lives, so long as we fail to develop our ideal possibilities as human beings.

2. THE NORMAL LINE OF PERSONAL DEVELOPMENT

Any account of the "normal" development and "ideal" possibilities of human beings must necessarily contain much that is not purely scientific. Science in itself knows nothing of norms and ideals; and the scientific study of human beings as they are cannot be expected to reveal the full range of the possibilities that are open to them. The study of the rudimentary behavior of young infants may reveal much about our physiological equipment, and about our most fundamental emotional responses; but it cannot be expected to reveal the full range of our ideal possibilities. The study of adult human beings, on the other hand, is complicated by the presence of all sorts of hampering conditions, both internal and external, which cramp human nature as in a strait-jacket, and give only a distorted image of its possibilities. We know that there are real natural limitations to our human abilities; the measurable limitations of the idiot, the imbecile, and the moron suggest to us vividly that the normal individual must have his limitations too; yet many of the actual limitations of human life are to be characterized as *unnatural*, abnormal, and unnecessary. Perhaps the best thing to do is to note the conditions under which original human nature appears to grow into the most robust and wholesome forms of character and personality, deriving from the study of this normal line of personal development some approximate notion of the possibilities which human nature might reveal in an ideal environment, under ideal educational conditions. In defining these "ideal" conditions, no assumptions need be made, except the common-sense judgment that health is better than disease, and growth is better than stagnation.

It is convenient to represent human personality as a

composite whole, built up out of simple reflexes by a process of "conditioning," and gradually integrated around some central object of devotion. Gestalt psychology protests that this is an artificial and arbitrary simplification of the facts, and the protest is certainly justified from a philosophical point of view. We may freely grant that the human being is from the very start a kind of *whole*, with a central drive corresponding to what later is called a will; yet it is not such a close-knit whole as it is destined later to become. Moreover, scientific analysis has won all its victories by obeying the motto, "divide and conquer"; and it is doubtless no more misleading to describe character as composed of conditioned reflexes, than to describe molecules as composed of atoms, or atoms of electrons. For simplicity's sake, then, and to avoid lengthy philosophical circumlocutions, we shall follow the usual scientific convention, and describe human personality as a complex aggregate "built up" out of simpler elements. Roughly speaking, we may say that childhood is the period in which the habits which are the elements of character become set in specific lines and patterns by a somewhat unconscious learning process; adolescence is the period in which character goes through a general melting-down and fusing-together, from which there emerges (if the operation is successful) an organized, conscious self, unified around some dominant interest or purpose; while mature life is the period when a man either becomes set in a fixed mold, determined by his specific place in the social order, or else adopts certain principles and methods of self-discipline which keep him malleable, and bring him more and more into harmony with his chosen ideal.

1. *Childhood and habit formation.* The infant is equipped at the start with a number of simple, unlearned reflexes, which furnish ready-made paths for the fundamental biological impulses; but the experiences of life

begin at once to alter both his impulses ("drives") and the paths ("mechanisms") on which they travel.[1] For example, it is natural for him to show symptoms of fear when he hears a loud noise; but by the principle of the "conditioned reflex," his native reaction can be altered until it becomes something entirely different. If the loud noise is regularly accompanied by some other stimulus, such as the presence of a furry animal, the child learns after a while to be afraid of all furry animals, with or without loud noises. Or if the noise be frequently repeated without painful consequences, the child learns to be indifferent to loud noises and may even learn to prefer a noisy city environment to a quiet country environment. Given a few original reflex paths and a few original emotional responses, and the possibilities of combination and recombination inherent in them through conditioning and unconditioning are almost limitless—as anyone may prove with the aid of a little simple arithmetic. The behaviorists, who have taken over the principle of the conditioned reflex from the great Russian psychologist, Pavlow, and made it the basis of their whole psychology, may perhaps be pardoned for uttering shouts of joy and voicing the most sanguine predictions as they contemplate its educational significance.[2]

But we are still only on the threshold of the enchanting world of possibilities which educational psychology opens to our view. The conditioned reflex is only the simplest and most elementary unit of learned behavior. Consider now the new and vaster realm of possibilities which appears when we begin to combine conditioned reflexes with one another to form those larger and more complex units

---

[1] For the distinction between "drive" and "mechanism," see Woodworth, *Dynamic Psychology*, Chap. II.

[2] Cf. Watson, *The Ways of Behaviorism*, p. 33 *et seq*.

which we call *habits*.[1] The principle of habit-formation is simply an expansion of the principle of the conditioned reflex: chain-connections between a given situation and a given reaction tend, we are told, "to grow strong by exercise and satisfying consequences and to grow weak by disuse and annoying consequences."[2] Yet if the principle is simple, the results are complex. The range of possible habitual connections between the simplest reactions of any two-year-old child is so vast as to stagger the imagination.

There are habits of all kinds: habits of perceiving, habits of thought and speech, habits of feeling, habits of acting. All kinds of habits are important as springs of action, for they carry with them, as it were, a charge of energy, a "will of their own," which rushes impulsively into activity unless inhibited by the activity of rival habits which impel in some different direction; but the most important of all habits are those complex habits called *sentiments*. Sentiments are systems or "constellations" of habits in which the central element is an emotional habit, focused upon a particular object in the environment, such as a parent, a pet, an enemy, a city, or even an abstract idea.[3] Each sentiment gives rise to a changing cycle of

---

[1] Cf. Burnham, *The Normal Mind*, pp. 170, 171: "A habit is a system of conditioned reflexes. . . . But we use the word habit in a loose sense referring to many instinctive reactions or to those developed pretty directly from the instinctive reactions as well as to more artificial responses like the conditioned reflexes. Again, habit usually connotes reaction tendencies of a rather stable and permanent character; conditioned reflexes are usually unstable and often temporary in character." Published by D. Appleton and Co., New York. (1924.)

[2] Thorndike, *Educational Psychology* (*Shorter Course*), p. 71. Published by Teachers College, New York.

[3] The concept of the *sentiment* was first elaborated in Shand's *Foundations of Character*, published by the Macmillan Company, New York, (1920), and McDougall's *Social Psychology*. Cognate terms used by other psychologists are *interest, disposition, complex*, and—closest of all—*attitude*. That there is an important shade of difference between the terms *sentiment* and *attitude* is suggested by the related words, *sentimental* and

emotions as the situation varies: "In the love of an object," says Shand, "there is pleasure in presence and desire in absence, hope or despondency in anticipation, fear in the expectation of its loss, injury, or destruction . . . joy in its restoration or improvement, and admiration for its superior quality or excellence."[1] The same applies, *mutatis mutandis*, to negative sentiments like hatred and aversion. Such sentiments, once established, have a tendency to grow in scope and power, putting forth tentacles in all directions, so to speak, and gathering to themselves subsidiary habits and habit-systems like railway corporations competing for a monopoly of transportation. In later childhood, one may discern the signs that a luxuriant crop of sentiments is sprouting and growing, and competing for predominance; and one may already predict with a fair degree of probability what type of character is to emerge; for the trend of a child's character is the resultant of the trends of his dominant sentiments and attitudes. It is his loves and hates that make his little world go round.

Formal education has as yet barely begun to attack the all-important problem of how to furnish children with right motives—that is, with right sentiments and attitudes. Public education is preoccupied with the establishment of memory-patterns and other intellectual habits. Moral education has too often contented itself with the establishment of habits of overt behavior which conform to certain preëstablished norms. Yet the deepest springs of human thought and action are to be found in the region of the emotions; and our emotional nature is sufficiently distinct, physiologically, from our intelligence and our overt

---

attitudinize. A "sentimental" person is one who cherishes an emotional disposition which does not correspond to his overt attitude; an "attitudinizer" is a person who strikes a pose which is meant to deceive people as to his real inner sentiments. We shall use *sentiment* and *attitude* interchangeably, however.

[1] Shand, "Character and the Emotions," *Mind*, N. S. 5 (1896), p. 218.

behavior to give rise to serious complications when no specific attention is paid to it. The physiological basis of emotion is found in the system of the ductless glands and other visceral organs, connected by the autonomic nervous system, whose very name implies its relative autonomy (independence) from the rest of our sensori-motor apparatus. And so while the child is learning to make correct answers and "behave like a good little boy" (on the surface), he may simultaneously be learning to loathe the school and the church and all that they stand for, from the very bottom of his soul—or his viscera, if one prefers to put it that way. Thus it happens that such noble sentiments as the child really acquires are picked up more or less by accident, in the home or on the street. Unofficially, the child is continually forming sentiments; and they tend to conform to the actual (not the professed) sentiments of the social group to which he belongs, provided only that he has learned to take real pride and satisfaction in belonging to that group. Not to be in emotional sympathy with one's own beloved social group is a painful state of affairs; and it takes more than a child's stamina to resist the pet prejudices of his family or his gang. Thus the actual sentiments of our imperfect social order tend to perpetuate themselves by a process of suggestion, and idealists who try to change them are put off with lip-service and outward conformity. When moralists come to understand as much psychology as advertisers and war propagandists, and begin to "make goodness attractive," then, perhaps, they will begin to realize the immense possibilities for good that are inherent in the process of emotional conditioning.

2. *Adolescence and the birth of the organized self.* It would be incorrect, of course, to give the impression that the self was born all at once. Throughout childhood, the elements of character are becoming more and more firmly

knit and the sense of individuality is being strengthened by frequent collision with other individualities. The tiny baby cannot distinguish between his own toes and other objects in his environment; but it is not many years before he begins to distinguish himself and his possessions from all mere "yous" and "theys," and to manifest a valiant will of his own when his impulses are thwarted. Psychoanalysts claim that the child's earliest "self-fantasies" influence all his later life. Still, his character remains volatile and unstable—always ready to be led off on a new scent by any stimulus that chances to cross his path of activity—and the highest permanent unity to be discerned in it is what is sometimes called the "behavior-pattern," that is, the habitual way in which the whole character reacts when it finds itself in a new and strange situation. The behavior-pattern is, so to speak, the outward expression of the childish self-fantasy; and it has great importance, for the reason that one tends to revert to it whenever some crisis joggles him out of his maturer habits; but a child with a well-marked behavior-pattern still falls short of conscious, organized selfhood.

The first effect of adolescence tends to be not so much to unify the character as to disrupt such unity as is already attained; not to give the youth a clearer sense of individuality but rather to make him seem a stranger to himself. The ripening of new and potent physiological drives upsets his whole equilibrium, and puts his half-formed character into the melting-pot again. Many a mother who prides herself upon the success with which she has instilled good habits into her small son is dismayed to find, when he turns fourteen, that the fixing of his character has all to be done over again—and this time she cannot do it without his consent. While the ripening of his passional nature enables him to individualize and appreciate other persons as never before, the ripening of his reasoning powers opens to him the whole world of abstract ideas; and between the wonders of the world of persons and the intricacies of the world of ideas he stands reeling and intoxicated. It looks very much like a return to helpless infancy.

Nevertheless, the final outcome of the adolescent crisis in the normal individual is the more or less sudden emergence of unified self-conscious personality. No doubt there are many young people like the coquettish flapper described by Mr. Tarkington in a recent novel,[1] to whom nothing less than tragedy could bring "the birth of an idea" or make her see herself through critical eyes; but it is more normal for youth to be acutely self-conscious, and fill the pages of its diaries with self-analyses and self-denunciations. Now self-criticism implies some ideal or standard of judgment; and it is in fact mainly by means of ideals—generally embodied in particular persons or institutions, and registered in particular decisions—that the unification of personality is achieved. Let us see more precisely how this momentous operation is accomplished.

The child, let us remember, has brought with him into adolescence a miscellaneous collection of habits, gathered into a series of large federations called sentiments, which are only loosely allied with one another by means of a general behavior-pattern. If his education has been bad, his habits and sentiments may be very miscellaneous indeed—so much so that it is hard to see how they can ever be reconciled with one another. If his education has been good, his habits and sentiments will be more harmonious with one another; and yet even in this case, the sovereign self-interest of the individual habits and sentiments constitutes a formidable obstacle to union. It is a law of political science that no sovereign body resigns its sovereignty

---

[1] *Claire Ambler.*

and becomes a member of a super-state without a good deal of internal resistance and external constraint; and the same law holds in, psychology. Were it not for the fact that the whole organism has as its most general tendency an *urge toward completeness*, the situation would be hopeless; and even with the aid of this powerful pressure, the youth must go through veritable birth-pangs before the self can be organized. He needs some new center of sovereignty in his world, some Geneva to which all his sentiments may resign their sovereignty and yield up their powers, with the assurance that no essential rights and interests will be lost in the process of unification; but where is that new center to be found?

Here it is that the rôle of ideals becomes significant. An ideal is a general plan of action which claims to be able, if adopted, to make us happy (i.e., to make us whole) by providing a central purpose through which all[1] our habits and sentiments may harmoniously fulfill themselves, emptying themselves into it like tributaries into a central channel. Many rival ideals urged by rival institutions and movements present themselves to the youth and put in their claims for his allegiance; and he hesitates before them, flirting first with this and then with that, as he flirts with the various maidens among whom he hopes to find the "not impossible She"; but when that ideal presents itself to which his habits and sentiments, taken as a whole,

---

[1] It is a question, of course, whether it is possible or desirable to integrate *"all"* one's impulses about *one* central purpose. Cf. Durant Drake, *The New Morality*, p. 30: "To exclude everything that does not contribute to the realization of one's dominating purpose would be to lose much of the incidental worth of living. . . . To pursue such a plan ruthlessly, without enjoying the many good things of life along the way, whether or not they contribute to the *leit-motif*, is not only to miss much, but is almost sure to lead to depression of spirit and make a man a hard person to live with" (by permission of The Macmillan Company, publishers, New York, 1929). This caution must be remembered whenever the problem of integration recurs. *Play* and *worship* are the two sovereign remedies.

approximately correspond, so that it promises really to satisfy the urge toward wholeness of life, then there is a stirring of that total responsiveness of the whole organism that we call the will—and with a mighty release of pent-up energies the self is born. Since the most ancient times, this crisis has been publicly recognized and celebrated in the form of ritual acts of initiation and confirmation, admitting the youth to the full privileges of the tribe or the church, hitherto enjoyed only by his elders. It is truly what many of these ceremonies symbolically represent it to be: a second birth.

In later adolescence, the birth of independent selfhood finds its consummation in what might be called the cutting of the umbilical cord which has hitherto bound the youth to his home and family. This is a painful and dangerous process. Dependence is more comfortable than independence; and between the clinging of parental affection and the shrinking of the new-born self from the chill of the great outer world, many never reach psychological maturity. Such people remain children all their lives, plaintively crying for some stronger and more competent being (God or man, they care not) to come and cuddle them in his arms. Others, revolting too fiercely against parental authority, assume a chronic attitude of bumptious defiance toward society and the universe, failing to recognize that absolute independence and absolute self-reliance are as impossible for man as for all finite creatures. Normally, however, the youth passes from the narrow environment of the home to the larger environment of college or the business world without experiencing any such violent revulsion; and passes from childish dependence on his parents, *not* into a state of chest-thumping, Henleyan, "captain-of-my-soul" independence, but into a state of manly dependence upon those social and cosmic resources in which the great leaders of the race have always put their reliance. The law of the land, or the principles of reason, or the Will of God now takes the place of parental guidance in the shaping of his character; and he is now an active and critical participant in the shaping process.

3. *Maturity and the education of the will.* If ever we are conscious of the full wealth of possibilities inherent in our human lot, it is at adolescence. It has long been recognized that most momentous issues hang upon the decisions made, the alliances formed at that time. The whole character is in a state of tremulous fluidity, and the slightest jar may precipitate its crystallization. Anyone who remembers his own youth with a fair degree of vividness will recall that all sorts of alternatives seemed open, and it was touch and go which should be chosen. For the youth, nothing seems impossible. He dreams of riding forth across the world at a gallop, to accomplish the most arduous feats single-handed. There is illusion in this, but it is not all illusion. There really is a wide range of alternatives open to him when his character is in this fluid state; and trifling influences may determine whether he is to crystallize into a priest or a burglar.

Once set in its mold, however, character tends to become much less adaptable. The passage from adolescence to maturity is marked by a series of specific decisions— marriage, choice of a vocation, etc.—which finally pigeon-holes the individual in a definite place in the social order, from which a single well-marked groove leads on and on, monotonously. If the problem of adolescence is the problem of achieving freedom from childish dependence, the problem of mature life is the problem of keeping free; that is, of remaining sufficiently critical of self and society so that one does not become the helpless slave of habit and convention, but continues to be conscious of life's unrealized possibilities, and to follow a moving goal in quest of greater fullness of life. This is the real problem of free-will; and theology would do well to eschew all discussion of metaphysical libertarianism and determinism until this practical problem has been faced and solved.

In a sense, of course, the stabilizing of character in mature life represents not a loss but an increase of freedom. We are never so much at the mercy of external circumstance as when we are in a state of indecision; never so free as when we have bound ourselves by a decision. Again, the limitations that we take upon ourselves when we assume some specific place in the social order are not all hampering limitations; in making ourselves the willing servants of society we become masters of circumstance as no solitary Promethean individualist could ever be. Yet no man is really free if he permits the whole of his later life to be determined by his adolescent decisions and the requirements of his chosen calling. He must remain capable of growth, capable of putting himself periodically into the melting-pot again, and coming out with a new will, focused upon new ideals.

How can this be? Can a man turn back the years and become a youth again? Can he by willing change his will, or wipe the slate clean of the results of his previous decisions? There seems to be no direct way of escape from this difficulty; but there is an ancient stratagem by which he may indirectly initiate a change in his own will. It is beautifully stated in one of the wisest books ever written, *The Education of the Will*, by Jules Payot. Payot points out that (ironically enough) we have no direct power over our emotions, which have great power over our actions, and we have direct power over our ideas, which have little power against our emotions. He finds the way out of this *impasse* in the practice of reflective meditation, which consists in holding certain ideas in the mind long enough to enable them to form emotional connections (i.e. to ripen into sentiments) and which tends in this fashion to break up the crust of habit and create a new will. Religious worship, which periodically withdraws the self from the exigencies of daily life and sets it in the presence of the highest idea it is capable of comprehending, accomplishes the same result in a preëminent degree. Some such practice is absolutely necessary, if the self is not to become completely mechanized, and completely mastered by the haphazard stimuli of its environment.

Are there any limits to this process of self-transformation and self-enrichment? Is there any age at which character must irrevocably harden? It used to be supposed that the learning process was confined to childhood and adolescence, and reached an absolute dead-line about the age of twenty-five; but the adult education movement has now demonstrated, both in theory and in practice, that it is possible—not only for the genius but for the average man—to go on learning as long as he lives, and learning more quickly and effectively as he grows older. This applies to the development of character and personality even more clearly than it applies to physical and mental development. With the coming of old age, bodily functions such as sight, hearing, and locomotion begin to be seriously impaired, and mental functions such as memory begin to fail; but there are cases known to all of us in which the growth of personality continued up to the last moment of consciousness, and the radiance of personality was never more brilliant than just before it was extinguished by death.

If we recognize the fundamental fact that personality develops by a process of social osmosis, that the self is at every moment of its existence a function of some particular other self or some particular aspect of its social environment, which communicates its character to the self, directly or inversely, simply by coming to dwell for the time being at the focus of attention,[1] then we must recognize that the development of personality is an essentially endless process; for the richness of our social heritage, embodied in great personalities and institutions, past and present, is an infinite richness, and there is no inherent limitation to the process of development which the self might pursue by setting itself successively in the stimulating presence of one or another aspect of this heritage. Only the accident of death can cut short such a process, when once it is well on its way; and—quite apart from the question of personal immortality, which we are not raising at this point—it is clear that certain great personalities have succeeded in leaping the gap of death itself and projecting their personal influence in ever-widening circles down the stream of time.

3. HUMAN NATURE: ASSET OR LIABILITY?

What, then, shall we conclude as to the potentialities of human nature? Is human nature to be regarded with hostility or with hope? Is it something which must be destroyed and overcome by supernatural influences before man can be restored to his true nature, or something inherently good in its fundamental tendencies? We cannot, of course, assume agreement as to what the "good life" is; but defining it provisionally as the life that is rich and full, free and masterful, harmonious within and without, our answer will be somewhat as follows:

Calvinistic pessimism about human nature is quite unwarranted; but Romantic optimism[2] is just as misleading.

---

[1] I am referring to James Mark Baldwin's "bipolar" theory of the development of personality, so beautifully expressed in the opening chapter of his *Social and Ethical Interpretations*—an old book, but still valid in its main contentions.

[2] As seen, for example, in Rousseau's deification of impulse, or in the contemporary cult of "self-expression."

Human nature is not inherently bad, but it is inherently ambiguous. It does not automatically push toward the goal of the good life; it is caught between the contrary pulls of what Freud calls the "pleasure-principle" and the "reality-principle": the one embodying the native inertia of the organism, the other embodying its native urge toward self-completion; the one leading inward, regressively and contractively, toward a life of cheap and easy satisfactions, on an animal plane of existence, or in a dream-world of wish-fulfillment, while the other leads outward, progressively and expansively, toward a life that is devoted to great and growing ends and in touch with ever-widening circles of reality. On the one hand, it is characteristic of man to seek his satisfactions with the least possible expenditure of effort, and to relax into comfortable inactivity as soon as possible;[1] on the other hand, it is characteristic of him to become restless and maladjusted after a short period of dreamy contemplation or lazy self-gratification. It is hard to say which is more fundamental in human nature: the impulse to save oneself, or the impulse to spend oneself; the impulse to follow the broad and easy path that pleasantly winds its way down to Avernus, or the impulse that leads men to risk and lose their lives in the ascent of Mt. Everest. Both tendencies are present; but we shall assume, from now on, that it is the first tendency which must be inhibited, and the second which must be released, if human nature is to fulfill its ideal possibilities. The pleasure-principle is not evil in itself; but it must be controlled by the reality-principle, and not *vice versa*, if man is to find the way to mental health and self-realization.

On the whole, then, we may conclude that if the facts of psychology tend to discredit the undue pessimism of

---

[1] Cf. the quotation from Dr. Hohman, *infra*, p. 84.

traditional theology and the undue optimism of contemporary "self-expressionists," they tend to justify the attitude which the Founder of Christianity took toward human nature—an attitude which combined the most serious concern over man's actual plight with the most audacious faith in his hidden possibilities. Jesus seems to have perceived that human nature is, as Professor Wieman puts it, "both God-bent and hell-bent, and for the same reason"; and in the face of that tragic paradox he dared to address to weak and willful men what have been called the bravest words ever spoken: "Be ye therefore perfect, even as your Father which is in heaven is perfect." We may well tighten our grip upon his faith as we proceed in our next chapter to examine the symptoms and causes of human ills and perversities.

The method of exact, discriminating diagnosis is now the regular way of dealing with difficulties and failures in every effective form of human endeavor. The mechanic tinkering with a knocking engine, the physician examining an ailing patient, the teacher dealing with a deficient pupil, the juvenile court referee probing into a case of delinquency, all have a direct and effective technique for locating the source of trouble. There seems to be no reason in the nature of the case why the greatest of all failures— failure to achieve one's personal destiny—should not be dealt with by a process of diagnosis at least remotely comparable in skill with the mechanic's skill in automotive diagnosis or the physician's skill in medical diagnosis. Urge, if you will, the complexity and subtlety of man's moral and spiritual nature, as compared with that of his physical organism; you will still find it hard to explain why the minister of religion should look so vague, so helpless and ineffective, when confronted with the brisk precision of other professional men.[1]

Why the contrast? The trouble lies, it seems to me, in the backwardness of theology, which has so far failed to furnish the minister with any adequate general theory of spiritual diagnosis. Such a theory should be based upon a body of exact knowledge concerning the varieties, symptoms, and causes of human ills and perversities, and should

---

[1] This judgment falls more heavily upon the Protestant ministry than upon the Catholic priesthood. It was a sad day for Protestantism when its clergy abandoned the science of casuistry and the art of spiritual guidance, and became mere purveyors of platitudes!

enable the minister to fit his gospel to human needs with precision, as the skilled physician fits his remedy to the disease, and the skilled juvenile court worker "makes the punishment fit the crime." Unfortunately, no such body of exact knowledge yet exists. While medicine and psychiatry list hundreds of specific diseases, each identified by characteristic symptoms, conservative theology still talks about Sin in general, traces it to a single cause (the Fall of Adam) and prescribes a single remedy (the atoning blood of Christ). Liberal theology has departed from this position in theory, but clings to it in practice. Imagine a physician telling his patient that he is afflicted with Disease, or tracing all disease to a single cause, or prescribing in every case one identical panacea! As a matter of fact, theology is still at the stage which is represented in the history of medicine by the theory that all diseases are due to demon possession, and all to be cured by exorcism.

This does not mean that there are no general principles which should govern us in our dealings with spiritual ills, and no general conditions which may be trusted to facilitate their cure. If there were not, we should be in a hopeless plight and there could be no general theory of spiritual ills and their cure. But such a theory, if the example of medicine means anything, needs to be built up inductively, on the basis of a vast number of case-studies, carefully analyzed and classified. As the knowledge of psychology becomes more widespread among the clergy, such case-studies will begin to accumulate; but meanwhile, the theologian will have to approach his problem indirectly, by way of analogy, basing his theory of spiritual diagnosis on those branches of applied science which come closest to his field; notably psychiatry, penology and education. Analogical reasoning of this sort is dangerous; and if we are to escape its dangers, we must begin by discriminating as clearly as we can between that class of human ills and perversities with which the minister of religion is directly concerned, and those with which he is only indirectly concerned. This accomplished, we shall proceed to analyze the symptoms and causes of this type of malady; and shall then discuss the problem of its prevention or cure.

I. THE PLACE OF "SIN" AMONG THE VARIETIES OF HUMAN MISERY

In one sense, religion is concerned with *all* the ills to which our flesh is heir, since its ultimate aim ("Salvation") is to overcome *all* the obstacles that beset the path which leads to the good life. Starvation, disease, and death; vice and crime; war and oppression; failure and disappointment—there is no sort of human ill to which religion is indifferent, and there is no sort of human ill with which religion has not attempted to deal in its own specific way. The prayers and rituals of primitive peoples are designed not merely to "save their souls from sin," but to procure for them, by the aid of the gods, release from all sorts of dangers and disasters: foreign conquest, early death, childlessness, the failure of the crops, the evil machinations of personal enemies, earthquakes, and volcanic eruptions. . . .

We must not criticize our primitive ancestors for conceiving the task of religion on such a broad and generous scale; we have, in fact, a right to demand of a completely adequate religion nothing short of a complete deliverance from all our ills; but experience has taught us that religion cannot attack all forms of ill directly with its own specific technique, which we call worship. In former days, the outburst of an epidemic of disease sent people thronging to the churches, to beseech Almighty God to let the plague pass by. Now, we close the churches, impose a strict quarantine, and make a determined attack upon the

germ-bearing rats or mosquitoes which medical science has
discovered to be the specific source of infection. We do
not—if we are wise—cease to pray about matters of sick-
ness and health; but we have ceased to expect results of
prayer alone. There is no human problem to whose solution religion may not make an important contribution, by
tapping sources of wisdom and courage otherwise inaccessible; but there is just one mighty problem which lies
in religion's own peculiar domain. It is the central and
crucial problem of human life, the problem of "personal
salvation"; and it might be stated in these terms:

How can we make the most of ourselves and the most
of our opportunities? How can we victoriously face life's
crises, and life's drab routine, and all the varying con-
tingencies with which our path is beset? How can we learn
to "carry on," not with *half* the courage and wisdom and
humor and generosity and hopefulness of which we are
capable, but with *all* of it? How can we lift our lives above
listlessness and fearfulness and ingrowing selfishness and
keep them consistently at that higher level? Or to sum
it all up, *How can we live like human beings:* not a
starved, anæmic existence, hardly rising above the vegetative level, but the rich and joyous life of a creature who
is not only a "child of earth," but as the old Orphic saying
has it, "the child of earth and of starry heaven"? This is
the one problem with which religion is prepared to deal
directly; and it is the key to all the rest. "Seek ye first the
kingdom of God, and his righteousness; and all these
things shall be added unto you."

I do not mean to imply that religion is to shut itself
up in its own domain, concentrating its whole attention
upon the pure art of worship for worship's sake; nor do
I mean to imply that ministers of religion are to preach a
"simple gospel" of personal salvation, avoiding all ref-
erences to questions of physical health or economic wel-

fare or social justice or scientific theory. Religion shut up in its own peculiar domain will surely suffocate; and whatever squeezes men's souls or impedes their personal development must be attacked and destroyed in the name of religion. But religion, the Mother of the arts and sciences, is now surrounded by a great family of grown-up offspring, each with a specialized task and a specialized skill of its own; and in relation to all these specialized arts and sciences, religion's rôle is simply to set them problems, to inspire them with fervor for their tasks, and to see that all their labors are coördinated in the interest of human welfare. Once, in medieval Europe, she attempted to tie them all to her ecclesiastical apron-strings and rule them with a heavy hand; they rebelled and won their independence. Now, she no longer attempts to be politician and scientist and economist and physician; when she speaks on these topics, she does not claim to speak with authority. She can rightly claim a respectful hearing only when she points out the bearing of economic conditions or habit-forming drugs or philosophical theories upon her own 'peculiar art and science, wherein she remains supreme: the art and science of the ideal life.

Positively, then, we may define the specific goal of religion as the fostering of the highest health and richest well-being of human personality through its adjustment, in the act of worship, to that on which its being and well-being depend and on which its loyal devotion ought accordingly to be centered. Negatively, this implies that religion is obliged to join in the fight against everything that stands in the way of the harmonious adjustment and full development of personality. But although every sort of human ill stands in the way of religion, there are many forms of human ill which should not be handled directly by the agencies of religion. We must therefore proceed to inquire, *What is that peculiarly religious form of mal-*

ady to which the peculiarly religious term "sin" may properly be applied, and which should therefore be referred for treatment not to the police court or the medical clinic, but directly to the pastor or priest? What is the relation between this peculiarly religious malady and the other forms of human ill?

Dr. Hadfield has contributed greatly to the advancement of our inquiry by discriminating clearly between the group of maladies which falls within the primary domain of religion, and three other closely associated groups which fall within what we may call the "secondary domain" of religion: organic disease, functional nervous disease, and moral disease.[1] His contribution lies chiefly in the invention of the term "moral disease," which applies to a group of disorders resembling organic and nervous disease in their involuntary character, but resembling sin or crime in their manner of expressing themselves. Kleptomania, uncontrollable ill-temper, and certain forms of sexual perversion would be cases in point. A person afflicted with one of these moral diseases can no more help himself than a person afflicted with "St. Vitus' Dance" or hysterical blindness: but *moral diseases are diseases as judged by a standard of conduct; nervous diseases as judged by a standard of individual health.*[2]

There can be no doubt that religious teachers have worked great mischief by treating morally diseased people as if they were sinners—blaming them for their conduct and threatening them with punishment here and hereafter. Blame and punishment may be the means of redeeming a healthy-minded sinner; but they may drive a morally diseased person to despair and suicide.[3] The unfortunate

---

[1] Hadfield, *Psychology and Morals*, Chapter VI. Published by Robert M. McBride & Company, New York.

[2] *Op. cit.*, p. 47.

[3] I do not, of course, mean to imply that responsibility for real, deliberate sin is all to be laid upon the shoulders of the individual sinner

person who is convinced that he has committed the "un-pardonable sin" is usually not a sinner at all, and should not be so treated. He should be sent to a psychiatrist, instead of being solemnly reasoned with by his pastor. Theology would be a far less dismal science today if it were not for the influence of persons like St. Augustine and John Bunyan—"sick souls," as William James rightly called them—whose meticulously accurate observations concerning their own uncontrollable obsessions has been erected into a general theory of the bondage and depravity of the human will. Before the rise of psychiatry, it was excusable to send such persons to jail or to subject them to a determined onslaught of prayer and exhortation. One had to do the best one could; and occasionally a reformation or a conversion really did result. It is noteworthy, however, that those who *did* get well (like St. Augustine and Bunyan) found salvation by themselves without much guidance or oversight; while the case of poor Cowper, who might have been moderately happy if it had not been for the officious services of the Reverend Mr. Newton, is probably more typical! Today, it is nothing less than a sin to subject a morally diseased person to unskilled religious exhortation; and religion must prepare to say good-bye to another one of her former domains, as she has previously done in the case of organic and nervous diseases.

What, then, is sin, and what makes a man a sinner? Dr. Hadfield, speaking from a purely psychological point of view, distinguishes between sin and its closest relative, moral disease, on the ground that sin is willful, controllable, and therefore blameworthy, while moral disease is

himself, nor that the morally diseased person is wholly irresponsible; but there is surely a great difference of degree between the kleptomaniac, who steals articles he does not need because of an irresistible impulse to steal, and the ordinary thief, who steals systematically with a view to profit.

"undesired, uncontrollable, and its cause . . . unrecognized." Sin is due to "wrong sentiments"; moral disease, to "morbid complexes."[1] This is a helpful distinction, and suggests at least one of the major criteria by which sin is to be differentiated from other maladies; namely, that it is *a disorder of the will*. But it is doubtful whether any purely psychological definition of sin could be an adequate definition; for sin is a religious concept, and religion (as we have seen) always involves something more than a psychological adjustment within a man's personality and something more than a merely social adjustment between the individual and his fellow men: it involves an attempt at an adjustment between the tiny, apparently helpless human creature and the vast, mysterious cosmic Reality on which his destiny depends. As it is most difficult (nay, impossible!) to determine the nature of that Reality with perfect precision, and still more difficult to know exactly how to come to terms with it, it is difficult to determine what religion is best and which conception of sin and salvation is nearest the truth; but this ought not to blur the undeniable certainty that Ultimate Reality is precisely what it is, and that for each living creature there is one, and only one, best possible attitude toward Ultimate Reality, which would result in that creature's fullest possible self-realization.

Sin must therefore be distinguished sharply from the *sense* of sin. It is an objective, cosmic maladjustment, *a pathological relationship between man and the source of his well-being*, which subsists whether the sinner is conscious of it or not—just as a man may have a cancer without knowing it. As there are countless ways in which the parts of the physical organism may become diseased, once they fall out of that harmonious coöperation which we call health, so there are countless forms of sin to which a man

---

[1] *Op. cit.*, pp. 48, 49.

may become subject, once he falls out of that perfect attunement to Reality that we call holiness. *Sin is any defect or perversion in a man's purposes, ideals, sentiments, or attitudes which tends to throw him out of harmonious adjustment with the Cosmic Reality on which his well-being depends.* It is not a single entity, to be spelled with a capital S, any more than disease is a single demonic force, to be spelled with a capital D. There is no single stream of Original Sin, flowing on like a hereditary curse from generation to generation; although when sins become embedded in social customs and institutions, they are contagious; and the interrelationship of these organized forces of evil gives them almost the appearance of a unified Kingdom of Evil, under the rule of a Satanic intelligence.[1] The proposition holds in general that *evil is plural*. It could not but be so, since evil is a form of disintegration or disorganization, preying like a parasite upon the unity of the good. Sin, therefore, is a collective term applicable to all disorders of the will which tend to destroy normal harmonious relations between the individual and those cosmic sources of energy and inspiration on which the health and vigor of the higher life depend. Sin isolates the individual, throws him out of connection with life-giving and health-giving influences, builds up a wall of defense about him which protects him against the efforts of those who seek his good, creates friction between him and his neighbors, and ultimately sets him at war with himself.

2. THE SYMPTOMS AND CAUSES OF SIN

It is evident that sin cannot be *absolutely* distinguished from crime, moral disease, or nervous disease; and the symptoms of sin therefore coincide in part with the symp-

---

[1] Rauschenbusch, *Theology for the Social Gospel*, Chap. IX, "The Kingdom of Evil."

toms of all the major ills and perversities, mental and moral. In primitive religion, one could distinguish sharply between sin and crime on the ground that sin was a wrong committed against the gods—as, for example, by failing to make sacrifice duly and correctly—while crime was a wrong committed against one's fellow men. Since religion has become ethical, no such sharp distinction is possible. It is recognized that it is impossible to be in right relations with God without achieving right relations with one's fellow men.[1] On the other hand, it is possible to live a moderately decent and well-adjusted life, so that one never becomes a "case" for the civil or criminal courts, or the social workers, or the psychiatrists, and still to be in a state of sin; that is, to be living according to low or perverted standards, whose immediate effect is to shut out the light of the higher life, and whose ultimate effect is to wreck personality. Such, in various degrees, is the state of most of us a good deal of the time; and the minister who takes this field of the milder disorders of personality for his specialty will not lack occupation! Indeed, it is essential for him to recognize that he is himself exhibiting symptoms of sin, in large areas of his life. When to this we add the fact that sin is often if not always a contributory factor in cases of moral, nervous, and even organic disease, which accordingly cannot be completely or permanently cured without the aid of the minister, we arrive at a conception of the minister's task which is almost staggering. He is not likely to be left idle in the immediate future—even if psychiatry and social case-work should take over large slices of his former domain!

There are many varieties of sin, each with its characteristic symptoms. In time, we may find clergymen special-

[1] Cf. the well-known saying of Jesus: "Leave there thy gift before the altar, and go thy way; first be reconciled to thy brother, and then come and offer thy gift." (Matthew 5:24.)

izing in the diagnosis and treatment of particular kinds of sin, as physicians now specialize in particular kinds of disease. At present, it is sufficient to note the fact that the symptoms of sin manifest themselves in all the major relationships of life—in our individual or "endopsychic" existence, where they appear in the shape of binding habits, conflicts, and weaknesses of all sorts; in our social relationships, where they appear as faults of character ranging from peevishness and lack of consideration for others to downright cruelty and malice; in our cosmic or superhuman relationships, where they appear in the shape of perverted attitudes and beliefs, ranging from ingratitude or sour defiance to a reasoned conviction that "God is on the side of the strongest battalions." Corresponding roughly to these three major spheres of life are three major classes of symptoms, which Professor Wieman characterizes in the following terms: "*social wrongdoing; mental misery* in the form of discouragement, worry, loss of confidence, nervous disorders of all kinds; or else *withdrawal from life*, narrowness, selfishness, meanness, misanthropy, callousness, insensitivity to all the lures that beckon on to fuller experience."[1] Social wrongdoing means that a man is maladjusted to his fellows; mental misery means that he is maladjusted within himself; withdrawal from life means that he has not achieved a right religious adjustment to Ultimate Reality. It is in this third and last sphere that the primary symptoms of sin are to be discerned. The social symptoms of sin are secondary; the endopsychic symptoms are tertiary; a marked development of these secondary and tertiary symptoms indicates an advanced stage of the malady.

There is one special feature of the condition of sin

---

[1] H. N. Wieman, *The Wrestle of Religion With Truth*, p. 112. By permission of The Macmillan Company, publishers, New York, (1927). Italics mine.

which demands special attention, as it seems to underly all the symptoms of sin, whether they take the form of mental misery, social wrongdoing, or impoverished life. The sinner is a[1] *"contractive."* His conduct is dominated by fear, or anger, or some other contractive emotion, which tends to isolate him from his fellow men and from his world and forces him into a self-centered, self-contained existence, cut off from all those nourishing, lubricating, expanding contacts upon which the health of personality depends. Having no center of devotion outside himself, he has likewise no reservoir of energy and inspiration outside himself, and is reduced strictly to his own resources —or so he feels. Of course, no one could live twenty-four hours strictly on his own resources. As we are constantly taking in physiological energy from our physical environment in the shape of oxygen and solar heat and food, so we are constantly absorbing the very stuff of which personality is composed from our social environment and what lies beyond it. The man who cuts himself off, through fear or anger, from normal dependence upon and coöperation with his larger environment becomes tense and convulsive in his behavior. The tension may visibly manifest itself in an anxious wrinkling of the forehead, a hostile, scowling, defensive attitude, or a general condition of muscular contraction extending from head to foot. In extreme cases, there may be functional paralyses and anæsthesias. The specialized symptoms of sin may be seen as more or less successful expedients for carrying on under this fearful handicap; while the sinner's philosophy of life may be seen as an attempt to rationalize and justify this state of affairs, on the principle that nothing better

---

[1] On the contrast between "contractive" and "expansive" attitudes toward life, see Professor Overstreet's *About Ourselves: Psychology for Normal People*, especially Chapter 10. Published by W. W. Norton and Co., New York. (1927.)

is really possible. The symptoms and the philosophy help to perpetuate the condition.[1]

Traditionally, the sinner has been chiefly regarded from the standpoint of his *guilt*. I do not minimize this element in the situation, since I define sin as a disorder of the will, for which, accordingly, a man is always to some degree responsible; but I prefer to look upon the sinner —as Christ did—from the standpoint of his *need*. He is maladjusted, he is miserable, he is sick, and he needs a physician. Our next task is to attempt to discover the causes of his wretched, contractive state.

The general conditions which make sin possible are plain enough. They are the same conditions which make the good life possible. When, in the previous chapter, we were discussing the "ideal possibilities" of human nature, we had our attention focused upon the possibilities for good which open out before the expanding personality at every stage in its development; but we must not overlook the fact that every possibility for good brings with it a corresponding possibility for ill.

Original human nature contains no elements that are wholly bad in themselves, and we may even say that it seems to have been "made" for communication with the Highest; but it contains powerful impulsive drives which easily get out of hand, to the destruction of all harmony of personal development; and those higher and subtler capacities which might become pathways to fullness of

---

[1] We are defining, of course, a "typical" case of sin, which means, of course, a purely imaginary case, in which all the symptoms are ideally clear and unusually acute. Most real sinners have some "saving grace" which makes their condition less miserable than this—and perhaps also less easily curable! A hundred per cent sinner could not endure his condition, and could not be endured by society; he would be obliged to repent; but a "grand old sinner," like the character depicted by George Arliss in Galsworthy's *Old English*, can be proud of himself and win a smiling toleration from society.

life may instead appear in the form of a bitter sense of frustration or a haunting and passionate but futile longing for something just over the horizon, forever eluding pursuit. Again, the process of "conditioning" and habit-formation opens up great possibilities for good; but as Professor Coe reminds us, "the laws of habit-formation are indifferent to social values."[1] Any impulsive action which is carried successfully through to its natural consummation gives a sense of satisfaction to the agent, and tends to become habitual; thus unless deliberate steps are taken by parents or teachers to attach painful consequences to cruel actions, habits of cruelty may easily be formed by young children. Adolescence, with its great upheaval of personality and its passionate idealistic attachments, offers great opportunities for the achievement of fullness of life; but it is easy to form degrading attachments and false ideals. Society, one might suppose, would see to it that antisocial habits and ideals were discouraged in the individual; and so it does; but society itself is partly corrupt and may seduce the individual to his own undoing. Personal influence and social pressure are the most powerful engines we possess for the molding of good character; but they, too, are ambiguous in their effect, and may become sources of perversion.

Thus, all along the line, the capacities and facilities which distinguish man from the animals and constitute his claim to supreme dignity—from learning capacity and linguistic ability to radio and moving pictures—all these capacities and facilities are precisely what make man the supreme sinner. When man starts to go wrong he shows himself a genius at it. For the squalid degradation of his organized and commercialized vices, for the hectic

---

[1] *Social Theory of Religious Education*, p. 165. Published by Charles Scribner's Sons, New York. The whole chapter gives an excellent account of the empirical conditions under which sin arises.

glamour of his follies, for the fiendish ingenuity of his cruelties, for the picturesque elaboration of his profanity and his obscenity, for the grotesque majesty of his insane delusions and obsessions, man stands alone. To call man "brutish" when he falls is to slander the "brutes." If there be some fallen angel, some Miltonic Satan, more godlike in his capacities than man, then he alone is capable of surpassing man in the dark splendor of his iniquities, and to him alone must man the sinner doff his hat.

Since the symptoms of sin are largely identical with the symptoms of mental disease, moral disease, and delinquency, we may assume that the causes are largely identical and avail ourselves of the results of the extensive studies which are being made in these neighboring fields. Setting aside for other specialists the major psychoses and the graver degrees of crime, let us study the causes of those mental and moral perversions which come closest to the minister's field: the common neuroses and the common forms of juvenile delinquency.

There are two well-marked types of neurosis: hysteria and psychasthenia. Both exhibit a deficiency of "drive" or "will-power," which causes the patient to "flee from reality" and dodge some difficult situation, instead of facing it and mastering its difficulties. The symptoms of both can be explained as "substitute reactions," taking the place of real adjustment to the situation, concealing from the patient (and often from the bystander as well) the real nature of his failure.

The one type of neurotic individual, the hysteric, adjusts himself to his lack of motive force by narrowing the field of his activity, so remaining intense in a narrow field, dissociated or split off from the rest of his life, to which he becomes indifferent. . . . The psychasthenic, on the contrary, is diffuse rather than narrow. He tries to keep hold of everything, but has not force enough to make anything go properly. He doubts, hesitates, repeats, ruminates, feels unreal and unsure of himself.[1]

We owe this distinction between hysteria and psychasthenia to Pierre Janet, who ascribes the patient's difficulty to a lack of energy, a deficiency of "psychological tension," which is ultimately traceable to a deficiency in a man's physiological heritage, for which he is no more to blame than he would be for a weak heart or poor eyesight. That a deficiency of drive is present is clear, but it is doubtful whether it should be referred in most cases to native physiological weakness. The fact that a psychasthenic can sometimes be cured of his fumbling ineffectiveness by falling in love, or enlisting in the army, or in general by finding some interest or purpose in life to mobilize his energies and "get his mind off himself," suggests that the trouble is not so much with his native equipment as with the lack of a stimulating motive about which his personality might be organized. The school of Freud suggests another important hypothesis concerning the underlying cause of deficient energy: it may be due to a conflict between some powerful drive and some "repressing" tendency, which wastes the patient's native energy in useless friction, and gives rise at the point of friction to what is called a "complex"—a sort of psychological analogue to an infected sinus or an ulcerated tooth, inaccessible to the consciousness of the patient, manifesting its presence only in bad dreams, obsessions, and other neurotic symptoms, and discoverable only by skillful psychoanalytical probing. Such complexes are generally traceable to some emotional shock experienced in early childhood or to some tragic frustration which the individual could neither conquer nor accept. In many neurotic cases there may be found *both* a lack of interests and purposes, making for general lack of

---

[1] Woodworth, *Dynamic Psychology*, p. 164. Published by Columbia University Press, New York. (1918.)

drive, *and* a crippling complex of some sort, wasting the patient's already deficient stock of energy in futile "stewing." An individual of this sort makes a mountain out of a molehill; his engine chokes and dies, and his car stalls hopelessly upon every little rise in the road which a normal individual would swiftly surmount by stepping on the accelerator.

The psychology of the delinquent is quite different from that of the neurotic individual. There are, to be sure, many border-cases, such as those collected and analyzed in Dr. Healy's *Mental Conflict and Misconduct*, where stealing, truancy, and other forms of juvenile delinquency are traced to genuine neurotic complexes, due to unfortunate sex experiences or other emotional shocks. Dr. Healy's cases must, however, be regarded as relatively exceptional, and belong in the category of "moral disease" rather than in that of delinquency. The typical delinquent child is thoroughly normal in his mental processes; his "conflict" is not with himself, but with certain conditions in his home, school, or community which have prevented him from expressing his normal impulses in normal ways. In that very enthralling autobiography, *You Can't Win*, by "Jack Black," there is presented the picture of a thoroughly normal and wholesome boy, neglected and misunderstood by his father, led by loyalty and generosity and a wholesome love of adventure into a chain of events which took him by slow degrees and almost by accident into a life of vagrancy, and finally into a career of professional burglary. Dr. Miriam Van Waters[1] of the Los Angeles Juvenile Court summarizes the attitude of the typical delinquent, and its causes, in very telling words:

---

[1] *Youth in Conflict*, pp. 149, 150, 152. Published by *The New Republic*, New York. (1925.)

The attitude of delinquency assumed by children is a compound of insolence, bravado, scorn, poise, wit, youthful cunning and resourcefulness in lying, impossible to describe unless witnessed. . . . Adult criminals would not dare to taunt or to defy the judge in this manner. Youth has more courage, less prudence. . . .

When the delinquent attitude is studied it is shown to be a defense-reaction built up of habits long used in self-protection. It is a natural product of a series of more or less "trifling" experiences with adults who have confronted, mocked, insulted, hunted, or set them apart. . . .

A symposium was held in the public schools on the question: "Why do children lie?"

The most revealing, the most deeply scientific answer was: "In order to get along with adults."

Although the attitude of the neurotic and the attitude of the delinquent are thus fundamentally different, the psychological principle underlying the formation of these diverse attitudes is the same. "As a broad principle it can be said that the general tendency of the organism is to avoid unpleasant stimuli and to get comfortable again as soon as possible."[1] This tendency easily leads to the formation of unwholesome attitudes. A child who is permitted to run away from all painful situations; a child whose parents give in to him whenever he cries and rages; a child who is persistently praised or punished, pitied or snubbed—all such children develop characteristic attitudes and behavior patterns which are the direct and inevitable consequence of the attitudes which their elders take toward them. They develop attitudes toward themselves ranging from strutting pride to cringing inferiority; they develop social attitudes ranging from hypersensi-

---

[1] Dr. Leslie B. Hohman, quoted in Murphy, *Outline of Abnormal Psychology*, p. 254. The whole chapter on "The Formation of Life Patterns" is worthy of careful study. Published by Modern Library. (1929.) (Reprinted from *Mental Hygiene*, vol. xi.)

tiveness to utter callousness; they develop attitudes toward the universe ranging from a feeling that "the world owes them a living" and will pay the debt if cajoled, to a bitter sense that "everything is against them." It is in the home, the school, and the neighborhood that these unfortunate life patterns generally take their rise; and the primary responsibility rests with the parents. It is hard to say which type of parent is the more blameworthy: the coddling parent who reduces his child to a state of helpless dependence, and dooms him to incompetence, or the harsh parent who induces in his child a mood of sullen resentment against society and life in general.

What we have said concerning the causes of neurosis and delinquency applies to the problem of sin. As we have seen, the symptoms of sin may take the form of "mental misery" (neurosis) or "social wrongdoing" (delinquency); or they may take the more subtle and pervasive form of a general "withdrawal from life," springing from a false attitude toward the universe. In dealing with the psychological roots of mental misery and social wrongdoing, we have already given a partial account of the causes of sin. We may now add that we have, in the conditioning process which goes on within the family circle in the earliest years of childhood, the key to the third class of symptoms also. Our attitudes toward God and the world grow out of our attitudes toward the family group. If an attitude of clinging dependence upon parental care is encouraged in the child, he will expect God to take care of him in the same fashion when he gets out into the world; and his trust is likely to be turned into querulousness when the heavens do not stoop at his command. If morals are taught in the family by the method of harsh censure, the child will acquire a positive distaste for moral goodness; and his attitude toward God, conceived as the supreme enforcer of moral sanctions, will partake of

Satanic rebelliousness. Josiah Royce, in his memorable lecture on "The Moral Burden of the Individual,"[1] has shown clearly how ordinary methods of moral discipline tend to inspire in the child not only a sporadic tendency to "kick over the traces" and offend the conventional order, but a deep-seated hatred of moral goodness as such, which may finally rise to the point where God, and society, and all forms of authority are both *recognized as good* and *detested*! "My will, not thine, be done," says the sinner; and though he dimly recognizes that he is fighting against his own good, as well as the common good, he persists in his contractive attitude of rebellion and remains inaccessible to all attempts at a friendly approach. The psychological genesis of such an attitude may perhaps be suggested by such observations as the following:

I know a little girl who responds quite automatically to any move on the part of her parents, even when it is for the purpose of doing what the child wants, with a rage-driven petulance. Putting on her coat so that she may go to the park, washing her hands so that she may eat candy, putting her on her chair to read her favorite book, all call forth shrieking. She has had fixed for her this primary pattern of rage, built on her instinctive avoidance of movement restriction, and she has been so securely conditioned that she cannot be released. She now responds with rage to the very things she wants.[2]

Perhaps if Dante had been a student of modern psychology, he might have had more sympathy for the rebels and traitors whom he placed in the lowest circles of the Inferno. He could more easily forgive the sins of the flesh, for he appreciated how easily habit, based on powerful impulse, may make slaves of us all; but he failed to appreciate how attitudes of rebelliousness or vindictive-

---

[1] Royce, *The Problem of Christianity*, Vol. I, Lecture III.

[2] Dr. Leslie Hohman, in Murphy, *op. cit.*, pp. 258, 259. Quoted by permission of the editors of *Mental Hygiene*.

ness may be formed in the home and the school by the self-same process. The cruel or malicious person is as much a slave, and as much to be pitied, as the drunkard or the adulterer. His life is just as "impoverished" as that of the timorous weakling, who shrinks from all human contacts.

3. THE CURE OF SIN

As the symptoms and causes of sin were found to be closely related to the symptoms of neurosis and delinquency, so the techniques which the social case-worker and psychiatrist employ will be found to be full of suggestion for the specialist in the "cure of souls."

In all cases, whether of neurosis or of delinquency, it is customary for case-workers to recommend a thorough medical examination as the first prerequisite to successful treatment. It would be foolish to begin by probing for a psychological complex when a medical examination might reveal that bad teeth and chronic autointoxication were at the root of the trouble. Another prerequisite in scientific case-work is an intelligence test; a third is a general study of the social background of the individual in question, including his family tree, his childhood environment, and the conditions under which he is living at present. The clergyman who really wishes to do his best for the more perplexing cases that he encounters should likewise begin by assuring himself that he is not dealing with a case of organic disease, mental deficiency, or mental disease; and he should endeavor to get a firm grip upon the environmental factors which make each case individual.

a. THE CURE OF MENTAL MISERY

The aim of the psychiatrist dealing with a neurotic patient is, in a word, to unify his patient's personality about some dominant interest or motive which is powerful enough to "take him out of himself"—out of his morbid inner world of fantasies and fears and resentments into the healthy outer world of active affairs. Perhaps the simplest of all the methods of psychotherapy, which is called the "work cure," ably advocated by Dr. R. C. Cabot, of Boston, is based directly upon this view of the matter. It is particularly successful in mild cases of psychasthenia or neurasthenia, where the patient's "tired feeling" and his general shrinking from decisive action have no real physiological foundation and no morbid psychological basis, but are due to a general lack of purpose and responsibility in life, and an excess of leisure.[1] Nothing does so much good to this type of patient as to set him (or more probably her) at some definite task, preferably manual at first ("occupational therapy"), which yields some tangible and worthful result and gives a sense of achievement. The patient can then be led from task to task until he finds some really satisfactory vocation in life, which enables him to proceed thenceforth "under his own steam."

The "work cure" is valuable as a *factor* in all therapeutic techniques; but it is usually insufficient by itself, for the patient is usually subject to powerful inhibitions and tensions from which he must be released before he is free to pursue any positive line of action. It is not enough to persuade him of the right path to pursue; it is neces-

---

[1] Burnham, *The Normal Mind*, p. 636, gives the following amusing case: "At a recent term of the court in a Massachusetts district it is said that one of the jurors drawn applied to Judge Webster Thayer to be excused on the ground of serious nervous breakdown. The judge thought the man looked better than the report would indicate, and refused to excuse him. As a result he was forced to serve for two weeks, and the result was so beneficial that when discharged he was a different man physically and mentally. He had gained eight pounds, and his nervous condition was so improved that the judge was said to be ready to recommend jury service as a remedy for nervous breakdown." Published by D. Appleton and Co., New York. (1924.)

sary to strike off his shackles and give him a gentle shove in the right direction by means of *suggestion*.

Before he can get "out of himself," and express his energies in health-giving activity, the patient must in such cases first *relax*, physically and mentally—relax all those conflicting tensions by which his powers are imprisoned and inhibited. The mere act of relaxation, mentally controlled by the patient under the skilled direction of the psychiatrist, is sometimes sufficient to effect a cure, since it breaks down the sense of insuperable barriers and convinces the patient that, at least in this particular case, while endeavoring to relax, he can exercise control over his own states of mind. If he can make himself relax, why can he not overcome his fears and change his habits?[1] Courtenay Baylor, of the Emmanuel Movement, has been particularly successful with this technique; he has cured a functional paralysis at the first interview, and given a man permanent victory over a long-standing habit of alcoholism, simply by the skillful use of relaxing exercises.[2]

Usually, however, the patient cannot escape from himself without assistance, even after the bars of inhibition have been taken down by the act of relaxation. He is ready and willing to be led or pushed; and since the relaxing exercises have put him into a receptive, hypnoidal state, he accepts without much question the advice of the psychiatrist, toward whom he is apt to develop that trustful, grateful, dependent attitude that is known as a *transference*. Advice given under these conditions of emotional attachment is more than persuasion; it is called *suggestion*, and has the effect of command—especially when delivered

[1] Hydrotherapy (i.e., the use of warm baths) is a useful adjunct to psychotherapy, since it induces relaxation. It is inferior to autosuggestive relaxation, however, since it does not give the patient a sense of his power of self-control.

[2] See Baylor, *Remaking a Man*, pp. 71-96 (Cases A, B, C).

in a calm, confident tone of voice, in the form of a prediction of future conduct. The cure is not complete, however, until this relation of dependence between physician and patient is gradually broken, and the patient does of his own volition, for good and sufficient reasons, what he first learned to do by force of suggestion.

Practically all the familiar symptoms of neurosis will yield to this method of relaxation and suggestion; and it constitutes the whole technique of some psychiatrists.[1] The trouble is that symptoms removed by suggestion often recur later on, either in the same form or in some equally distressing form. It is evident that in such cases the underlying causes of the symptoms have not yet been destroyed, and deep drilling seems to be in order. It is for such cases that the technique of psychoanalysis, the most elaborate of psychotherapeutic methods, has been devised. Stripped of its Freudian mysteries, and simply stated, it consists of the following steps:

1. *Relaxation.* As in the technique of suggestion, it is first of all necessary to get the patient into a passive, trustful, effortless state of body and mind, which may approach the verge of hypnosis. A whirring fan or some other soothing, monotonous sound may facilitate this.

2. *Analysis, or probing for the complex.* The patient's memory is explored in search of the original incident which occasioned the emotional shock which is assumed to be at the root of the trouble. Word-associations, and free, un-

---

[1] There is some confusion in the use of the terms psychiatry, psychotherapy, psychoanalysis, and cognate terms. Some writers draw a contrast between the *psychiatrist*, whose interest is purely in diagnosis, and the *psychotherapist* or *psychoanalyst*, whose interest is in therapeutics. Others distinguish between the two on purely sectarian lines: the psychiatrist being non-Freudian, the psychoanalyst being at least slightly tainted with Freudianism! I am using the terms *psychiatrist* and *psychiatry* in a more inclusive sense, applying both to diagnosis and to treatment, both to Freudians and to non-Freudians.

critical associations of ideas are used as clues. Whenever undue emotion is exhibited, the analyst feels he is getting "hot"; but the patient is not urged to make any *effort* to remember, since the most troublesome memories are precisely those which have been forcibly forgotten, as too horrible or disgusting to be faced. Such memories have to be coaxed out of their lairs by strategy and indirection; but tactful questioning will finally locate them.

3. *Abreaction, or draining off the complex.* The patient is encouraged to rehearse the forgotten incident in all its details, bring it back to consciousness as fully as possible and tell the physician all about it. The poisonous and festering emotions which have been accumulated about it are thus drained off, as one drains off an ulcer; and the bare fact is left—often a trifling and unimposing fact, when viewed from the perspective of the adult. The mature understanding of the forgotten incident and its effect upon one's later history sometimes closes the case. Usually, however, a further step is necessary.

4. *Reëducation, or disposing of the elements of the complex.* This is sometimes divided into *reassociation* and *sublimation.* Reassociation takes the incident which was the nucleus of the complex and associates it, by the familiar principle of the conditioned reflex, with wholesome instead of unwholesome emotions. Sublimation takes the desire or the impulse whose frustration made the incident so painful and finds for it some normal outlet in activity, so that its energies are released instead of being repressed. At this stage, as at the first, the technique of psychoanalysis coincides with the technique of suggestion, and its general effect is identical with that of the "work cure": it takes the individual out of himself and enables him to devote himself to some worthful activity. Only the second and third stages of psychoanalysis are peculiar to this technique.

b. THE CURE OF SOCIAL WRONGDOING

Since the coming of the psychiatrically trained social case-worker, it is hard to draw a sharp line between the methods used in the cure of the neuroses and those which are used in the treatment of delinquency. The case-worker has all the psychiatrists' tools and tricks at his disposal, and occasionally makes use of all of them. In dealing with mentally normal delinquents, however, he finds himself using a technique which is *analogous to* rather than identical with psychiatry. The analogy and the difference both stand forth clearly in Miss Van Waters' account of her method, which she summarizes under four heads:[1]

1. *"Insight."* This corresponds to the first three stages in psychoanalysis, when the causes of the patient's trouble are located through analysis and he is led to an understanding of his own case. The difference is that the case-worker ranges more widely than the psychiatrist in his search for causes. The conflict he is seeking to resolve is not merely a mental but a social conflict; and he accordingly explores not only the mind of the delinquent, but his whole social background. When he has sympathetically understood the motives which have driven the delinquent into trouble, and the social conditions which have led these motives to express themselves in undesirable ways, he shares his understanding of the case with the delinquent himself—and often gets a reaction of insight, gratitude, and energetic resolution parallel in its intensity to the "blowing off of steam" which occurs in "abreaction":

"Gee! I'll never do *that* again. I see it in a new light now; wait till I get out of here, you'll see I'll make good."[2]

2. *"Transference."* In psychiatry, this term applies to

---

[1] *Youth in Conflict*, pp. 178-187.

[2] *Ibid.*, p. 181.

an emotional attachment between patient and physician. In social case-work, it applies to any sort of emotional attachment which gives the delinquent some object of love and devotion beyond himself. Like "sublimation," it gives his personality a positive set toward mental and moral health, which mere insight into the causes of his difficulty cannot give by itself.

3. "*Development of personality* (growth of skill, clear ideas of new behavior-goals, and the *wish* for social esteem)." The analogy to the "work cure" is very evident here. Nothing develops personality like success in a task. It equips the individual with self-confidence, and prepares him for social relationships.

4. "*Development of new social relationships.*" Here the border-line between psychiatry and social work is clearly passed. The psychiatrist is content with creating harmonious patterns in the individual personality; the social worker endeavors to create harmonious patterns in and between social groups. This is even more marked in "social group-work" than in social case-work; here the effort is not merely to restore the delinquent individual to a condition of normal (average) social adjustment, so that he ceases to be a "case"; the effort is to bring out all his latent potentialities through intimate coöperative fellowship.

It is evident that the pastor, without overstepping the bounds which mark off his proper professional field from that of psychiatry and social case-work, can learn much from the methods that are employed in dealing with neurotics and delinquents. Religious maladjustment often takes forms that approximate to the neurotic or delinquent pattern. For this reason, it is desirable that *some* pastors should specialize in psychiatry or the study of delinquency, and render an unusual type of service, perhaps connected with hospitals, asylums, and prisons. For the average pastor, however, such specialization is unnecessary and undesirable. What he needs is just enough acquaintance with the symptoms of mental disease to enable him to distinguish normal from abnormal cases; just enough acquaintance with the technique of psychotherapy and social case-work to enable him to utilize certain broad general principles of mental and social hygiene in dealing with ordinary people. He should not attempt an amateur psychoanalysis of serious mental disorders, nor should he attempt perilous experiments in suggestion and hypnosis; but he may very properly use the general method of "talking things over and talking them out,"[1] of which psychoanalysis is a special application, and it is his main business to "take people out of themselves" by presenting aims and ideals that are fitted to mobilize their energies. When he meets with the "attitude of delinquency," he is as able as anyone (once he understands the principle of the thing) to pierce behind the external appearance of bravado to the frustrated motives which are at the root of the trouble and, by sympathetic understanding of these motives, to release the perverted energies of rebellious souls into more wholesome channels.

C. THE CURE OF SIN ITSELF

In an unpublished series of lectures on "Redemption," delivered some years ago at Union Theological Seminary, New York, George Herbert Palmer classified the agencies making for the cure of sin under three main headings:[2]

1. *"Agencies of Restraint."* These are necessary when the sinner is not disposed to recognize his sin; when he rebels against the moral world, and uses its orderly ar-

---

[1] See Mackenzie, *Souls in the Making*, p. 30.

[2] The following three paragraphs, without aiming at literal fidelity, contain much of the substance of these lectures. I am very grateful to Professor Palmer for permission to use this material.

rangements for his individual advantage, to the detriment of others. Here is the legitimate place of blame, punishment, and even—in extreme cases—of violent coercion. When society sends a man to prison, it says to him, in effect, "You want an isolated life, do you? Very well, you shall have it!" All such measures tend to "arrest" the sinner in his career, and make him realize his *actual smallness* and worthlessness. By themselves, however, they cannot redeem him; they may only harden him in his rebellious attitude unless he is simultaneously made conscious of his *possible largeness*.

2. *"Agencies of Enlargement."* These might be summarized under the general head of "new environmental influences." The measures to be employed will vary with the condition to be remedied. The sinner may be in such a state that he is incapable at first of responding to moral influences; it is necessary, then, to begin by improving his physical health, his social attachments, his economic status. In and through these more concrete benefits, there must be conveyed to him the sense that there are those who care for him and believe in him, and expect eventually to be able to approve of him. The sense of being cared for and the hope of social approval—here is the greatest of all the agencies of enlargement. Formal instruction in the good life is needed to clinch the gains of habit and unconscious imitation; but it should come only after the sinner's coöperation has been secured; and even then, example should come before precept.

3. *"Agencies of Consecration."* Up to this point, the sinner's mind has been turned selfward; he has been concerned with the saving of his own soul. But no man is truly redeemed until he becomes a redeemer—until he finds some object of devotion beyond himself, for the sake of which he is ready to forget himself. Love of some individual person will probably be the turning-point for

him; loving is infinitely superior to *being* loved, as an agency of redemption. Next above private affection on the ladder of ascent come professional responsibility and public spirit, which broaden the scope of a man's disinterested love until it includes the community, the nation, and at length all humanity. Last of all—a stage which some never reach—comes the recognition that the moral order against which the sinner had rebelled, and which he now seeks to obey, is more than human in its basis and offers a field for loyal service that is literally universal and endless in its scope. "When we recognize Duty as not arbitrary and mechanical, but friendly, we believe in God."

Religion has often aimed at carrying the sinner suddenly, at a bound, from the depths of his impotence and degradation to the heights of God; and the amazing conversions which sometimes occur in rescue missions and revival meetings most plainly give the lie to those who claim that this is impossible. When deep human need meets with deep religious faith and Christlike compassion, it is rash to say what may not occur. But ordinarily, the cure of sin is a gradual and difficult process, like the cure of insanity and crime. The religious worker must be prepared to exercise patience and must master the details of his case with the same care that is required of the psychiatrist and the social case-worker.

A comparison of the three techniques which have been successively reviewed will reveal the fact that the same general principles govern the cure of neurosis, the cure of delinquency, and the cure of sin. Insight, sympathy, and the presentation of a compelling object of devotion are in all three cases essential. But the cure of sin is a more difficult and more comprehensive undertaking than the cure of neurosis or delinquency. Really to be cured of his sin, a man must incidentally be relieved of his mental miseries and abandon his social wrongdoings; but he may be cured of his neurotic and delinquent tendencies and still remain a sinner. Only a life alternating perpetually between discerning worship of the Supreme Object of Devotion, and loyal service of the ends which such worship revealed, could be wholly without sin. To rise at least occasionally to that transcendent level of existence is the goal of the religious life.

4. RELIGION AND MENTAL HYGIENE

We are now in a position to face once more, with a broader perspective and a more adequate body of information, the question with which Part I of this book is chiefly concerned: *What is the place of religion among the agencies making for the alleviation of human ills and perversities, and (more positively) for the full and healthful development of human personality?*

As we saw in the earlier part of this chapter, religion can no longer be regarded as a cure-all. One by one, the agencies of human betterment—medicine, education, social work, psychiatry, and all the rest—have won their independence of religion, and developed specialized techniques of their own. Yet it is noteworthy that, of recent years, these highly diversified agencies have been drawing closer together, and becoming conscious of their common aims. Especially since the rise of the Mental Hygiene Movement, artificial barriers and distinctions have been crumbling with amazing rapidity. Starting in 1908 with a vigorous attack upon the abuses then prevalent in the care of the insane,[1] it has rapidly extended the scope of its program, until its attack has come to bear upon moral and social as well as mental disorders, and its emphasis is upon prevention rather than cure. Medicine, education, psychol-

---

[1] See the article entitled "Twenty Years of the Mental Hygiene Movement," in *Mental Hygiene* for July, 1929.

ogy, psychiatry, criminology, social work, social science, and other formerly separate enterprises have coalesced in this movement into one great army, bent upon a single objective: the scientific study and elimination of every form of human maladjustment, and the furthering of the highest possible development of human personality. In the presence of this remarkable tendency, the problem of the function of religion in relation to the whole quest of human happiness can be stated in concrete terms: *What is the place of religion in the Mental Hygiene Movement?*

There are some who would answer, "No place at all. Religion has now been replaced by more effective agencies. Psychiatry and psychotherapy in particular (as the literal meaning of both words[1] might well suggest) have now undertaken to perform, in truly scientific and reliable fashion, the very work which the pastor and the priest have been attempting to perform in an ignorant and blundering fashion." No less a personage than Pierre Janet, the dean of modern scientific psychotherapists, the pupil of Charcot and the teacher of Freud, has lent his authority to this view. In the concluding lecture of a course on the psychology of religion, delivered at the Collège de France in 1921-22, he went so far as to predict that as psychotherapy advanced, religion would gradually disappear, because it would no longer be needed.[2]

There is much to give support to this view, radical as it sounds. The similarity of the methods traditionally employed by pastors and priests, and those employed today by psychotherapists and psychoanalysts, is striking at many points. The analogy between confession and "abreaction," repentance and "insight," conversion and "integration,"

---

[1] Psych-iatry and psycho-therapy both mean, literally, "cure of souls."

[2] Cf. my report of these lectures in the *American Journal of Psychology* for January, 1924, and my discussion of this view in *Religious Education*, January, 1928.

sanctification and "reëducation," is too close to be accidental. Many of the specialized psychotherapeutic techniques such as "work cure," "faith cure," etc., were first discovered by religion. William James's famous definition of religious conversion, as "the process, gradual or sudden, by which a self hitherto divided, and consciously wrong, inferior and unhappy, becomes unified and consciously right, superior and happy," would serve just as well as a definition of the process through which psychotherapists and psychoanalysts hope to assist their patients; and there can be no doubt that many people are getting more help along these lines from professional psychiatrists than they could get from religious evangelists.

Yet it is doubtful whether psychiatry—sharing with religion as it does the ideal of helping men to achieve a perfectly integrated, well-adjusted and highly developed personality—is competent, by itself, to carry men all the way to this goal. Pierre Janet himself admits that the psychotherapist has neither the "time nor the means" to take the patient who comes to him demanding treatment for some twitching of the face or other nervous symptom, and "alter his will as a whole," even though that, fundamentally, is what he needs, and "such a transformation should have the happiest effects on the pathological symptoms."[1] Gardner Murphy, in his *Outline of Abnormal Psychology*,[2] suggests that while there is an almost irresistible temptation for the psychiatrist to "give the patient the psychiatrist's own system of values," the temptation should be resisted; for "we know altogether too little about the meaning of life to try to fit people to a given norm." Dr. Oliver, who approaches the problem both as

[1] *Principles of Psychotherapy*, pp. 111-112. Quoted in Wieman, *The Wrestle of Religion with Truth*, pp. 120-121.
[2] Page 315.

a priest and as a psychiatrist, expresses himself, rather picturesquely, as follows:

The psychiatrist . . . has to exorcise the devils of fear, of inhibition, of obsession; the lesser demons of worry, and tenseness, and self-pity. Then, having got the devils out of the house of the mind, he must do something at least to clean the house. And after cleaning it, he has got to furnish it with new habits of thought, new interests, new ambitions. But here his work stops. He has nothing to say as to what kind of people are to be, by the owner, invited to enter in and dwell there. . . . Plenty of psychiatrists burn their own fingers in such attempts. I have learned to avoid them. For this particular part of the job belongs not to the specialist in mental diseases, but to the specialist in human souls, to the minister or to the priest.[1]

To summarize the view of the relation of religion to psychiatry, which emerges from such statements as these, we might say that while religion cannot possibly take the place of psychiatry as a means of clearing up specific pathological conditions which block the normal development of personality, psychiatry cannot possibly take the place of religion as an agency for stimulating man's deepest potentialities and awakening his highest aspirations. "Psychiatry looks at a man analytically; religion looks at him synthetically. Psychiatry takes him to pieces, removes his inhibiting conflicts and complexes, oils his works, and then, unless guided by religion, puts him together again without giving him a new mainspring, or, at best, with an ordinary standardized mainspring: ambition, or the love of a woman, or the desire to be comfortable in one's old age. Religion takes him into the presence of what is noblest and most awe-inspiring, kindles in him new loyalties, reverences, purposes and enthusiasms, adjusts him to what is deepest in the nature of the universe, and so re-

[1] Oliver, *Foursquare*, p. 174. By permission of The Macmillan Company, publishers.

leases floods of warm energy within him, which often melt down and sweep away those obstructions and inhibitions which psychiatry removes by more mechanical methods."[1]

Here, in the positive promotion of mental and moral health, is religion's great contribution to the task of mental hygiene; and one finds this contribution more and more clearly recognized by the leaders of the movement. In Dr. Burnham's classical exposition of the general principles of positive and preventive mental hygiene,[2] religion is given a place of central importance. The first of his twelve principles of mental health is "Sufficient unto the day is the evil thereof"—religious trust. The eleventh is the necessity of a normal sense of religious dependence. The most fundamental emphasis throughout the book is the need of a supreme object of devotion to "take a man out of himself," mobilize his energies, and unify his life. Dr. R. C. Cabot's four principles of mental hygiene—Work, Play, Love, Worship[3]—might be taken as a fair summary of Dr. Burnham's twelve; while if one prefers the still simpler formula to which other writers on mental hygiene have given currency—"stimulus plus security"—in either case, the contribution of religion to mental health is obvious.

If, as current developments lead one to suspect, religion is shortly to become an integral part of the Mental Hygiene Movement, I believe this will be to the advantage both of religion itself and of all the other component elements in the movement. From contact with scientific psychiatry, social case-work, pedagogy, and other professional techniques, religion will learn precision and exactness in methods of diagnosis and treatment. The Catholic

---

[1] Quoted from my article in *Religious Education*, January, 1928.
[2] *The Normal Mind*, especially Chapter XX.
[3] *What Men Live By.*

confessional and Protestant pastoral counsel will become conscious of their psychological crudities and may eventually rival the medical clinic in professional skill, while they surpass all specialized techniques in their capacity for getting at the very root of the human problem. Evangelism might become much more effective if it adopted the case-work approach.[1] But if religion would thus benefit by contact with scientific technique, all the other branches of the Mental Hygiene Movement would benefit by contact with religion; for religion pursues the common, central aim of the movement with an inspiring zeal which none of them can equal; and, as Miss Van Waters points out, the success of all these enterprises depends ultimately not upon technique alone, but upon the personal qualities and attitudes of the men and women who carry them on— attitudes like love, self-control, patience, humor, which religion with its high enthusiasm is peculiarly fitted to foster. The task of religion, broadly defined as the cure of sin and the development of personality, is the task not alone of religion, but of the whole Mental Hygiene Movement. It will take nothing less than a complete program of mental health, curative and preventive— counting religion in—to accomplish it.

Thus far, our discussion has been concerned exclusively with the problem of *individual* self-realization, and the aid which may be expected towards its solution, not from Christianity or any other particular religion, but from *religion-in-general*. Our conclusion has been that the in-

---

[1] Cf. Zahniser, *Case-work Evangelism.* What power might be achieved by an evangelistic movement which used such methods is illustrated by the vast influence of the Buchman movement, with its almost psychoanalytic program: "Confidence, Confession, Conviction, Conversion, Continuance." On the Buchman movement, see Harold Begbie, *More Twice-Born Men.* For a severe criticism of it, see the chapter on "Buchmanism" in Ferguson's *Confusion of Tongues.*

dividual personality needs religion in order to maintain its health and fulfill its highest potentialities. But, for at least two reasons, it is now necessary to pass beyond this point of view, and broaden the field of our investigation. In the first place, as we have seen, individual personality cannot be understood from a purely individualistic point of view; it grows by a process of social osmosis, absorbing the very substance of its being from the surrounding social *milieu*. In the second place, "religion-in-general" is a pure abstraction: all that really exists is a series of concrete, historic religious traditions, embodied in great social movements and institutions, and each different from all others in the effect which it exercises upon the human personalities that come under its influence. We have been maintaining that religion makes for mental health, meaning by this that, if religion fulfilled its ideal function, it *would* make for mental health; but it must candidly be admitted that not all religions come up to this standard. Indeed, it can plausibly be maintained, with plenty of historical data to support it, that, far from being a means of adjusting oneself to reality, religion is a way of escaping from reality, into a dream-world of comforting illusions.[1] "Religion is the opiate of the people!"

It is necessary for us, therefore, to move out beyond the field of individual psychology into the field of social psychology, and to inquire whether Christianity, the particular religion which we here in the Occident have inherited, is capable of aiding human nature to develop its ideal potentialities, as a good religion ought to do. This may seem to be carrying us beyond the strictly psychological sphere; but if it be true, as writers on mental hygiene affirm, that a personality can develop only by entering into relations of harmonious adjustment with other

---

[1] Cf. Everett Dean Martin, *The Mystery of Religion.*

personalities, and by finding some ideal objective that "takes it out of itself" in loyal devotion, then it is necessary to enter into the social realm in order to find the key to the solution of the individual problem with which we began.

Part II
Christianity and Personal Development

In which the Christian tradition is examined from the psychological point of view; and Christ is found to occupy a central place among the historic religious resources making for personal development.

FRANCIS: I would show thee Christ, Soldan. Or if by that name thou know Him not, then by His other name which is Love, wherein also dwell Joy and Peace. This I have come to show.

SOLDAN: Yea; speak!

FRANCIS:

Oh, hearken for this is wonder!
Light looked down and beheld Darkness.
"Thither will I go," said Light.
Peace looked down and beheld War.
"Thither will I go," said Peace.
Love looked down and beheld Hatred.
"Thither will I go," said Love.
So Light came and shone.
So came Peace and gave Rest.
So came Love and brought Life.
And the Word was made flesh and dwelt among us.
—LAURENCE HOUSMAN: *Little Plays of St. Francis.*
Published by Jonathan Cape & Harrison Smith, Inc.,
New York

Like every great religion, Christianity has three main aspects: an ideal of the good life, a "way of salvation" that leads to it, and a theory of the universe that supports it. In our discussion of the psychological adequacy of Christianity, we shall deal successively with the Christian ideal of life, the Christian way of salvation, and the Christian attitude toward the universe.

I. THE CHRISTIAN IDEAL OF LIFE

Ideals spring from want, need, and disappointment; or as Felix Adler says, they are "pang-born." They arise under the pressure of circumstances and reflect the character of the specific pangs that gave them birth. In primitive religions, idealism is of a low and meager order, since the horizon of the savage is limited by his half-starved, precarious manner of existence. Hunger, exposure, and privation; fear of wild animals, human enemies, and the mysterious powers of nature—these are the pangs that stimulate such idealistic dreaming as he has time for. His gods are gods of vegetation and reproduction, guardians of the crops and herds, or gods of battle; his heaven is a happy hunting-ground. But with the organization of tribal life and the gradual mastery of the means of subsistence, other cravings begin to be felt. Man discovers that he wants not only to live, but to live well; and so the endless quest of the good life begins. The flicker of a light that never was on land or sea begins to appear on the far horizon; and that glistening mirage[1] lures man on forever after, growing brighter as his fate grows darker, and faithfully reflecting, in the language of dream-fulfillment, precisely that which his life is *not*— but might possibly become. It is at this higher level that we first meet with the Christian ideal of life.

If one ask what specific "pang" lies at the root of the Christian ideal, the clue may perhaps be found in Nietzsche's famous characterization of Christianity as "slave morality." Historically and psychologically, that is exactly what it is: the ideal of an enslaved and downtrodden people, perpetually subjected to the taunts, insults, exactions, and cruelties of their masters and oppressors. Some great ideals bear the visible imprint of the mentality which Nietzsche so admired; the mentality of the freeman, the warrior, the nobleman, the aristocrat; in short, the master-mentality. Such was the Greek ideal of courage, temperance, wisdom, and justice, conceived by the proud and self-reliant masters of a social order based upon helots and slaves. Not so the Hebrew ideal, nor the Christian which grew out of it. Palestine formed the natural bridge between the valley of the Nile and the valley of the Euphrates; and that bridge echoed constantly to the marching feet of conquering armies. From the enslavement in Egypt to the Babylonian captivity, and from the rebuilding of the Temple under Nehemiah to its destruction by Titus, periods of political independence were few and troubled. The perpetual problem of the Hebrew was how to maintain his self-respect in the face of intolerable oppression; and his perpetual dream—sometimes conceived

---

[1] By the simile of the mirage, I do not mean to suggest that ideals are illusions; but I do mean to suggest that they involve great danger of self-deception. There are true ideals and false ideals. False ideals born of fierce desire may lure one, like will-o'-the-wisps, into a quicksand; true ideals represent unexplored possibilities that are really inherent in this actual world.

in sober political terms, as a program of restoration or reform, sometimes despairingly projected into the heavens, as an apocalyptic vision of another world—was of a great Day of the Lord, in which justice and peace should be established amongst the sons of men, and war and oppression should be no more. Meanwhile his morality, at its best, was motivated by the remembrance of his undeserved sufferings, and the determination not to wrong others as he had been wronged:

Love ye therefore the stranger: for ye were strangers in the land of Egypt. . . .
Thou shalt not pervert the judgment of the stranger, nor of the fatherless; nor take a widow's raiment to pledge: but thou shalt remember that thou wast a bondman in Egypt, and the Lord thy God redeemed thee thence. . . .[1]

It is against this general background that we must view the specific contribution of Jesus to the Christian ideal. He stands upon the shoulders of his predecessors, the great prophets of the eighth and seventh centuries B.C., and he dreams their dream anew. Never was the problem of oppression more acute than in his time; never was the nation nearer to destruction, either through succumbing to a feeling of inferiority and tamely submitting to Romanization or—what actually happened—through yielding to blind hatred and committing collective suicide in a futile struggle against overwhelming force. It was at least a part of the great significance of Jesus that, in facing and solving this peculiarly Jewish problem, he rose to such heights of emotional elevation, such universality of human compassion, that his solution has become, to multitudes in every part of the world, the key to the whole human problem. He found a new path to spiritual serenity, sanity, and self-respect: the path of a love so universal that

---

[1] Deuteronomy 10:19; 24:17; cf. 16:11 and many similar passages.

it included the oppressor himself, and was readier to serve than he was to coerce; the path of a selfless meekness so profound that nothing could wound or insult it. There was nothing yielding in this love or this meekness; unconquerable loyalty to the cause of the triumph of righteousness burned steadily within it; but it was purged of all hatred and all bitterness, and it viewed every son of man as potentially capable of reciprocating in kind and becoming himself a willing servant of the same spirit of invincible good will.

The psychology of Christian love—who is competent to discuss it? Those who have fully explored its nature are few indeed. The example of Christ has been more honored in the breach than in the observance. Christian love has usually been concentrated upon "the household of faith"; the heretic and the infidel have been put beyond its scope; and ever since the rise of the Christian Church to a position of influence and power, it has shown a disposition to persecute and oppress in which there is little enough of "slave morality"—except in this sense, that the emancipated slave is often noted for his bumptiousness and cruelty. Today, our prosperous, conservative, cautiously benevolent Protestantism, separated by a barrier of class-consciousness from the proletarian masses, presents a curiously inverted contrast to the broad humanity of the Founder. One finds Protestant preachers carefully explaining away those troublesome passages about turning the other cheek and going the second mile, and Protestant scholars urbanely concluding that there is nothing really original in the teachings of Jesus. Yet from time to time there appears a man—a Francis of Assisi, a George Fox, a Tolstoy, a Gandhi—who catches a glimpse of the true meaning of Christian love, and dares to follow his vision. To analyze the attitude of such men, and through them to get at the spirit of their Master, is the primary task for a psychology of the Christian ideal of life.

Some significant attempts have been made to ground Christian love in biological instinct—thus justifying the saying that the soul is "naturally Christian." Henry Drummond, in his Lowell Lectures on *The Ascent of Man*, identifies Christian love, in its first beginnings, with the parental instinct which impels all the higher animals to struggle and sacrifice to secure the welfare of their offspring; and Professor Coe, in his *Social Theory of Religious Education*, treats the parental instinct as the central drive around which every distinctively Christian character must be organized. McDougall, in his much-discussed and much-criticized *Social Psychology*, makes this instinct the source of that "tender emotion" which we feel toward children, pets, and weak and helpless creatures of all sorts —the emotion of pity or sympathy, in other words, which Nietzsche himself considered to be the essence of Christianity, and which he bade his followers suppress as ministering to a weak and slavish state of mind.

These attempts are almost certainly on the right track. The psychology of instinct is now in a state of confusion. Many psychologists scoff at the idea of a "parental instinct," while others lump it together with sex in one primordial "libido"; but so long as hunger and sex are listed as elemental human drives, so long, I believe, must a parental impulse continue to be listed as something different from either, and almost equally deep in its biological rootage. Whether this impulse be viewed as an "instinct" or consigned to some other pigeonhole, Christian thought must continue to view it as the best element in human nature, and the most promising point around which personality can be integrated. It is important to remember, however, that human impulses are much more flexible and adaptable than animal instincts, and are readily reconditioned and combined to form tendencies of the greatest variety and subtlety. Christian love, as one finds it in Jesus or Francis, is certainly not to be identified with raw, naïve, unpremeditated parental affection—the kind of affection portrayed in Miss Anne Parrish's brilliant novel, *The Perennial Bachelor*, where we see it cursing them that give and him that takes. It has ceased to be narrowly selective and become universal; it has ceased to be solicitous about the immediate comfort of the person loved, and become solicitous about his ultimate welfare. At its best, Christian love is a highly refined variety of parental love, grown wise, disinterested and farsighted.

If one asks what are the special conditions under which this specialized variety of love may have developed, one meets with the suggestion that it is in the family, the neighborhood, and other intimate "primary groups" that this type of disposition naturally originates. Christian character, from this point of view, is characterized by the persistent adherence, in all relations of life, to those friendly and truthful attitudes which prevail in family and neighborhood life at its best; and the Christian ideal of a universal Kingdom of God is the ideal of a world family or a world neighborhood.

There is much historical evidence to support this view. The Jewish people have always been noted for strong family loyalty, and for a strong sense of neighborly solidarity. The teachings of Jesus are full of illustrations drawn from family and neighborhood life. They have, accordingly, what can only be described as a feminine note and a feminine appeal; since the ethics of the family and the neighborhood, as distinguished from the ethics of the market-place and the military council chamber, have always been profoundly affected by that ancient division of labor which decreed that woman should stay at home to look after the household and rear the children, while man went abroad to hunt and barter and stave off the assaults of the enemy.

Here emerges the crucial question, on whose answer our whole attitude toward the Christian ideal depends: Can an ideal which developed within the relatively simple and sheltered environment of the family and the neighborhood possibly hold good under the more complicated conditions which prevail in the economic and political spheres? Can an ideal whose primary appeal is to gentle, womanly souls ever claim the honest, unhypocritical allegiance of aggressive and pugnacious males? Or to return to Nietzsche's formulation of the same question, Should rulers and freemen permit their moral fiber to be weakened by succumbing to the soft seductions of an ideal invented by cringing slaves?

A case can be made out for the view that the Christian ideal is too one-sided and partial to be able to deal effectively with the task of integrating all the characteristic drives and interests of human beings; that it is so deficient on the side of the civic and manly virtues, as to be fit only for women, children, and slaves. There is little said in the Gospels concerning public and civic duties; the hope of a swiftly approaching millennium so absorbed the Christians, throughout the first few centuries, that they had no interest in public affairs; and when, to their own surprise, they found themselves triumphant in *this* world and elevated to positions of authority in the Empire, they had to borrow their conceptions of social ethics from the Greeks and Romans, for they had none of their own. The first Christian treatise on ethics, St. Ambrose's *De Officiis Ministrorum*, was simply an adaptation of Cicero's *De Officiis*. Later on, when St. Thomas Aquinas built his delicately balanced system of Christian thought, he found it necessary to supplement the feminine virtues of faith, hope, and love (the gist of the Christian ideal) with the masculine virtues of courage, wisdom, temperance, and justice (the gist of the Greek ideal). It must be admitted that when Christianity runs to seed, it generally declines in the direction of that undiscriminating charity and mawkish sentimentality which Nietzsche so rightfully detested.

Yet it is a fundamental misconception of Christian love to see in it nothing more than womanly soft-heartedness. There is manly courage in it, and manly self-control, and farsighted sagacity. Love has far-reaching social and civic implications. If these were not explicitly stated in the Gospels, they are nevertheless dynamically present in the Christian spirit and attitude, and manifest themselves whenever the message of the Gospel is taken in hearty earnest. The abolition of private war in Italy under the influence of the Franciscan movement, the promotion of prison reform, social legislation, and many other forms of humanitarian effort in England under the influence of the Wesleyan movement, and the recent achievements of Mr. Gandhi in South Africa and India: all these testify that Christian love is "a power, not a platitude," in public as well as in private life. Miss Maude Royden is right, I believe, when she argues that the Christian graces rest implicitly upon a basis of pagan virtues like courage, honesty, and self-respect; and that when this solid pagan basis is removed, the superstructure falls to the ground, and Christianity turns into a grotesque and repulsive caricature of itself.[1] This means that when Christian philosophy strikes an open alliance with pagan philosophy, as in the system of St. Thomas, it is not so much repairing deficiencies in the Christian Gospel as it is making explicit its own underlying presuppositions. I think it not unfair

---

[1] See her article, "Pagan Virtues and Christian Graces," in the *Atlantic Monthly*, June, 1926.

to say, with Studdert-Kennedy,[1] that Christianity represents, not the woman-ideal alone, nor yet the warrior-ideal alone, but the two locked in "creative conflict"—the woman venturing forth unarmed to do battle with the warrior, the slave to do battle with the master, the conflict issuing in no taming of the warrior's valor, no destruction of the master's self-respect. "In Christ there is neither male nor female, bond nor free." Surely, as one listens to our most radical contemporary exponent of Christian love, Mr. Gandhi, one cannot justly accuse him of a soft and slavish disposition:

Where there is only a choice between cowardice and violence I advise violence. . . . I would risk violence a thousand times rather than emasculation of the race. . . . But I believe that non-violence is infinitely superior to violence, forgiveness more manly than punishment. Forgiveness adorns a soldier. . . . Strength does not come from physical capacity. It comes from an indomitable will. Non-violence does not mean weak submission to the will of the evil-doer but the putting of one's whole soul against the will of the tyrant. . . . Non-violence is the law of our species as violence is the law of the brute. The dignity of man requires obedience to a higher law—the strength of the spirit.[2]

I am not claiming that the Christian ideal is "perfect." Perfection, in this universe of flux and change, is only a vanishing-point to aim at. Neither am I claiming that the Christian ideal embodies, implicitly, every value that any of its rivals possesses. The Christian ideal has not only become more explicit by contact with other ideals, but has

---

[1] G. A. Studdert-Kennedy, *The Warrior, the Woman, and the Christ.* Cf. Professor Hocking's argument, in *Human Nature and its Remaking,* to the effect that pugnacity, sex-love, and ambition are not destroyed, but only sublimated, in the highest type of Christian character.

[2] Rolland, *Mahatma Gandhi,* pp. 65-68. Published by The Century Co., New York. (1924.)

been greatly enriched thereby as well;[1] and this process needs to continue as long as the world lasts, since the changing exigencies of the times require alterations of emphasis and perspective. All that I claim for the Christian ideal of love is that it is fundamentally on the right track. More fundamentally than any other, it strikes at the root of the problem of life; and hence it is capable of gathering to itself, as subsidiaries and allies, all the values of all the great ethical and social ideals which mankind has conceived on its toilsome way toward the goal of a full and satisfying life. Since this process of assimilation is perpetually going on, the Christian ideal takes on a variety of forms in the course of history—the monastic ideal, the ideal of chivalry, the Puritan ideal, the Evangelical ideal, the humanitarian ideal of modern "social Christianity"— but in all these forms (in spite of much corruption and decline of the original Christian principle and much infusion of hostile and incongruous elements) Christ, the animating spirit of the Christian movement, "fulfils himself in many ways." And his manner of fulfilling himself, in every age, with due allowance for diversities of vocation, nationality, age, and sex, is to create harmony in the individual soul, peace among men, and a sense of being at home in the universe.

2. THE CHRISTIAN WAY OF SALVATION

We have come to the conclusion that the Christian ideal is fundamentally on the right track, and that it points to a goal that is both supremely desirable and ultimately

---

[1] For example, it would be quite artificial to trace our modern emphasis upon the *athletic*, *æsthetic*, and *intellectual* virtues to any Hebraic source. These virtues represent our debt to ancient Greece—although they have now become so much a part of the Christian ideal that they are preached from Christian pulpits, and even deduced from Scripture texts, without any sense of incongruity.

accessible. Can we now go on to assert that Christianity has been just as fundamentally right in its teachings concerning the ways and means of reaching that goal? Not, I fear, without grave reservations. The story of Christianity's attempts to whip human nature into shape, and bring in the Kingdom of God among men, is not without its bright chapters; but it is, more largely than one might wish, a story of humiliating defeats and pyrrhic victories.

We are assuming, be it noted, that the "way of salvation" and the "means of grace" have to do with the ways and means of getting ahead on the path that leads from the contractive and self-centered life of sin toward the full and satisfying life of loving fellowship in a coöperative social order. This is not what the Church has always meant. "Salvation" has sometimes been defined, quite selfishly, in terms of the individual's escape from the unpleasant consequences of his wrongdoing, here and hereafter; or it has been defined as a metaphysical change in his essence, whereby he is changed from a human to a divine being without necessarily undergoing any observable change in his character; or as an inward state of joy and peace, which may or may not be accompanied by its appropriate outward expression in deeds of kindness.[1] All such conceptions of salvation may be dismissed as unpsychological or unchristian. From a truly psychological and truly Christian point of view, "salvation" means fullness of life, personal and social, and "grace" means the sum of those stimulating influences which tend to release men from their constricting inhibitions and perversions and increase the harmonious richness of their communal life. Only a man who is really becoming better is being saved; and no one is fully saved who is subject to bad temper or

---

[1] For a good survey of the varied meanings which the word "salvation" has borne, see Professor Richards' *Christian Ways of Salvation* or Professor George Cross's *Christian Salvation.*

morbid fears, or given to tyrannizing over his associates, no matter how great a prince of the Church he may be. This, after all, has been the main continuous strand in the teaching of the Church, however poorly it has been expressed. Salvation from sin, not salvation from its penalties, has been the main concern.

Judged from this higher point of view, all of the historic Christian ways of salvation seem to fall woefully short. For purposes of this discussion, these historic ways of salvation may be reduced to three: the Catholic way, the Puritan way, and the Evangelical way.

The Catholic way of salvation is based upon a double standard of attainment: one for the saint, and one for the common man. Early in its history, the Catholic Church found itself invaded by a host of purely nominal adherents—"rice Christians," they would be called on the mission field today—who entered the Christian fold *en masse*, with their eyes on some purely selfish advantage or blindly following the lead of some semi-converted ruler like Constantine or Clovis. The Church dared not evade the responsibility of doing whatever could be done for this ignorant and irresponsible multitude; but her true ideals and preferred methods are rather to be seen in the strict regulations of the various monastic orders, which were founded for the benefit of those who wished to take the Christian Gospel in deadly earnest, and found it necessary to flee from the Church as well as from the world in order to do so.

The achievement of the Catholic Church in civilizing a horde of wild and untutored barbarians during the Dark Ages and bringing them up to the level of culture represented by the Age of Charlemagne should be reckoned to her eternal credit. Nevertheless, it must be insisted that the methods which she then employed, and still employs, in dealing with the masses are not calculated to bring men

up to the "measure of the stature of the fulness of Christ."
A strict, inquisitorial system of supervision, culminating in
the confessional; an authoritarian discipline based on the
fear of hell and the hope of heaven; a cunningly devised
scheme of penance and indulgence, whereby the reins of
government can be tightened or slackened as necessity may
dictate—here is a marvelous technique for enforcing
obedience and outward conformity, but no adequate means
for lifting the masses above the plane of childish irrespon-
sibility and investing them with the dignity and freedom
which comes of responsible self-direction. A certain freedom is possible in the ranks of the Catholic Church, and a
thousand happy converts bear witness to it; but it is the
freedom of the child or the soldier, under parental or
military discipline, freed from the necessity of making his
own decisions.[1] The great mass of "good Catholics," thus
condemned to live their whole lives in a state of childish
dependence and conformity, can hardly be reckoned
among the "saved."

It is different, generally speaking, with the Catholic
religious orders. Some of them, it is true, employ an elaborate technique for breaking the will of the novice, and
all of them include *obedience*, along with poverty and
chastity, among the primary vows that must be taken; yet
the monastic way of salvation, once entered upon, turns
out to be a solitary path of self-discipline, leading to lonely
heights of mystic exaltation, where the soul at last is freed
from its dependence, and sees God directly, without intermediaries. It may in fact be plausibly maintained that
the Catholic saint stands at the opposite pole, psychologically, from the Catholic masses. He is as much an in-

---

[1] The testimony of converts to and from the Catholic Church forms a
fascinating body of material for psychological study. To my mind, one
of the most revealing of all these human documents is Mr. Stanley B.
James's *Confessions of a Spiritual Tramp.* See especially p. 51, where
he compares the effects of army discipline with those of Catholic discipline.

dividualist as they are collectivists and conformists; and his overstrained other-worldliness, expressing itself in asceticism and mysticism, is the negative counterpart of their complacent worldliness.

Asceticism of some sort—what Mr. Walter Lippmann calls the "discipline of desire"—is a necessary element in all serious religion; and mysticism in the broad sense of the word (i.e. the discipline of concentrated thought, the "practice of the presence of God") is equally essential; but Catholic asceticism and Catholic mysticism, in spite of many noble exemplars, have so signally failed to understand human nature and to control its driving forces that the very words "asceticism" and "mysticism" have come into disrepute. "Ascetic" suggests to us an emaciated, ill-kempt creature in a hair-shirt, struggling to suppress all his normal human impulses and buffeting his poor body as if in it lay the root of all evil. "Mystic" suggests to us a wild-eyed enthusiast, given to trances, visions, and ecstasies, and incapable of using his rational intelligence. Both of these views caricature the truth; but the *Lives of the Saints* furnishes a real basis for the caricature.

Yet the greatest error of Catholic monasticism is neither its asceticism nor its mysticism; it is the error inherent in the distinction between the saint and the common man: the error of supposing that saintliness thrives best in solitude and that the ideal life can be best lived apart from the storm and stress of everyday existence. The progress of monasticism and its eventual discredit were both brought about by the gradual recognition of this error. At first, the monks lived alone, as hermits, in caves or in the desert; then, finding that (by the law of negative suggestion)[1] the temptations of the flesh became all the more

---

[1] Professor Münsterberg used to illustrate this law by solemnly averring that anyone could turn dish-water into molten gold if he would stir it for fifteen minutes, *Taking care that the word "hippopotamus" never*

seductive the more one attempted to combat them by solitary meditation, they banded themselves together in little communities and imposed austerities mutually upon one another. In the West, these communities came to devote less and less of their time to the direct cultivation of piety, and more and more of their time to work and study and other useful occupations. Finally, with the coming of St. Francis and St. Dominic, the barrier between the monastic communities and the rest of the world broke down; the friars mingled freely with the life of the common people, sharing their burdens and their joys with no sense of superiority or exclusiveness. It was noteworthy that as monastic life became more normal and human, it gained rather than lost in the quality of sanctity it produced. The way was thus paved for the Protestants, who repudiated the double standard altogether and asserted that there was but one way of salvation for all.

If the Protestants agreed in asserting that there was but one way of salvation, they differed in their definition of it. Into their multitudinous differences it is impossible to enter here; but we may safely take the Puritan and the Evangelical ways of salvation as representative of the two most persistent types of Protestantism: the one seen at its best in Geneva under Calvin, Scotland under Knox, England under Cromwell, and New England down to the time of Jonathan Edwards; the other seen at its best in the religious experience of Martin Luther and John Wesley, and the evangelistic endeavors of Dwight L. Moody and General Booth.

Puritanism does not deserve all the opprobrium which is being heaped upon it at present. It produced some of the most stalwart and fearless characters of whom we have historic record; and an examination of their letters and

came into his mind. The poor hermits used to take care that fleshly desires never came into their minds!

diaries will prove that they were by no means so deficient in æsthetic appreciation and tender emotion as it is now the fashion to assert. Nevertheless, it is clear that Puritanism, with its belief in the total depravity of original human nature and the sinfulness of all spontaneous joy in life, has consistently failed to handle human impulse in any constructive and effective way. Whenever the Puritans have got the reins of government into their hands, they have embarked upon a program of prohibitory legislation which has threatened to rob life of all wholesome relaxation, all diverting nonsense, and reduce it to a weary round of duties, grimly performed for conscience sake. The result has in every case been a revolt so violent that it has tipped society over into the opposite extreme, of libertinism and frivolity. Such was notably the case in the Stuart Restoration, after the death of Cromwell. In our Anglo-Saxon world, where Puritanism has been most influential, it would almost seem as if it had condemned us to rush forever from prudery to licentiousness and back again to prudery, never able to stop at any golden mean. Surely, a way of salvation which provokes human nature to revenge itself so violently is no real way of salvation.

Evangelical Protestantism stands in sharp contrast to Puritanism. It is as buoyant and joyful in spirit as Puritanism is repressed and dour; it is full of the sense of moral power as Puritanism is full of the sense of moral strain. A typical Evangelical conversion tended to clear away all those haunting scruples and anxious doubts which plagued the soul of the Puritan and to give a man, instead, the full assurance of his salvation. Only let the sinner make a "full surrender"—let him take God's will unreservedly as his guide in life, and trust in His redeeming love, revealed in the Cross of Christ—and he would find all his burdens rolled away and a stream of inexhaustible power welling up within him. Such, at least, was the pros-

pect which the great Evangelical preachers held out to
their hearers; and it has been verified in thousands of
lives.

It is hard for one who has been touched by the enthusiastic spirit of Evangelicalism to view its merits and
defects with a cool, appraising eye. He knows he is saved;
and the only question that he stops to ask is, "Brother,
are *you* saved?" To inquire whether personality has been
fully integrated and sanely balanced by the conversion
experience, and whether a less catastrophic transformation
might not in many instances prove more wholesome, seems
to him a sacrilege. Nevertheless, the psychologist cannot
help asking these questions; and his verdict is likely to be
something to this effect: that while Evangelicalism at its
best has produced a succession of noble, dynamic personalities, lifted above strain and fear, and wholly consecrated
to the service of God and man, Evangelicalism at its worst
has produced a succession of unbalanced fanatics, narrow-
minded and censorious, lacking in social vision and Christian charity.

Perhaps the best way to understand and evaluate the
Evangelical way of salvation is to see it as the more or less
faithful reflection of the religious experience of St. Paul.[1]
The great problem of St. Paul's life was, how to get

---

[1] Consider the symbolic circumstances under which John Wesley experienced his Evangelical conversion: it was in a little Moravian chapel
in London, *during the reading of Luther's commentary on Paul's Epistle
to the Romans*, he tells us, that he "felt his heart strangely warmed," and
found his assurance of personal salvation. Remember that Luther was an
Augustinian monk; remember that the Moravians were the most radical
of those German Pietists who kept alive the devout spirit of Martin
Luther in an age of barren theological dissipation. The line of succession
is complete: St. Augustine repeats the religious experience of St. Paul;
Luther, an Augustinian monk, rediscovers it; the Pietists propagate this
experience in Germany; Wesley and his successors propagate it in the
Anglo-Saxon world. The strength and weakness of Evangelicalism are
the strength and weakness of St. Paul himself.

power to do what he believed to be right. As a Pharisee, he seems to have set himself to the task of observing the Jewish Law with fanatical scrupulosity, as if nothing less than a grade of one hundred per cent and a degree of *summa cum laude* would satisfy him—and his remorseful summary of his failure is well known: "The evil that I would not, that I do." Like St. Augustine and Luther, centuries later, he found that sheer will-power furnished no adequate dynamic to drive one along the path of duty; and the turning-point in his life came when he ceased to trust in himself and committed the direction of his life wholly to the power of the indwelling Spirit of Christ, which, he believed, "possessed" him very much as one might be "possessed" by a demon. From that moment on, the problem of moral power was solved for him; he became a personality so terrifically dynamic that his influence has been projected unimpaired across nineteen centuries; but he did not at once, if ever, achieve a *well-balanced* personality.[1] He could endure unbelievable hardships and persecutions, and thrive upon them; but he never overcame a certain personal touchiness, and a tendency to be censorious. How could he, who had his Gospel directly from the seventh heaven and who had Christ as his spirit-control, be tolerant of the opinions of those who opposed him? How could he err or sin, being divinely guided? . . . He must have been a hard man to get along with, as Peter and John Mark and many others could testify! Something of the same perfectionistic pride and intolerance is to be noted—with less excuse—in his modern followers; and by so much, the claim of Evan-

---

[1] Or as Dr. Mary Ely Lyman once put it to me, Paul's religion had *power*, without any of that *peace* and serenity which characterizes Johannine Christianity. With the passage of the years, his personality seems to have mellowed greatly. He trusted less and less to private, mystic revelations and spiritual ecstasies, and more and more to the promptings of the Spirit (of Fellowship in love) which he found manifested in the Church.

gelicalism to have discovered the true and perfect way of salvation must be denied.

It may be asked whether Liberal Protestantism cannot offer a way of salvation of its own, different from any of the ways just described, and superior. The answer, I fear, must be in the negative. Liberal Protestantism is a theology, not a religion; a way of thinking rather than a way of living. It represents, not a new religious impulse, but an endeavor to adapt the Evangelical way of life to a new view of the world. On the speculative side of theology, its achievements are great; on the practical side, it has at best contributed a set of critical footnotes to the classical ways of salvation. It has protested, with much force and much justice, against Evangelicalism's tendency to define salvation in purely individualistic and unwholesomely emotional terms; it has insisted that religion is something normal and natural, which can be gradually learned and cannot be rightly acquired in one convulsive crisis of conversion. And yet, so far, its gospel of "salvation by education" remains a mere prospectus, alluring to the eye but unsupported by any substantial accomplishments. The founders of the Religious Education movement and the Social Gospel movement were themselves Evangelicals, formed and inspired by the faith against whose inadequacies they were protesting; they have yet to produce in the younger generation a religious passion and a stalwartness of character comparable with their own. As matters now stand, there is more to be hoped from a slow and cautious liberalizing of Evangelical Protestantism, which would overcome its limitations without destroying its fervor, than from any dynamic movement which is likely to arise among Liberal Protestants. It is easier to tame a fanatic than to put life into a corpse!

Is there, then, no effective way of salvation in the Christian religion? Such a verdict would not be justified by the facts. From Zacchæus the publican to the latest convert of the Jerry McAuley mission, there stretches the long, unbroken line of those who have found freedom from sin and power for great living in the Christian Gospel. Beneath the peculiar tenets which distinguish the Catholic from the Protestant, the Puritan from the Evangelical, the liberal from the conservative, there lies something which they all have in common, and which is more important than their differences: a sense of the "constraining love of Christ." A tremendous faith in the inherent worth and infinite possibilities of men, even the worst, and a love of men that did not stop at the extremest sacrifice, if only thereby an answering spark of devotion could be evoked: this it was that gave the Founder of Christianity his inimitable power over men; and wherever his spirit lives in his followers—as, for example, in the Salvation Army, with its saying that "a man may be down but he's never out"—there men respond today as much as they ever did. There is no moral stimulus comparable in power with that of being loved and trusted beyond what we deserve; and when to this there is added the effect of membership in an intimate fellowship, cemented by common loyalty and mutual affection, it is no wonder that under these circumstances the moral life can be lived on a plane of high enthusiasm, where the sense of struggle vanishes completely.[1]

The tragedy is, that a religion armed with such weapons as the constraining love of Christ and the sustaining power of Christian fellowship should not be more consistently victorious in its struggle with human nature. The trouble has been that, ever since the rise of monasticism,

---

[1] Psychiatrists are beginning to stress the therapeutic value of *intimate fellowship* and *mutual affection*. To be *singled out* as friend and comrade is often enough to remake a man.

the Church has tended to look upon human nature as something inherently fleshly, worldly, and evil, an enemy to be subdued, not an ally to be won; and, believing evil of men, has appealed to lower motives like fear and self-interest instead of staking all upon their responsiveness to love and trust. How great a mistake this is can easily be seen, when one notes the tremendous success which attended the preaching of a man like Dwight L. Moody, who had neither education nor eloquence, nor any weapon in his armory save the single weapon of the constraining love of Christ.

Dare one hope that in our day, the old misunderstandings about human nature being laid at rest and the secrets of human motivation being laid bare as never before, the Christian way of salvation may at length find its full and adequate expression? That would be unduly optimistic, no doubt. It takes more than new *knowledge* to create a new Gospel of salvation. Yet I know of nothing which is more likely to give a new glow and a new touch of reality to religion in our generation than the effort, on the part of lovers of mankind,—whether in the regular ministry or in the cognate ministry of social case-work and psychiatry, —to employ the new knowledge of human nature in such a way as to bring it directly home to the specific problems of individual self-realization which their friends and clients bring to them. Love by itself offers no way of salvation; psychological technique by itself offers no way of salvation; but love working through psychological technique is *the* way of salvation for the individual, as love working through sociological technique is *the* way of salvation for society. It is just at this point, in its bearing upon the Christian way of salvation, that the psychological approach to theology may be expected, in the long run, to make its greatest contributions.

3. THE CHRISTIAN ATTITUDE TOWARD THE UNIVERSE

Theories of the universe, as such, lie beyond the scope of our psychological approach to theology. Einstein and Eddington, Whitehead and Lloyd Morgan, all have their contributions to make to contemporary theology; but it would demand another book, of quite another sort, to deal with these questions. From the psychological point of view, what matters is not how men picture the universe, but what attitude they take toward the universe they picture. If their attitude is sane and wholesome, their religion may be adjudged a good religion, even though their theology may be riddled with false assumptions about the nature of the physical world; and they need not greatly alter the vital core of their faith, though Copernicus and Darwin may transform their universe from center to circumference. The crucial question with regard to Christianity is not whether its cosmology is correct, but whether its cosmic trustfulness represents a sound and workable attitude. Christianity's cosmology is borrowed; its attitude toward the world is its own.

A careful examination of most religions and philosophies of life will disclose that their cosmic attitude is closely related with their ideal of the good life. Whatever is regarded as good, the universe is believed to support. Thus Lao-Tze believes that Nature is gentle and non-violent, as the good man ought to be; while Nietzsche finds in the "will to power" not only the ideal human motive, but the central cosmic urge. Occasionally, as in the contemporary "humanist" movement in religion, one finds a fundamental disharmony between the ideal of the good life and the attitude toward the cosmos; but where this occurs, it is safe to predict that one or the other must give way. As I have said elsewhere, "A cold and suspicious attitude toward the cosmos is hard to combine with a trustful and affectionate attitude toward human beings. Either trust and affection will radiate out into nature, or what we may call 'cosmic imperialism' will trickle down into human relations."[1] Even the Russian Communist, with all his professed materialism, exemplifies this almost irresistible necessity to make one's ethics square with one's metaphysics, and *vice versa*; for when hard pressed in an argument, he is as apt as anyone to thump the table and assert that the "nature of things" is on the side of the Communist ideal.

The Christian attitude toward the universe is absolutely in harmony with the Christian ideal of life. To put it quite simply and naïvely, the Christian assumes that human brotherhood is possible because the universe is already in some profound sense a Home, and because this Home is presided over by a Father. The first rule of Christian ethics is, to have toward our brothers the same patient and forgiving disposition which the Father constantly exhibits toward us. Christian piety is dominated by the grateful sense that, while we were yet undeserving, all manner of gifts were showered upon us, as parents shower gifts upon their children. By grace, says the Christian, we are born into a world and into a social order that we did not create. By grace we are fed and clothed and housed and educated. By grace we enter upon the possession of all manner of goods—laws and institutions, literature and art, and the wealth of hallowing influence that streams from noble lives—all of them there before we arrived, bought by the bitter toil and sacrifice of those who have gone before us. Surely, says the Christian, our attitude toward the universe ought to be one that is inspired by grateful recognition of "The love that, from our birth,

---

[1] *Theism and the Modern Mood*, p. 82. Published by Harper & Brothers. New York. (1930.)

over and around us lies"; and this attitude should find practical expression in a desire to share with less privileged brothers the undeserved blessings which the Father, out of pure generosity, has bestowed upon us.

"How idyllic! How childlike—not to say infantile!" murmurs the modern sophisticate. But stop! there is another side to all this. The world as it is, is not home for the Christian. "We are but strangers here; heaven is our home." "The world passeth away, and the lust thereof." The very fact that the Christian prays that God's will may be done on earth as it is done in heaven proves that he does not regard this world, in its present state, as God's world, but rather as Satan's. There is no rosy optimism about the Christian attitude toward the existing world order; it is grimly realistic, to the point of bitter cynicism. "God's in his heaven; all's right with the world!" is a lovely Victorian sentiment; but it would probably have been received with a wry face by the Christian Fathers. *Their* sentiments were better expressed by the saying that "this world is a vale of tears."

This dual attitude toward the universe—grateful confidence in its governing spirit, combined with stern disapproval of the actual state of affairs—has been graphically expressed in popular theology by the theory of the "two worlds." "This world" is evil; the "world to come" will be good; and its prototype already exists above us, in heaven, where God sits upon His throne, ruling and overruling. There is nothing in the attitude itself to tie one down to this popular anthropomorphic symbolism; it does not necessarily involve belief in a dualistic, supernaturalistic universe, or a personal Devil, or perhaps even a personal God. All that is essentially involved in it is what Professor Macintosh calls "moral optimism": "a fundamental attitude of confidence in the cosmos, together with a full sense of man's responsibility, . . . expressed in the conviction that if only a person's will is right, he need have no fear of anything the universe can do to him; no absolute or final disaster can come to him whose will is steadfastly devoted to the true ideal."[1]

While this attitude of "moral optimism" may go almost equally well with many different cosmologies and philosophies, it does tend to rule out the extreme forms of pantheism and the extreme forms of naturalism or humanism. It rules out extreme pantheism because the pantheistic attitude is one of "non-moral optimism": a perpetuation of that quietistic mood of relaxed adoration which the sight of a glorious sunset is apt to induce, for the moment, in all of us. It rules out extreme naturalism, because naturalism involves an attitude of well-nigh complete pessimism —the kind of attitude expressed in Mr. Bertrand Russell's famous essay on "The Free Man's Worship," where man is represented as a "weary but unyielding Atlas," sustaining, all by himself, the ideal world which his own dreams have created, against the relentless onset of "omnipotent matter." Professor Macintosh thinks it also rules out the "mere meliorism" of William James. Strictly speaking, it does; but I prefer to define the Christian attitude a bit more broadly and inclusively than Professor Macintosh defines it. Wherever one finds a man who refuses to bow the knee before "the God of things as they are," but who in his struggle for a more brotherly world feels sustained by a power vastly greater than himself, and cosmic in scope, there one may recognize the Christian attitude toward the universe.

The Christian ideal of life and the Christian attitude toward the universe stand or fall together. If the Christian ideal is discovered to be impracticable, then the Christian attitude is jeopardized. If, on the other hand,

---

[1] *The Reasonableness of Christianity*, p. 46. Published by Charles Scribner's Sons, New York. (1926.)

an attitude of fundamental confidence in the universe is found to be justified in experience, then it is fair to conclude that the Christian ideal has more than a fighting chance to be realized. These are issues too vast and too complicated to be settled by any single argument; they must be fought out in the arena of universal history. The Christian world-view has never yet been stated in thoroughly defensible form; it has always been hampered with erroneous assumptions about astronomy or biology or what-not. Yet I think it is significant that, as between the Christian attitude of "moral optimism" and its two chief rivals, it is the Christian attitude which seems to be most in accord with the general principles of mental hygiene. Pantheistic religion, with its "non-moral optimism," fosters an attitude of infantile dependence, an unwillingness to face reality in its grimmer and more repulsive aspects, a tendency to take refuge in a world of dreams, where the sun is always shining, and evil can be abolished by calling it an error and thinking it away. Naturalistic or humanistic religion, with its cosmic pessimism, puts man under an unbearable nervous strain. Man is not built for the rôle of Atlas. The world is too great a load to strap upon his little back. If his back does not break under the load, his nerve is sure to break under the strain of attempting to maintain his heroic pose. To live under the constant impression that "the world is against me" is to become an easy prey to inhibiting fears and delusions of persecution. A child normally reared will escape this Scylla and this Charybdis; he will realize that he lives in a world where there are genuine obstacles to be grappled with, but where there are vast sustaining forces of all sorts—sunlight and the recuperative powers of the organism, friendship and the sense of social justice—which can be counted upon to come to his aid, if he rightly adjusts himself to the con-

ditions laid down for their release. This, essentially, is
the Christian attitude.

We saw in Chapter III that health of personality, de-
pending as it does upon devotion to ideal objectives that
enlist its energies and focus all its interests, can be greatly
aided by religion of the right sort. Our verdict must now
be that Christianity, as judged from the psychological
angle, is emphatically "religion of the right sort." It is
not "perfect," or "final," or "absolute," for it has committed serious tactical blunders in dealing with human
nature; but it has repeatedly demonstrated its ability to
set men at peace with themselves, their neighbors, and
the universe—thus passing the fundamental psychological
test.

Supposing, now, that Christianity, without losing those
ideals and attitudes wherein its power lies, should perfect
its technique for dealing with human nature; would it then
become the "final" religion, to which all mankind must
gravitate in the future? This question must inevitably be
faced, for in our rapidly shrinking world a religion incapable of serving all of us will eventually be incapable
of serving any of us. The religion of the future must be
a world religion, adapted not only to meet the needs of
civilized Occidentals, but to meet the needs of all sorts
and conditions of men, in every part of the globe. It can
be said today of Christianity, as of every other religion,
that it must either expand to world proportions or con-
tract into insignificance. Can we imagine Christianity thus
expanding to universal dimensions?

Frankly, it must be admitted that, in this form, the
question almost irresistibly suggests a negative answer.
The word "Christianity" (not without reason!) has gathered psychological associations which make it, to the rising self-consciousness of the Orient, not a symbol of all

that releases and enriches human personality, but of all that oppresses and exploits it. Modern Christianity, split into a million sectarian fragments by its own internal dissensions, inextricably entangled with Western commercialism and Western imperialism, is fiercely denounced and violently resisted as a menace throughout the Orient today. And yet, paradoxically enough, the name of Jesus is held in growing reverence by the same people who abhor the name of Christianity! Evidently, we have not one question on our hands, but two, when we seek to determine the future of Christianity: "How will it fare with organized Christianity?" and "How will it fare with Jesus?"

It is doubly necessary to distinguish between Jesus and Christianity, since no discussion of Christianity can be complete which fails to recognize the unique significance which Christianity attributes to its Founder. No other religion has given to the person of its founder so central a place. Buddha was content to be forgotten, so long as his principles were remembered. Christianity feels, on the contrary, that the person of Christ somehow contains more than the sum of his principles. Ask a Christian, "What must I do to be saved?" or, if you prefer to turn it into modern phraseology, ask him, "What must I do to release and develop my personality?" The answer will not be, as a rule, "Take up Christianity"—as one might say, "Take up Pelmanism, or Theosophy, or Christian Science"—but, however modern the terminology, the answer will be in substance the same which Paul gave to his jailer at Philippi: "Believe in the Lord Jesus Christ and thou shalt be saved!" It is almost as unreal to discuss Christianity-in-the-abstract, apart from all reference to the person of Christ, as it is to discuss religion-in-general, apart from all reference to specific historic religions.

Our next chapter, on "Christ and the Future," thus advances the "state of the argument" in two ways: (1) It proceeds to estimate the place of Jesus himself—as distinct from the ideas and institutions which have attached themselves to his name—among the forces which make for the redemption and enrichment of human personality; and (2) it proceeds to estimate the place which Christianity in both senses—both as the religion *of* Jesus and as the religion which has grown up *about* him—is likely to occupy in the world religion of the future. The test by which both Jesus and Christianity are to be judged is the psychological test: ability to call out the devotion, mobilize the energies, unify and enrich the personalities of all men everywhere.

If it were possible to take the Christian estimate of Jesus as a fair indication of his real significance, we should have to conclude at once that all saving, enlightening, and enlarging influences were so completely summed up and embodied in his personality that there could be, in effect, no other conceivable candidate for the position of Leader, Saviour, and Master of Mankind. For traditional Christianity, Jesus is the focal point of world history, the central actor in the drama of salvation, and the cosmic principle "through whom all things consist." He is the Second Adam, who undid the damage caused by our first father's fall; his coming splits all time into B.C. and A.D. Only through him, our sinless exemplar, can we know what a human life ought to be; only through him, our saviour, can we be redeemed from our guilt; only through him, our mediator, can we meet the Eternal God. Every religion has some center, some palladium in which all its teachings are symbolized and summarized, and its deity is made manifest. For Judaism, it is Torah, the written Law of the Lord; for Christianity, it is the Person of Christ. Christ is to the Christian what Torah is to the Jew. About him the whole Christian universe revolves.

But if Jesus is the center of the *Christian* scheme of things, that very fact makes one hesitant about attempting to define his place in the *real* scheme of things and about predicting the place he will occupy in the religion of the future. Whenever a book, or a ceremony, or a man becomes the center and palladium of a religion, mass psychology begins to weave about it a web of secondary accretions which eventually conceals the simple truth under a glistening vestment of romance. The Jewish Law is surrounded by a ring of commentary, this by a ring of commentary on the commentary—the encircling rings may be seen with the naked eye on any page of the Talmud—and these again are surrounded by endless homiletic amplifications and allegorical interpretations. One sees the same process beginning in China and Russia today, where the well-nigh sacred writings of Sun Yat Sen and Karl Marx are becoming the subject of endless disputation between the partisans of rival interpretations.[1] By a similar process of accretion, amplification, and (mis)interpretation, the simple agnostic philosophy of Gautama Buddha has grown into the elaborate ceremonial cult of the Great Vehicle, the Lord's Supper has grown into the Sacrament of the Blessed Eucharist, and Washington and Lincoln have grown into legendary heroes. Dare one assert that this has not occurred in the case of Jesus? If it has occurred, how is one to pierce through the obscuring vestment of romance which Christian piety has woven about him and get at the naked truth about him? How are we to determine what Jesus really accomplished for mankind? How are we to be sure that the name of Christ is anything more than a "stereotype," a mere blank X into which everyone puts the value he chooses?

There is a serious psychological obstacle which makes it difficult even to attack this problem. When anything becomes a religious symbol, it cannot be subjected to analytic scrutiny without evoking a furious palpitation of the heart which makes critical judgment almost impossible. When a Christian critic of the New Testament begins to sift the documents bearing upon the life of Jesus, and finds the familiar Jesus of popular mythology beginning to dis-

[1] I am told that there are already four different versions of the *text* of Sun Yat Sen's writings, each claiming to be authoritative.

appear, he cannot help feeling that sinking at the pit of the stomach which proverbially comes to the man who discovers that he is "sawing off the limb he's standing on." If the critic is a Christian first and a historical scientist afterward, he will unconsciously rationalize his dilemma in such a way as to produce a triumphant "vindication" of the popular view about Jesus. If he is a scientist first and a Christian afterward, or if (like the Ritschlian theologians) he keeps his Christianity and his science in "logic-tight compartments," he will nevertheless not escape the effect of his profound emotional attachment to the object of his investigation. Like a surgeon operating upon his own daughter, he is apt to strain so desperately after scientific coolness that he botches the job and kills the patient. Like a husband faced with the scientific problem of the faithfulness of his wife, he is unable to find any middle ground between warm assertion of undying trust and . . . an attitude of quite a different sort.[1] Nor is it any satisfactory solution to hand the question over to non-Christian critics. Their judgments may, to be sure, provide a valuable counter-check to those of Christian critics; but Christianity has become the object of so much furious antipathy, and so much of that antipathy has been transferred by association to the person of Christ, that no one who has ever heard of Christianity can be guaranteed to be free of prejudice about Christ.

There is only one way to approach theological questions successfully: to begin by showing that they are not so important as they seem! So long as a particular theological conviction is held to be a matter of life and death; so long

---

[1] I have noticed this leaning-over-backward effect in some of the greatest scholars under whom it has been my privilege to study. In their courses on the history of Christianity, they managed to combine the critical attitude with the appreciative attitude when dealing with the Hebrew prophets, or the Fathers, or the Reformers; but when dealing with Jesus they were utterly cold and unappreciative.

as it is really so fundamental to a man that he finds in it the whole stimulus of his life, and would be faced with the alternative of suicide if he lost it—and that it is not at all a fanciful dilemma!—under such circumstances, the conviction simply *cannot* be examined candidly. The man will use abusive language, willful falsehoods, and any other weapons he can lay his hands upon—a history of theological controversy would reveal that it has rarely been conducted according to the polite principles of good sportsmanship!—and the only way to make him rational is to convince him that the matter is not really so fundamental, after all. Convince a man that the main articles of Christian faith would remain substantially unimpaired if the doctrine of the Virgin Birth should be given up, and he can then discuss the question fairly; otherwise not. Convince him that if he were to give up the particular conception of God which he has inherited, he would not plunge inevitably into gross immorality or utter despair, and he can then fairly consider the question of the existence of God; otherwise not.

If, therefore, one wishes to estimate, fairly and objectively, the place which Jesus really deserves to hold in the estimation of all mankind, it is necessary to begin by distinguishing between the historic Jesus and the glorified "Christ" of Christian faith; and it is necessary to point out that all would not be lost, religiously, if it should be proved that Jesus of Nazareth was a wholly mythical character who never lived at all. Other great religious leaders, past and present, would remain; and the teachings commonly ascribed to Jesus, together with all the beautiful sentiments which have gathered round the name of "Christ," could still be judged and tested on their own merits. Christian love would be just as compelling a force among men, whoever first discovered it. As a matter of fact, we all get our first impressions of the truth and value of Christianity, not from any historical figure but from our immediate contemporaries. Destroy the original ground-plans, and the castle still stands. Once this has been perceived, and the worst has been faced with equanimity, it becomes possible to discuss the problem of the place of Jesus dispassionately, as one would discuss the place of Confucius or the place of Buddha; and it is in this spirit, let us hope, that we now approach it.

I. WHAT DID JESUS OF NAZARETH ACCOMPLISH FOR MANKIND?

The view that Jesus never lived at all may be dismissed as unhistorical. Such a view could never have arisen except as a protest against the frenzied excesses of adulation to which the followers of Jesus have sometimes given way. It may be regarded as an exaggeration of a truism: that the myth-making process has been at work upon the person of Jesus from the very beginning. The real question is, "Was Jesus such a person as to *deserve* to have myth and legend cluster about him, or was it all a historical accident?"

The question is entirely parallel to the question whether Socrates *deserves* his position as patron saint of the life of reason in the Western hemisphere, or owes his prominence solely to the fortunate circumstance that he was idolized by an eminent line of successors. In both cases, the historical facts cannot be precisely determined, for they have been thickly overlaid with idealizations. We see Socrates only through the eyes of Xenophon and Plato—the malicious caricature of Aristophanes can surely be dismissed—and the two pictures are quite as unlike as are the portraits of Jesus in the four Gospels. In the *Dialogues*, especially the later ones, it is clear that Plato puts his own sentiments into the mouth of Socrates, as the

author of the Gospel of John puts his own sentiments into
the mouth of Jesus. Neither in the case of Socrates nor
in the case of Jesus will it ever be possible to write a de-
tailed biography, with full confidence that it contains no
inaccuracies; yet in both cases it is plain that there came
into history, either through them or through their immediate successors—the former alternative is far the more
probable—a revolutionary and creative impulse whose
force has gone on increasing rather than diminishing with
the passing of the centuries. In the case of Socrates, one
may say that, if his successors created great philosophic
systems, he epitomized in his life and heroic death the
philosophic spirit which has animated them all, down to
this day. In the case of Jesus, one may fairly claim that
the following contributions to posterity stand out clearly
as his real achievements:

1. *Jesus inaugurated a new era in the history of Western morals.* Hitherto, for Jew and Greek alike, the *lex
talionis*, "an eye for an eye and a tooth for tooth," had
been the basis of the whole social order. The duty of
vengeance, and the unmanliness of forgiveness, were commonly recognized. There had been those, both in Israel
and in Greece,—Hosea, for example, and Plato,[1]—who
had pointed out a more excellent way; but they had failed
to catch the imagination of mankind. The best formulation
of ancient common-sense morality is to be found in the
Ethics of Aristotle, where it is quite plainly stated that
meekness is a slavish quality and the great law of retaliation underlies the whole structure of society.[2] So long as
vengeance was thus legalized and consecrated, mankind
was trapped in a vicious circle; for if retaliation does tend
to restrain injustice, it also tends to provoke further re-

---

[1] Notably in the *Gorgias*.
[2] *Ethics*, IV,5 and V,5.

taliation, eventuating in the feud or vendetta. It was Jesus who effectually broke this vicious circle for the Western world, as Gautama the Buddha broke it for the East.[1]

2. *As the historic source of multitudinous influences making for the transformation and liberation of human personality, Jesus is perhaps the greatest single redemptive force at work in the Western world today.* He is not only a moral leader but a moral savior. He seems to have been quite conscious of his rôle as "friend of sinners"; he knew that it was an original rôle and was prepared to be criticized for it. "Not he that is well hath need of a physician, but he that is sick"—such was the tactful and, one suspects, slightly ironic defense which he offered to his orthodox critics for his unconventional conduct in fraternizing with publicans and harlots. Whatever his intention, there can be no doubt of the result: as a consequence of contact with his dynamic personality, crooked men like Zacchæus became straight; weak, vacillating men like Peter became strong; and sick men were actually cured of their mental or physical disorders. Faith, health, and moral power exuded from him wherever he went; and the initial impulse which he communicated to the world through his little group of followers has never died out. Whenever men like Francis of Assisi have brushed away the accumulated débris of the centuries from his figure and so got a fresh perception of his personality, they in turn

---

[1] Felix Adler thus describes his first impressions of the Gospels, which he first read after his open break with the Jewish faith in which he had been nurtured: "I was particularly struck with the originality of Jesus' teachings, a quality in them which to my amazement I had found disputed, not only by Jews, but by representative Christians. . . . The impression of novelty which I received in reading the Gospels was definite and striking. . . . To put my thought briefly, I came to conclude that the ethical originality of Jesus consists in a new way of dealing with the problem of evil, that is, of evil in the guise of oppression." (*Ethical Philosophy of Life*, pp. 30-32.)

have become vitalizing centers of faith, health, and moral power, saviors and Christs to their generation.[1]

3. *By the boldness of his trust in God, and the indefatigability of his love for men, Jesus has become the living symbol of what many believe to be the deepest truth about the universe: that it responds to such trust, and expresses its very essence in such love as his.* It is impossible, of course, to prove the validity of this judgment by any simple test, either historical or psychological. Only the final outcome of all human experience will prove whether Jesus was a revealer of the one true God or a deluded enthusiast; whether he has shown us the right attitude to take toward the universe or betrayed us into a false trust in a universe which is really hostile or indifferent to us. But so long as anyone continues to believe in a God of love, he must continue to think of Jesus as the truest revelation and supreme incarnation of that God—the greatest Word that he has spoken in his effort to make himself intelligible to man.

The three contributions of Jesus just named correspond to the three aspects of historic Christianity discussed in the previous chapter. They reinforce the impression that what is most fundamentally important in Christianity can be traced to its Founder. But were we to stop here, as if the meaning of Jesus to posterity could be estimated by adding up the sum of the influences which he set afloat, we should fall short of the truth. The supreme "contribution" of Jesus is the story of his own life and death; and it will be hard for posterity, East or West, to refuse to accept *him*, whatever posterity may think of his teachings.

---

[1] Montefiore, the eminent Jewish scholar, finds in Jesus' attitude toward the lowly and the lost, in his out-going, aggressive concern for "sinners," the chief characteristic which differentiates him from the Rabbis and the prophets who were his contemporaries and predecessors. (*The Religious Teachings of Jesus,* end of Chapter II, on "Jesus and the Law.")

I would go so far as to say that there is no figure in history who belongs to the whole human race as does the figure of Jesus of Nazareth; and I would, therefore, contend that there is none so fit to serve as a rallying-point for world unity in religion. There are others, of course, who approach him in universality of appeal. Lincoln, bearing on his shoulders the weight of a great social conflict "with malice toward none and charity for all," belongs (or will eventually belong) to all Americans, North and South; and he is beginning to be appreciated far beyond our boundaries. Socrates, dying for pure love of truth, belongs to all truth-loving men in every place and time. The Buddha, turning back from the peace of Nirvana to share his great secret with suffering humanity, belongs in a very real sense to all of us, whether we accept his religion or not. But Jesus belongs to all of us in an even more poignant sense. *He belongs to all of us because, deliberately and with a full counting of the cost and the risk, he gave himself to all of us*—gave himself in so dramatic and tragic and compelling a fashion that no man to whom the gift is fairly presented can refuse it, unless he is blinded by prejudice or unless his soul is so narrow and constricted that it cannot expand to take in and comprehend so great a boon.

What does it mean, to say that Jesus "gave himself to all of us"? A swift survey of the dramatic story of his career should suffice to make the meaning plain.[1]

Imagine a young Jew of humble birth, growing up in a troublous time and brooding much over the fate of his

---

[1] In this brief sketch of the life of Jesus, I am relying upon the results of scientific New Testament criticism, as far as I have been able to assimilate them; but I am passing over all controversial matters that might obscure the simple, stark lines of the picture. In spite of many vagaries —such as the theory that Jesus and Judas had a secret understanding!— I find Middleton Murry's *Jesus: Man of Genius* the most convincing literary portrait of the Nazarene so far produced.

oppressed compatriots, and the strange, sad destiny of humankind. Imagine him reading the religious literature of his people—not under rabbinical instruction, but freshly for himself—and, brushing aside all irrelevancies, pushing straight to its fundamental and universal elements; then, turning upon life as it is about him, piercing its insincerities and hypocrisies at one swift glance, so that the whole existing order of things stands condemned in his eyes, a rotten fabric ready to fall in pieces, too far gone for patching and ripe for destruction.

At this juncture, word comes to him that a new prophet has appeared in the desert, proclaiming that the times are fulfilled and the end of the age is at hand. The young man finds the message plausible, and enrolls himself among the followers of the prophet; but he soon outgrows his instruction. John's message is negative, grim, ascetic; Jesus launches out for himself, preaching a message that deserves (far more than Nietzsche's!) to bear the name of "The Joyful Wisdom." Put aside hatred, pride, and fear, he says; let love impel you to abandon all privileges and share your brothers' lot; see life clear-eyed and simply, like little children, and you may take the Kingdom of Heaven by storm. Even great sinners, if they change their attitude, may enter that Kingdom, here and now! The common people hear him gladly; many are healed of their ills and many lives are changed; and in exultation he cries, "I have beheld Satan fallen as lightning from heaven!"

But soon comes a turn of the tide; and he finds himself repulsed, left alone with his joyful wisdom, his gift rejected. The civil and religious authorities, with that sensitiveness to their own interests which all organized groups exhibit, instinctively feel that the whole established order is being threatened at its very core by this young teacher; and they band themselves together against him. His own kinsfolk, alarmed at his temerity and thinking him mad, try to induce him to come home and keep quiet. Finally he is forced to flee from his native country to escape arrest at the hands of Herod the Tetrarch, who has already put the prophet John to death.

What shall he do now? He might conceivably, even yet, make his peace with the authorities, settle down quietly and become a learned rabbi—as disillusioned prophets in our day become harmless scholars and literati. Or if he could not placate Herod, after once defying the "old fox," he might at any rate live peaceably in exile, philosophically resigning himself to his failure. But he does none of these things. Instead of taming his spirit, failure only deepens his sense of mission. Misunderstood, lonely, thrown back upon himself, he becomes only the more convinced that God has entrusted to him a message for mankind which must somehow be delivered. It looks as though he could not give the message without giving his life. Very well; so be it!

What did Jesus have in mind when he "set his face to go up to Jerusalem"? No one knows; no one will ever know. It is plain that his followers did not understand him at the time; how should we pretend to understand him now? But it is evident that he was playing a bold game, single-handed against all his adversaries. He did not mean to be caught like a rat in a trap, like poor John; if he must die, he would die as publicly as possible, in the capital city, on the great festal day of the Passover. That year, he would be the Pascal lamb! Or perhaps God would publicly vindicate him in some dramatic fashion, and *so* his message would be delivered.

If he expected any such divine intervention, he was disappointed. He played his game skillfully, to the very end. By appearing in public only when the presence of the multitude insured his safety, he escaped arrest until the very eve of the Passover; then, after a last terrific struggle with himself, questioning whether this were really God's will for him or no, he permitted himself to be betrayed and captured. The authorities made short work of him. Next day, he hung in his death-agony upon a cruel instrument of torture, ignominiously flanked by two thieves. Hours passed. God did not intervene to vindicate him. The whole tragedy and bitterness of human existence whelmed down upon him. "My God, my God, why hast thou forsaken me!" he cried; and soon after, with a loud shout, he expired. He had risked all, and lost!

And yet he had not lost, and he has been vindicated. From the ignominious eminence of the Cross, he has caught the eye of the world, and won the heart of the world. He has *given himself to the world*, in a fashion that makes it almost impossible to refuse the gift or to undervalue it. The disturbing influence of his joyful wisdom and the magic of his personality are now the common property of mankind, forever. His friends have been his worst enemies. They have wrapped him about with a tissue of pious legend and theological speculation; and many have rejected the gift because of the wrappings. Jews, in particular, have been restrained from taking their greatest son to their heart, because his name has been upon the lips of their persecutors. But as these wrappings and false associations are torn away by critical historians, and the simple human story of Jesus stands forth in all its power, it is becoming harder and harder to resist him.[1] Sooner or later, men accept the gift of himself which he proffers with tragically extended arms—and give themselves to him in return.

---

[1] I am inclined to agree with Rabbi H. G. Enelow, who closes his book called *A Jewish View of Jesus* with the prediction that Jesus may yet prove to be a bond of unity between Jews and Christians. This could never be, so long as Christians obscured the simple historic facts of the life of Jesus with their anti-Jewish theology.

In its doctrine concerning the Person and Work of Christ, Christianity has gone to the utmost limits of metaphysical subtlety and speculative daring; and, exceeding even those limits, has plunged into a sea of magic, mystagogy, and mummery. To many modern minds, this frantic, boundless adulation of the Founder of Christianity has become so distasteful that they are unable to see in him anything more than a second-rate fanatic, deified by the superheated imagination of his followers, who managed to persuade themselves that he had risen from the dead. "If this faith of the Apostles in their Master's restoration to life had not been published abroad," says Guignebert, "*there would have been no Christianity*"; [1] and the implication apparently is, that had the figure of Jesus not been advertised to the world in this extraordinary way, it could never have deserved the world's attention. Yet, it seems to me, a more discerning eye must see in the resurrection-faith itself, and the constantly increasing weight of divine and miraculous attributes under which the Church has buried (and too effectually entombed!) the figure of its Founder, a deeply moving evidence of the exalted affection which he had the power to inspire in his friends; [2] and even in the most daring and fantastic speculations of theology concerning the Incarnation and the Atonement,

---

[1] Guignebert. *Christianity*, p. 47. Published by The Macmillan Company, New York.

[2] Cf. Montague, *Belief Unbound*, p. 17: "To have discovered and proclaimed the way of absolute beauty and at the same time to have shown that it is free to all, and then to have lived gently and ardently and died terribly as a supreme exemplification of his own teaching, is enough for a son of God born of woman. For us to try to better the picture by ornamenting its frame with biological and psychological anomalies, such as a virgin birth and a miraculous absence of all sin and ignorance, verges on the tawdry. For his immediate successors, however, it was understandable and pardonable enough, for they could see no better way of honoring their friend and celebrating the glory and solace of his message, than by following the well-worn path of mythological custom. . . ." Published by Yale University Press. (1930.)

the literal truth about his uniquely fascinating life can still be traced.

The doctrine of the Incarnation sounds, indeed, as if it had no basis at all in religious experience: it teaches that Christ was a preëxistent spiritual being, "who, existing in the form of God, counted not the being on an equality with God a thing to be grasped, but emptied himself, taking the form of a servant, being made in the likeness of men."[1] Yet there can be no doubt that this exalted conception of Christ had its roots in the religious experience of St. Paul—not only in his experience of the risen Christ upon the Damascus road, but also in his appreciation of a certain divine quality of self-impartation in the earthly Jesus: "For ye know the grace of our Lord Jesus Christ, that, though he was rich, yet for your sakes he became poor, that ye through his poverty might be rich."[2] Irenæus put the matter still more simply: "He became what we are, that he might bring us to be what he is."[3] These words are applicable to the myth of a celestial spirit stooping from high heaven, and taking upon him human flesh, "for us men and our salvation"; but they are equally applicable to the literal facts of the earthly life of Jesus, who identified himself with the lowly and the outcast and the lost that he might bring them back to themselves and back to the divine Source from which he believed they sprang. The doctrine of the Incarnation is but a poetical and metaphysical amplification of these bare facts—an amplification such as they must needs receive whenever their impact falls upon grateful human hearts.

The same may be said of the doctrine of the Atonement. Formally, it appears to deal with a mysterious legal transaction between the persons of the Trinity, a bargain

---

[1] Philippians 2:6, 7.
[2] II Corinthians 8:9.
[3] *Adv. Haeres. V, præf.; cf. Athanasius, c. Arianos,* i. 39.

concluded in heaven, whereby Christ, the righteous one, has his righteousness transferred to sinful man and has man's guilt and punishment artificially transferred to him. Actually, it is an attempt to express the significance of the sense of cleansing, reconciliation, and infinite indebtedness which came to the first Christians as they considered the grim fact of their leader's tragic death. Tragic it was, but grandly tragic; tragedy that made the world better for its occurrence; tragedy that purged men's souls as only great tragedy can do; tragedy that somehow overcame and atoned for the wickedness that caused it.[1] All theories of the Atonement—wooden and incredible as they may sound—are more or less successful efforts to suggest what this great tragedy has actually done for human beings; and the most highly metaphysical theories are perhaps the truest! To the modern mind, what has been called the "moral" theory of the Atonement has the most immediate appeal, according to which Christ bore man's sins by "sympathy," and the effect of his death was not in any wise to change the eternal relationship between God and man, but only to exemplify God's suffering love in such a way as to win man to repentance. To all who can believe in a God of love, this is highly rational and satisfactory; and yet, to one who studies attentively the awesome tragedy of the Cross and its impact upon human experience, it often seems that the older, "transactional" views of the Atonement, with all their legalistic absurdities, expressed the plain historical truth of the matter more fully than the "moral" theory. It is not enough to say that Jesus bore the sins of his contemporaries by "sympathy"; he bore them, as Walter Rauschenbusch puts it,

---

[1] It is precisely this kind of tragedy which, according to Mr. Joseph Wood Krutch, is forever unachievable and unbelievable (except by naïve self-deception) in our modern mechanized world! (*The Modern Temper*, Chapter on "The Tragic Fallacy.")

"in their impact on his own body and soul,"[1] as Arnold von Winkelried bore the Austrian spears in his breast. He met, was overcome by, and overcame the massed attack of the evil that pollutes the whole stream of human history, in which we all participate by social solidarity; and his tragic victory has somehow—as conservative theology always insists—made things different "once for all" and forever afterwards. Through his life and death there has flowed into human history a kind of valorous, sacrificial love which was radically new, and which has the power to reconcile men not only to their hard lot in life, but to their own past failures and traitorous deeds; for it carries with it the conviction that, in the words of Royce, *"No baseness or cruelty of treason so deep or so tragic shall enter our human world, but that loyal love shall be able in due time to oppose to just that deed of treason its fitting deed of atonement."*[2]

In a word, the supreme achievement of Jesus of Nazareth has been to make the existence of a good God seem credible and almost tangibly real. It is not for us to say, at this stage in our argument, whether that is a service to mankind or not. If belief in God is a primitive superstition, which man must outgrow before he can fulfill his true destiny, then Jesus of Nazareth is not to be named among the benefactors of mankind; for he is the greatest single obstacle in the way of the advancement of atheism! But if there truly exists a Cosmic Mind that participates in our human sufferings, but enables us to transcend them, then the crowning evidence of God's existence must be seen, not in the orderliness of nature or the general trend of human history, but in the life and death of an untutored

---

[1] Rauschenbusch, *Theology for the Social Gospel*, p. 258. Published by The Macmillan Company, New York.

[2] Royce, *The Problem of Christianity*, Volume I, p. 322. By permission of The Macmillan Company, publishers, New York. (1918.)

young Jew who brought God's love and power near to us two thousand years ago.

It may be that the religion of the future will be more concerned with general principles, abstract ideals, technical problems of ways and means, and less concerned with the values enshrined in great personalities than religion has been in the past. It may be that men will cease to turn to the past for inspiration and guidance, and come to regard the good life as a simple problem in social engineering, to be faced in a matter-of-fact mood, as one builds a bridge or plans a budget. In that case, Jesus will have no significance for the religion of the future, for the general verdict will be that the reading of biography is to be severely discouraged. But so long as man feels the need of the power that comes from great lives—and that, I venture to say, will be for a long time to come—so long will the figure of Jesus loom up in the midst of the host of the great and the good as the dome of St. Paul's looms up among the church spires of London. The longer one's glance rests upon any of the others—and there are many worthy of prolonged attention—the more surely is it led back to him.

This is, of course, a value-judgment, like that which acclaims Beethoven as the supreme musician. Such judgments cannot be forced upon anyone; they must be the product of spontaneous appreciation, and there will always be those who cannot honestly subscribe to them. It is possible to consider the life and teachings of Jesus and remain unmoved, as it is possible to be bored at a performance of the Fifth Symphony or the Sonata Appassionata. But if any one person is to become the flag, the emblem, the organizing center of world unity in religion, I am convinced that it is most likely to be Jesus. Mahatma Gandhi is witness enough that this is more than a Christian prejudice.

2. THE JESUS OF HISTORY AND THE LIVING CHRIST

Thus far, we have been exclusively concerned with Jesus the Nazarene, a historical character who lived and died in the first century of our era. Brushing aside so far as possible the web of romance and pious legend which mass psychology has woven about him, we have found that the simple human record of his life and teachings must be counted among the great and lasting resources of mankind. But it must be confessed that no mere historical character, no mere figure in the pages of a book, however attractive and inspiring, can ever perform the redemptive functions which Christianity attributes to Christ. As a matter of fact, it has never been seriously maintained (except by certain modern theologians of the Ritschlian school) that the Jesus of history could, so to speak, jump out from between the covers of the New Testament and, leaping across the intervening centuries, save sinners and make saints in modern New York. When the Salvation Army invites sinners to "Come to Jesus," when it announces that "Jesus saves," *it does not mean simply the Jesus of history; it means the "Living Christ": a living spirit whose imperfect body is the Church, whose immediate presence and healing power can be experienced by men today.* If, therefore, we are to penetrate to the heart of Christianity, we must study the psychology of this most characteristic Christian experience and seek to estimate its significance for the development of human personality.[1]

---

[1] In conservative circles, this experience of the Living Christ is often used as the distinguishing mark of a true Christian. For example, Mr. Gandhi, the foremost living exponent of the Sermon on the Mount, is considered to be quite correct in refusing to call himself a Christian, because he has never "accepted Christ as his personal Saviour." Cf. the following significant passage from a review of Pringle-Pattison's *Philosophy of Religion* in a conservative periodical: "One says it humbly and

Historically speaking, this experience first manifested itself in the disciples' vision of the risen Jesus, and in the "descent of the Holy Spirit" upon the Jerusalem church on the day of Pentecost; but it was Paul's conversion experience upon the road to Damascus which did most to impress the belief in the Living Christ, accessible to all Christians, upon the consciousness of later centuries.[1] Christ was there revealed not only *to* him, by some rending of the heavens, but "in him," as he tells the Galatians[2] in describing his conversion. In other words, it seems likely that Paul conceived of Christ as both transcendent and immanent—an indwelling cosmic spirit, in the same category of existence with the angels and demons who peopled Paul's universe. As a man could be possessed by a demon, so he could be possessed by Christ. To the end of Paul's life, there remained in his inner consciousness a definite object called "Christ," which was the controlling center of his activity. Paul felt that all he had to do was to let this possessing spirit act through him and he could not go wrong. He was unable to live up to his ideals through his own strength; but now that difficulty was over, for he was not Paul any longer, but Christ, just in so far as he remained united in intimate fellowship

---

sadly, the author has surely never known, in his own personal experience, the Lord Christ, Who is the daily companion of those who love Him. Professor Pringle-Pattison writes as an appreciative but rather disinterested appraiser of a historical character, long since dead, whose history is largely obscured through the later speculations that have warped the only records we have of His life. Any humble Christian could give a more worthy and true account of Christ in the course of a few minutes than this learned professor gives in several chapters." (The quarterly *Register* of the Louisville Presbyterian Seminary, XIX, No. 4, p. 17.)

[1] At this point begins the first of a series of quotations from an article of mine entitled "Shall We Discard the Living Christ?" (*Biblical World*, May, 1919). Since the quotations are rather numerous and much amended, I am not making use of quotation marks. I have permission of the *Journal of Religion* (successor to the *Biblical World*) to use these quotations.

[2] Galatians 1:15, 16.

with his guiding spirit. This experience seems to have been the source of his amazing energy, self-confidence, and influence; and in one form or another it has been a part of Christianity ever since.

The conception of the Living Christ is different in the Catholic and Protestant churches; but the experience is not fundamentally different. For the Catholic, Christ is closely associated with the Church, and the sense of his "Real Presence" is conveyed by visible and tangible symbols: by the bread and the wine of the Holy Eucharist, which in some mysterious sense are his veritable body; and also by the hierarchical rulers of the Church, who are his earthly representatives and functionaries. For the Protestant, Christ is not so closely associated with the Church; he is thought to be immediately accessible to mystic experience, apart from any intermediaries whatsoever. As Schleiermacher puts it, the Catholic comes to Christ through the Church, while the Protestant comes to the Church through Christ. Yet if one compares the Christ mysticism of St. Bernard or Thomas à Kempis with the Christ mysticism of Zinzendorf or Wesley, one becomes at once convinced that, beneath their differences, Catholics and Protestants share an underlying unity of experience: a sense of power and guidance springing from communion with a spiritual Presence which is at once the communal mind of the Christian Church, the connective tissue which holds Christian history together, and in some sense, the continuation of the life of the historic Jesus. It is this "communal Jesus"[1]—not the historic Jesus—who is, to Catholic and Protestant alike, "the joy of loving hearts"

[1] For an interesting distinction between *seven* senses of the word "Jesus," see the remarkable article on "The Significance of Jesus" by A. C. McGiffert, Jr., in the *Journal of Religion* for January, 1931. The article also contains an excellent psychological analysis of the significance of the historic Jesus.

and the source of saving grace. It is he who converts and regenerates men in the Bowery Mission; whose spirit moves men to engage in daring missionary service; who is the source of moral power to millions of humble Christians the world over.

What is this experience of the Living Christ, psychologically speaking? I suppose it might be described as the reinforcement of the individual will by conscious and continual submission to the influence of a personified ideal—an ideal which, moreover, the believer feels to be grounded in the nature of things and really as well as imaginatively present in power. This ideal may have little to do with the actual character of Jesus of Nazareth. Often, if not generally, the ideal is derived from elsewhere. What seizes and transforms the drunkard is the ideals he was taught in childhood. What a youth embraces when he joins the Church is the moral standard prevalent in his church—often copied from the popular morality of the district. Sometimes conversion is an even more fundamental overturn than this, a recrudescence under some favoring stimulus of the deep-lying social instincts, too long suppressed under a mass of selfish impulses and habits. In such cases the Christ who redeems is the parental impulse itself, the spirit of love that lies dormant in us all, the "light that lighteth every man that cometh into the world." In one or another sublimated form this motive is present in practically all experiences of the Living Christ that are ethically fruitful like Paul's, and not merely mystical. It is powerfully or feebly fostered by the more or less vigorous moral consciousness of the local church.

The Living Christ, then, is a composite photograph of the best Christians the new convert sees about him. He is the embodiment of that group consciousness of the Church which—when in times of stress it is sufficiently aroused to ardor—is known as the Holy Spirit. He is the more or less perfect incarnation of the Spirit of Love, which results when a man comes under the influence of the Holy Spirit speaking through the Church. This incarnation begins when something in the Gospel that is preached, or lived, strikes home; it is progressively extended through the continual influence of the ideal upon the actual. The ideal of yesterday is the actuality of today; the ideal of today is a new and more glorious thing. This ever actualized, ever glorified ideal is the Living Christ. "And all of us, with unveiled faces, reflecting like bright mirrors the glory of the Lord, are being transformed into the same likeness, from one degree of radiant holiness to another, even as derived from the Lord the Spirit."[1]

We are ready now to consider whether the name "Living Christ" is appropriate; in other words, whether the historic Jesus is in any sense to be found in this ideal figure. That is a hard question to answer unequivocally. In the first place, even if one happens to attribute to the Living Christ a character precisely like that of the historic Jesus, it is hard to see any literal connection between the ideal figure of today and the historic figure of the first century. In the second place, the subjective variations between the diverse conceptions of the Living Christ actually held by Christians are so great as to make it difficult to believe in his veritable reality. "Christ" is simply the reflex of local moral codes, if we are to judge from appearances; and often enough he is made to act as the protagonist of pharisaic ideals that the Jesus of history fought against all his life! I should like to observe, nevertheless, that the same variation of subjective judgment exists in other fields—in our conception of Nature, for example, and in our opinions of our neighbors—and in

---

[1] II Corinthians 3:18, Weymouth's translation.

such cases we do not necessarily conclude that no objective reality gives rise to these fluctuating subjective estimates. I am strongly inclined to assert that there is a present reality working in the world, through the Church, which is substantially identical with the personality of Jesus of Nazareth. The lines along which identity can be traced are the following:

1. With a considerable proportion of Christians the basis of their conception of the Living Christ is the picture of Jesus which they find in the Gospels. Jesus thus lives in their minds substantially as he lived in Galilee, though of course the picture is very imperfect. If there be no such thing as personal immortality, Jesus has at least this immortality of influence.

2. So great was the initial impress of Jesus' personality upon his followers that its effects have never wholly ceased. Even when we do not consciously go to the Jesus of history for guidance and inspiration we are getting from a thousand sources his own personal influence, transmitted from generation to generation of Christians.[1]

There is, then, and I believe there always will be a place for an idealized portrait of Jesus, in which are embodied the best Christian ideals of our own day, as well as the qualities which we admire in the historic Jesus. If we have such a concept and recognize its distinctness in certain respects from the historic Jesus, we shall not be led into the error of reading our later ideals back into the historic Jesus. We shall be able to give credit where

---

[1] It is impossible to read any narrative of the work of the Salvation Army, such as Hugh Redwood's *God in the Slums*, without feeling that in the divine compassion of these simple, unsophisticated Christians, the life of Christ is literally continued. In cases of conversion which occur under their ministry, the "Christ" who saves is the Christ embodied in the Christ-like faith, hope, and love of the Army, working upon any vestiges of early religious training or any divine spark that may glow in the sodden breasts of drunkards and harlots.

credit is due—to Greek philosophy and the modern scientific temper, as well as to all other ideals which Christianity has assimilated in its long career—and we can treat Jesus as we treat the Bible, with perfect intellectual candor, not requiring him to conform to our ideals, but giving him liberty to be what he may be. If personal immortality is a fact, and Jesus is working in the world today, we must suppose that his ideals have developed to meet the changing vicissitudes of history, just as the conception of the Living Christ, the embodiment of the Christian ideal, has developed in the consciousness of the Church.

The question is indeed open whether it be not better to discard the historic Jesus than to discard the Living Christ. The Living Christ is immediately accessible, as the historic Jesus is not. The Living Christ is a safe guide for today, for he embodies ideals that have been painfully achieved since the time of Jesus; but the historic Jesus has nothing definite to say to us on some of the greatest questions of our day—international questions, social questions, and the like. It may be that he lived an ideal life two thousand years ago, but how does that help us, who have to live under such different conditions?

Actually, of course, it is necessary to keep both conceptions, if either is to retain its force. The historic Jesus helps us at two vital points where the Living Christ fails us:

1. It makes a tremendous difference that Jesus really lived; that the ideals which he represented in his teaching were really proved practicable in his life. It is this in part that makes men call him Saviour; that under typical human conditions he met and mastered the forces of evil to which most of us yield. Conditions have changed, it is true; but the fundamental evils that killed Jesus are with us today, as Rauschenbusch makes so plain. At critical points in our moral history, when we are tempted to give

up our ideals and yield to expediency, it is the historic Jesus who can give firmness to our wavering wills and minds. If the Living Christ can do this also, and with more intensity, it is only because we are firmly convinced that none of the new ideals associated with his name is out of harmony with the ideals which the historic Jesus successfully incarnated. Without the historic Jesus as its firm foundation, the conception of the Living Christ is powerless to help us in such crises.

2. It is to the historic Jesus that we go for new ethical insight into new social situations. Herrmann is quite right in his observation that as a rule the Living Christ does not free our souls and lure them on to new heights of perfection as the historic Jesus does. The Living Christ gives us a vivid realization of the ideals we already hold, and helps us to live up to them; but when new moral issues arise he cannot help us. It is an easily observable fact that members of evangelical churches, who make most of the doctrine of the Living Christ, are remarkable for moral vigor but lacking in ethical discrimination. What they need is a more intensive study of the character of the historic Jesus. If that will not convict them of sin and make ethical reformers of them, nothing will; not even the study of ethics will do it so well, for there is more in the personality of Jesus than ever has been or ever can be crammed into a system of ethics. "What would Jesus do in this situation?" is an excellent rule of conduct, even though the historic Jesus never found himself in the situation in question; for as the classic embodiment of the attitude of love there is something authoritative about the ethical pattern of his life, about the attitude in which he stands over against his environment. He is not to be taken as an arbitrary authority; his example is opposed to such a procedure; but he is to be made an inspiring counselor and guide in our efforts to solve our own ethical problems.

Experience has taught many of us that in Jesus are to be found truths that we afterward discover running all through life and blazoned across the face of the heavens —but we should never have found them in life if we had not first found them in Jesus. Experience has taught us that on the whole it is safe to trust Jesus' principles—his central principles, that is—even when it is impossible at first to verify them in life; for many times a persecuted sect like the Quakers, by steadfast adherence to ridiculed and apparently impracticable ethical principles which they believed they found in Jesus, has at length proved that these principles *are* practicable. As long as Jesus continues to do this for us he is our supreme prophet.

I must still insist, however, that alongside the conception of the historic Jesus, and constantly interacting with it, we need to retain the conception of the Living Christ; for it keeps before our minds in vivid form the whole body of ideals that have developed in the course of Christian history as the necessary result of the reaction of Jesus' spirit upon changing social environments, and it—or rather, the Reality it represents—gives us moral power to live up to them. If there is one thing that we miss in the liberal Christianity which more and more prevails, it is that sense of the presence of a great sustaining moral power which used to be the glory of the evangelical churches. Ethical sensitiveness is here aplenty in the liberal movement, but I am not so sure about moral power. If this diagnosis be correct, liberalism needs to recover the experience of the Living Christ. It must, of course, be constantly corrected by comparison with the Jesus of the Gospels, as conscience is constantly corrected by reflection; but it cannot be replaced by any mere historical portrait of Jesus. The experience of the Living Christ is the most vital and intimate form in which the experience of God comes to us; and his voice—which is at once the voice of Jesus, and of the Spirit in the Church—should be heard with reverence.

From the purely human and social point of view which we have adopted as our provisional platform in Part II of this book, it is impossible to settle all the fascinating metaphysical questions which cluster thickly about the conception of the Living Christ. Until the problem of belief in God and in immortality has been faced in Part III, we can only say, "*If* there is a God, then one may find a true revelation of him in Jesus of Nazareth, continued and expanded in the constantly enriched experience of the Living Christ. And *if* immortality is a fact, then one may conceive of the Living Christ as the conscious continuation of the life which apparently ended on the Cross. Already, however, we may assert positively that the experience of the Living Christ is not merely a subjective illusion, for we have seen that in most instances it is traceable to external stimulation, in the shape of some actual contact, present or past, with Christian tradition and the Christian spirit.[1] Provisionally, we may describe the external reality

---

[1] For an apparent negative instance, consider the conversion experience of Mr. S. H. Hadley, cited in James's *Varieties of Religious Experience* (Longmans, Green and Co., 27th impression, 1916), pp. 201-203: "As I sat there thinking, I seemed to feel some great and mighty presence. I did not know then what it was. I did learn afterwards that it was Jesus, the sinner's friend. I walked up to the bar and pounded it with my fist till I made the glasses rattle. Those who stood by drinking looked on with scornful curiosity. I said I would never take another drink, if I died on the street, and really I felt as though that would happen before morning. Something said, 'If you want to keep this promise, go and have yourself locked up.' I went to the nearest station-house, and had myself locked up. . . ."

". . . When I arose the following Sabbath morning I felt that day would decide my fate, and toward evening it came into my head to go to Jerry M'Auley's Mission. . . . There I saw the apostle to the drunkard and the outcast—that man of God, Jerry M'Auley. He rose, and amid deep silence told his experience. There was a sincerity about this man that carried conviction with it, and I found myself saying, 'I wonder if God can save *me*?' . . . I said, 'Dear Jesus, can you help me?' Never with

which evokes this experience as a great broadening stream of hallowing influence or "grace," taking its rise[1] in the actual life and teachings of Jesus of Nazareth, enriched by many tributaries in its course across the centuries, but having its chief historic channel in the Christian Church, and its irrigating sluiceways in the generous outpourings of Christ's spirit from the Church—symbolically in the sacraments, more literally in the preaching of the Word, and *most* literally in the *living* of the Gospel by Christ-filled men and women.

Such a conception makes it possible, even without delving into ultimate metaphysics, to settle many puzzling theological questions which have vexed the Christian Church. It shows that the Catholics are right in their contention that we come to Christ through the visible Church —just as we come to an appreciation of Washington and Jefferson through the medium of the American civilization which they helped to create—but it also shows that the Protestants are right in their objection to the Catholic

---

mortal tongue can I describe that moment. Although up to that moment my soul had been filled with indescribable gloom, I felt the glorious brightness of the noonday sun shine into my heart. I felt I was a free man. Oh, the precious feeling of safety, of freedom, of resting on Jesus! I felt that Christ with all his brightness and power had come into my life; that, indeed, old things had passed away and all things had become new." (Quoted by permission.)

The "Jesus" who saved Mr. Hadley from drunkenness and suicide appears to be a purely subjective or endopsychic urge for larger life; and Professor Leuba so interprets the case. Yet there was clearly, even in this case, the objective stimulus of Jerry M'Auley's testimony; and the subjective urge was probably traceable to early religious instruction.

[1] I do not mean to assert that the life of Jesus was an absolute "new beginning," with no historic antecedents or sources. All that was noble and life-giving in the Jewish heritage helped to produce the character of Jesus; so that the river of grace did not, strictly speaking, "take its rise" in him, or "flow down from heaven" through him alone. Yet in the river of grace that waters and fertilizes our Western world, he represents the ever-living and ever-abundant spring (nourished, of course, by subterranean connections with remoter sources) to which one most naturally points when asked where that river takes its rise.

tendency to find Christ literally, materially, and perfectly
embodied in the ritual, dogma, and government of the
Church. The Church is the central channel through which
the life of Jesus is connected with the life of today; and
it is important to maintain its continuity unbroken (as the
Catholics insist), lest the Living Christ be severed from
the Jesus of history; but its continuity does not depend
upon the maintenance of an unbroken line of prelates,
descending in due legal succession from the apostles by
virtue of the official laying on of hands. The true Apostolic
Succession is nothing so legal and formal as that. It maintains the unbroken continuity of the Church not through
episcopal ordination, but through the contact of life upon
life—a vital sacrament which the layman is often more
competent to perform than the clergyman! The Quakers
are wrong, of course, in their theory that they can com-
mune with Christ directly, through the "Inner Light,"
without the mediation of Christian tradition; but as a
matter of common observation, they have more of the
genuine, healing, redemptive Spirit of Christ than most
High Churchmen.

The doctrine of the Real Presence of the Living Christ
in the Church, his Living Body, is a great Catholic doctrine which Protestants could perfectly well appropriate,
from this point of view; but they would have to continue
to protest against the view that Christ's Real Presence is
supremely made manifest in the bread and the wine of the
Eucharist; *Christ's Real Presence is primarily to be found
in the individual and corporate life of Christlike people.*
The sacrament of Christ's body and blood is a beautiful
symbolic expression of the dependence of all Christians
upon Christ, and the organic fellowship which results
from that common dependence; but to confuse the sacrament with the fellowship it represents is as bad as con-

fusing the church edifice[1] with the true "temple of the Holy Ghost." We need visible, tangible sacraments and symbols, like baptism and the Eucharist, for we are men of flesh and blood; but we must not become so attached to the sign that we miss the thing signified. "This is my body," in the eleventh chapter of First Corinthians, must not be understood literally; the true Body of Christ, which the Eucharist symbolizes, is described in the next chapter: "Together you are the body of Christ, and individually its parts."[2]

Since the influence of Christlike men and women constantly penetrates beyond the Church into the surrounding civilization, Christ's body cannot simply be identified with the visible Church, although the continuity of the Christian tradition is chiefly maintained by the Church. The Living Christ works as truly through the home, the school, the hospital and the settlement as through ecclesiastical channels; and so if we are to identify the Church with the Body of Christ, we must vastly expand the conception of the Church, to take in many persons and institutions that hardly know the name of Christ. All who have been drawn into the Apostolic Succession through the kindling touch of Christian life upon non-Christian life become thereby parts of the living, growing Body of the Living Christ. They are not a very adequate body for the great Spirit that informs the Christian movement; but they are the best he has. Some day he will have a better body: a Christian world civilization.

---

[1] Of course, there is a real sense in which Christ is present in the church edifice. Any place, any art, any custom may be sanctified by Christian usage; and one might truly claim that Gothic architecture, Italian painting, Bach's chorales, and the poetry of Dante and Milton "embodied Christ." Yet the embodiment of Christ in ritual, art, and preaching must always be held as secondary to his embodiment in life.

[2] I Corinthians 11:24; 12:27. (Translation of the latter taken from Twentieth Century New Testament.)

3. JESUS, CHRISTIANITY, AND THE RELIGION OF THE FUTURE

It seems but a step from the conception of the Living Christ to the conception of the Living God. It is but a step, *for Christians*. If the Christian world were the whole world, we could now pass directly to the discussion of those great metaphysical questions whose mystery we have already confronted in our analysis of the experience of the Living Christ. But in a world where provincialism of all kinds is being crowded out by a new sense of planetary unity, it is impossible to ignore the existence of other great religious (and anti-religious) traditions, and impossible to assume, without discussion, that the pathway to God (if God there be) lies through the Christian tradition alone. The test by which we have been judging Christianity is the psychological test—capacity to free men from all that impedes the full and harmonious development of their personalities, and capacity to release their deepest potentialities. Judged by that same test, the Living Buddha must be admitted to have done for the East very much what the Living Christ has done for the West; and Russian Communism, with its passionate devotion to the task of destroying religion, must be rated high as a channel of saving grace! To be sure, primitive Buddhism was fundamentally a negation of the whole quest of fullness of life, and Russian Communism seems to deny the very existence of any spiritual potentialities in man; yet Buddhism in its developed form is charged with a human compassion and an æsthetic richness which make it a noble vehicle of personal development, while Communism in practice produces a powerful type of personality, based on absolute self-devotion in the presence of a great social ideal, beside which our average American "Christian," grown flabby with prosperity and self-indulgence, looks pale and anæmic indeed.

What attitude shall we take in the presence of these and other rival faiths? It is impossible, from the psychological point of view, to rule everything but Christianity out of the picture. All the great surviving faiths, in various degrees, are real resources for the development of personality and must, therefore, he regarded as expressions of that hypothetical Supreme Resource called God, whose existence and nature we are shortly to investigate. All, including Christianity, have serious defects as they actually stand; and all, in their spurious or degraded forms, are positive *hindrances* to the development of personality. Some forms of Christianity are far worse than some forms of Buddhism, and *vice versa*. Once this has been admitted, we seem to be led to the conclusion which Rabbi Silver has recently defended with such power: universality in the field of religion is forever out of the question, and the hope of the future is that all should learn tolerance enough to "enable them to meet in joint, coöperative enterprises without losing their individualities."[1]

With some features of Rabbi Silver's argument one must unhesitatingly agree: that "artificial uniformity" in religion is both undesirable and impossible, now that freedom of conscience and the "right of non-conformity" have been won after centuries of struggle; that religions may meet and coöperate without endeavoring to swallow one another up; that religion can never be universal in quite the same sense as science; that there are in every religion precious values which are necessarily private and distinctive, and which would be lost to humanity if that religion permitted itself to be dissolved in some general melting-pot; that Christ can never mean quite the same thing to

---

[1] *Religion in a Changing World*, p. 113. Published by Richard R. Smith, Inc., New York. (1930.)

the Oriental or the Jew that he does to the Occidental Christian, any more, one might add, than Lincoln can ever mean the same thing to an Englishman or a Southerner that he does to a man whose father was killed in the Union army. Yet when all these admissions have been made, it must still be insisted that the religion of the future, if it is to be adequate to meet the psychological needs and claim the allegiance of our descendants, must be something far more unified, much closer to what might properly be called *a world religion*, than anything we know at present; and in the making of that world religion there is reason to believe that the *spirit* of the Living Christ—whatever may become of his *name*—will play a central rôle.

The whole world is today much smaller than was the Mediterranean basin in the first century A.D. A century ago, it was still possible for the Eastern and Western worlds to live their lives separately, untroubled by the fact that Eastern civilization denied all the basic assumptions of Western religion, and Western civilization denied all the basic assumptions of Eastern religion. A generation ago, with increasing contacts, the difference between East and West began to be felt more acutely, but was accepted fatalistically, as something inevitable, and not without its conveniences! Kipling was the great interpreter of this phase of thought:

Ship me somewhere East of Suez, where the best is like the
    worst,
Where there ain't no Ten Commandments, and a man can
    raise a thirst.

Today, the East and West confront each other more critically and less tolerantly, conscious of their wide divergencies of outlook but conscious also of the necessity of finding some common basis of understanding, if they are not to come to blows and batter each other to pieces. In the angry accusations which they are hurling back and forth at one another, there is an implicit appeal to a common scale of values and a common outlook on life, non-existent as yet but needing desperately to be created—or discovered.

We *must* have a world civilization, if we are not to cut one another's throats; but what is its basis to be? I believe that if we are ever to have a world civilization, we must have a world religion as its basis. That is, we must at least come to some common understanding, acceptable both east and west of Suez, concerning the general nature of the world in which we live and the basic laws which should govern human conduct. Such a common under-standing has been arrived at before, on a smaller scale—in Athens during the Age of Pericles, in Medieval Europe, in China during many centuries—and wherever this has occurred, civilization has flowered into culture. As Everett Dean Martin puts it:

A culture comes into being when the manifold interests and activities of a people can be made to derive their deepest sig-nificance from a common understanding of the meaning and value of human life. It is a coöperative answer which men give to the riddle of their existence. . . . I believe this to be the greatest task and function of religion. And when a religion is a living faith, it is so by virtue of the fact that it is the nucleus of a culture.[1]

Mr. Martin is of the opinion that, this time, a purely secular and non-religious basis of civilization may be found. Let us not quibble about terms. Let us define religion broadly enough to take in the kind of secularistic faith which he suggests, and proceed to discuss the ques-tion, "What *kind* of religion is most likely to succeed in

[1] *Liberty*, pp. 88, 89. Published by W. W. Norton & Company, Inc., New York. (1930.)

creating world unity and furnishing a basis for world civilization?" Several possibilities suggest themselves:

1. There is, in the first place, the possibility that the world may be united in the acceptance of a secular, humanistic creed, based solely upon the hope of man's mastery over nature and his own destiny, through science and the machine. This is a possibility which is being seriously entertained and explored, by those who are guiding the reconstruction of civilization in Russia and Turkey, and to some extent in China. At the Jerusalem Missionary Conference, it was generally recognized that "secularism" constituted so formidable a rival of all the great historic religions that they might quite conceivably be led to form a defensive alliance with one another.

There can be no doubt that science and technology have still to reveal their full consequences for religion and civilization. Negatively, they are sure to continue their corrosive influence upon all the great religious traditions, eating away all vestiges of magic and superstition. Positively, they are bound to exert a powerful influence for world unity, since scientific principles are, by definition, universal, and machinery tends to create a common type of civilization wherever it comes into use. Yet a purely scientific and technological civilization, based upon a purely humanistic and rationalistic religion, is hardly likely to satisfy men's deeper needs. Once before, in the eighteenth century, the experiment of a purely rationalistic and humanitarian creed was tried, on a small scale; and the results were instructive. In the very midst of the "Age of Reason" there burst out the Wesleyan revival, and the greatest orgy of religious emotionalism that has occurred in the Christian era swept through the Anglo-Saxon world. This, to be sure, affected the masses more than the intellectual classes; but at the beginning of the nineteenth century, they too were caught in the rising tide of the great anti-intellectualist movement which goes by the name of Romanticism; and so the "Age of Reason" came ignominiously to a close, and an age of religious faith and exuberant philosophical speculation came in. Such, I believe, would once more be the result, if Russian Communism or American humanism should sweep the world. The spirit of disillusionment is as contagious as the spirit of faith; and as the fruit of faith is mental peace, the fruit of disillusionment is neurosis—leading at last back to faith by way of a violent emotional revulsion. Man does not live by bread alone, nor by creature comforts alone, nor by art and literature alone. He demands an answer to many questions which science cannot even raise, and feels many needs which science cannot meet. He craves light upon the mystery of his destiny, and he needs objects of devotion higher than himself, capable of quickening his deeper emotions and flooding his existence with meaning. Any religion which starves this side of his nature will taste to him—as some one maliciously said of President Eliot's sketch of the religion of the future— "like a soda-cracker: perfectly wholesome as far as it goes; but you need something to take with it."[1]

2. Shall one, then, adopt the opposite alternative, and predict that some one of the existing organized religions —Christianity or Buddhism, let us say—will become universal? Admitting for the sake of the argument that Christianity has a better chance than any of its rivals,[2]

---

[1] In Turkey, where the secularistic experiment has now been under way for some years, critics are beginning to point to a "great void" in the national life, and the government is becoming alarmed at the rapid increase in the number of suicides. Judged by the psychological test, secularism has failed again.

[2] In spite of the gradual abandonment of its original pessimism and life-denial, Buddhism cannot be said to have completely overcome that initial handicap, which from the psychological point of view was wellnigh fatal. On the other hand, Buddhism is definitely superior to Chris-

what existing form of Christianity is fit to inherit the earth? None of the Protestant sects, surely; the notion of the whole world becoming Baptist, or Presbyterian, or even Protestant-in-general is simply too grotesque to be entertained for a moment. The rise of Protestantism coincided with the rise of nationalism and the rise of the "middle" or merchant class; its spread has largely followed the line of the expanding influence of that class, within certain national boundaries; and it has remained a class movement, subject to the characteristic prejudices and petty provincialisms of the tradesman—now exalted, in the age of capitalism, into the merchant prince; subject, in addition, to certain nationalistic limitations which have made it difficult for Protestants to attain a genuine world outlook. It has never touched the masses, on a large scale, except perhaps at the time of the Wesleyan revival; and Methodism seems now to have become as hopelessly middle-class as any other Protestant sect. A workingman simply does not feel at home in a Protestant church.

Catholicism, on the face of it, seems to have a better chance of becoming a world religion. It has repeatedly shown its power to absorb elements from its cultural environment, and build them into a rich yet harmonious whole, a unity in diversity. It is as cosmopolitan as Protestantism is provincial; and it has always known how to appeal to the masses. Yet it has one fatal defect: it apparently cannot reconcile itself with the modern spirit of free inquiry; and it accordingly seeks to create religious unity by coercive authority rather than by free consent. The great enemy of Catholicism is not Protestantism, but the scientific spirit. So long as the scientific spirit continues to exert an authoritative dominance over our intellectual classes—and I believe that dominance will endure, al-

tianity at some points—notably in its *wider* feeling of compassion, extending to the whole animate world.

though there may well be a reaction against the exaggerated claims of scientific dogmatism—so long will it be impossible for the Catholic Church to bring the world under its sway. If there could be a revival of Catholic philosophy, which would purge the Church of popular superstitions and bring about a genuine reconciliation of science and religion, then there might be some chance of a Catholic world hegemony. If the Protestant churches could overcome their contentious divisiveness,[1] recognize the narrowness and one-sidedness of classical Protestantism, and lay claim to that great Catholic heritage which ought to belong equally to all Christians, then there might be some chance of a Protestant world hegemony. As it is, neither Catholicism nor Protestantism has even a fighting chance to become the religion of mankind—and we may well be thankful that it is so!

3. The only remaining possibility of world unity in religion would seem to lie in a process of religious syncretism and amalgamation, which would result in a "peace without victory." This is the prospect which the Theosophists and other religious syncretists have long been urging upon our attention. All the religions teach essentially the same truths, they urge. Let the differing terminologies of the world religions be studied, and they will be found to express a common mystic experience, and a common faith in the Absolute Being who is the ground of all existence. Actually, however, the Theosophists (like their ancient prototypes, the Gnostics) attain religious unity

---

[1] I do not mean to say that sectarianism is an unmitigated evil, from the psychological point of view. Pratt in his *Religious Consciousness*, M°Comas in his *Psychology of Religious Sects*, and William Adams Brown in his *Imperialistic Religion and the Religion of Democracy*, have shown that religious sects correspond roughly to certain well-marked psychological types. The religion of the future must be sufficiently multiform to make room for contrasting psychological types; but it needs to overcome the spirit of factious contentiousness which has been so rife in Protestantism.

only by choosing one form of religion (Hinduism) as the norm and arbitrarily interpreting all other religions in terms of it. If Christianity and the other great historic religions are to make their full contribution to the religion of the future, they must resist premature absorption into such amorphous syncretisms as Theosophy and Bahaism.[1] They must, as Rabbi Silver insists, keep true to their distinctive messages, and not tone them down for the sake of being ingratiating and polite to other religions. To attempt to follow Buddha, Christ and Confucius all at the same time is to lose one's sense of direction and decision. The religion of the future is not to be found by taking the Least Common Denominator of existing faiths, but by pushing coöperatively toward a faith that lies somewhere in the region to which the highest and most vigorous affirmations of the greatest religions seem to point. Each must follow its own interior logic, while respecting the obligation of the others to do the same.

All of the great world religions must, therefore, continue to exist for a long time; but they will all be profoundly influenced by one another and by the scientific spirit. It will be the business of all religions to learn as well as to teach. In the world religion toward which we are slowly moving, elements of all the great religions will survive. It would be a pity to have all variety and local color in religion abolished, just as it would be a pity to have all cultural differences vanish in a completely standardized and mechanized civilization. Not all the elements in any religion are capable of being universalized; in

---

[1] Bahaism is not in the same class with Theosophy. It does not require one to secede from his own religion in order to join the new movement; and its fundamental principles almost certainly embody some of the fundamentals of the world religion of the future. Yet there is some danger that, like Theosophy, it may lead one to minimize the contribution which the historic faiths can make by remaining stubbornly true to their own highest insights.

matters of worship, church architecture, speculative philosophy, etc., variety is desirable. Yet the core of the world religion will consist of the *universal* elements in the great religions of the past, which will survive because of their inherent worth and truth. As Christians, we naturally hope that Christianity will contribute more than others to the new faith; and we fail to see any figure comparable with Jesus as a rallying-point for humanity; but we must recognize that the world religion, when it comes, will be much richer and more manifold than any existing form of Christianity, just as the Christianity which conquered the Roman Empire was richer and more manifold than the Jewish Christianity which first entered the Mediterranean melting-pot.[1]

Whether the world civilization produced by such a world religion would be Christian in name or not, it would surely be Christian in spirit. Its animating principle would be to the Living Christ of today what the Living Christ of today is to the historic Jesus: a natural expansion of the original Christian impulse, combined with and nourished by all sorts of congenial materials from foreign sources. But if Christians could speak of this civilization as "Christian," others might with equal right call it by other names. When Rabbi Krass's congregation offered Dr. Fosdick's congregation the use of their synagogue, during the construction of the Riverside Church, one of Dr. Fosdick's parishioners impulsively said, to one of Rabbi Krass's parishioners, "That was a very Christian thing for you to do." The Jew smiled. "We thought," he said, "that it was a very Jewish thing to do." What we (and all humanity) want is a religion capable of gathering up all sorts and conditions of men,

---

[1] See Professor Macintosh's remarkable articles on "The New Christianity and World Conversion," where a similar view is developed. (*American Journal of Theology*. Vol. XVIII, pp. 337 *et seq*., 553 *et seq*.)

of every race and clime, and giving them supreme satisfaction through participation in a common human task, great and worthful enough to summon out their deepest potentialities. That is what we want; and that is what we would prefer by any name, to an inferior religion that bore the name of Christ. Until all the other religions have assimilated everything implied in the word "Christ," we must continue to maintain the Christian Church as an independent organization. Jews and Moslems must do the same. But perhaps the day may at last come of which St. Paul speaks[1] when Christ shall "deliver up the Kingdom" to his Father, that henceforth "God may be all in all." Moses and Buddha must surrender their leadership at the same time.

To put the same thought more concretely, consider what the Bible of the future is likely to be. Our present Christian Bible very early became inadequate to express the full richness of the Christian tradition. If it were to be brought down to date, it ought to have two Old Testaments, a Greek as well as a Hebrew, including the dialogues of Plato and the discourses of Epictetus as well as the prophecies of Amos and Isaiah; and its New Testament ought to be extended to include: (1) such Catholic classics as the *Confessions of St. Augustine* and the *Imitation of Christ*, (2) selections from Luther, Fox, Bunyan, Wesley, and other Protestant leaders, and (3) something —let us say, from the writings of Henry Drummond—to represent the fusion of Christian tradition with the modern scientific temper. But the Bible of the future will have to be still more manifold. It will have many Old Testaments, among which the Hindu Old Testament and the Chinese Old Testament will stand out prominently;[2] and

---

[1] I Corinthians 15:24-28.

[2] I do not mean, of course, that every one will make use of this whole body of literature; but Hindus will make use of the Hindu Old Testa-

its New Testament will portray not merely the spread of the direct influence of Jesus, but the confluence of the whole Christian tradition with the other great religious traditions of the world.

Already, as Professor Pratt points out in his *Pilgrimage of Buddhism*, there is visible a convergence of the Buddhist and the Christian traditions, originally so diverse. In present-day Buddhism and Christianity, the Living Christ and the Living Buddha touch hands for the first time. In the religion of the future, they will have joined forces with one another and with a multitude of influences streaming from other sources. All this multiplicity must, of course, be reduced to unity by some simple controlling principle. Christians have reason to hope that this will be found in the spirit of Christ; but they are bound to join in the quest for a world religion in all open-heartedness, sharing both their hopes and their misgivings with their brethren of other faiths and of no faith at all. The task of surmounting the barrier between East and West, and finding a faith in which all men can unite, is a task which demands the coöperation of every human being.

Such, at any rate, would be the ideal line of religious progress. No one can at present predict whether it will actually be followed, or whether there will occur, instead, one of those great cultural catastrophes which have from time to time turned the clock of world history back for a century or two. There is certainly no guarantee that history will follow the path of rationality, as Hegel believed, it would always do. Armed fanaticism often cuts across the path of human betterment. At the present juncture, what is most to be feared is that the intolerant secularism of Soviet Russia, clashing with the social conservatism of the great historic religions, may make orderly progress

---

ment, Chinese will make use of the Chinese Old Testament, and Christians will make use of the Christian Old Testament (our present Bible).

impossible for the next century or two. This would be a tragedy; for Russian Communism is essentially religious in spirit, while Christianity, at least, has much more in common with the Soviet ideal than might appear from a casual glance at American Christianity. It is to be hoped that the religious forces of the West may come to appreciate the real greatness of the Communist faith, and respond to it as a challenge rather than as a menace, thus paving the way to an appreciation of religion on the part of the Communists. On the plane of war and violence, a conflict between Communism and religion would be a calamity for mankind; on the plane of discussion and emulation, such a conflict would tend to bring out the best in both contestants.

If it be asked whether Christianity would ever consent, without a struggle, to "sell out" to any hypothetically superior world religion, the answer is that no sudden capitulation is contemplated, but only a continuation, on a grander scale, of a process of expansion and adaptation which has been going on throughout the whole history of the Church. The council of Jerusalem, A.D. 1928, repeats the crisis of the council of Jerusalem, A.D. 45. In both cases, the church was faced with the necessity of sloughing off provincialism, if the essential message of the Gospel was to be made available and intelligible in an enlarging environment; and in both cases, the Church rose to the emergency. Since 1928, Christianity stands committed to a new conception of the missionary enterprise. No longer is "heathenism" the enemy at which the missionary onslaught is aimed; the enemy is human misery and sin, wherever it is to be found, and the ethnic faiths are regarded as valuable allies in the warfare. Christianity does not henceforth cease to preach its Gospel to the adherents of other religions—exporting thenceforth nothing but the visible and tangible goods of Western civilization, in the shape of medical, educational and other secular forms of service!—but it does its preaching hereafter at a general Round Table[1] or Parliament of Religions, where each religion is invited to press its own cause, as statesmen at Geneva press the interests of their own nation. Since each great religion claims to have the interests of all humanity at heart, each is morally bound to appropriate whatever is universally true, or good, or beautiful, wherever it finds it; and out of the debates of the Parliament of Religions is bound at length to emerge what we do not yet possess: a religious consciousness that is not merely sectional, provincial, or imperialistic, but grows out of the common consciousness of all mankind.

Christian thought is quite prepared for such an extension of intellectual hospitality. In fact, it may be said that if Buddhism and Confucianism are not destined to contribute anything of vital significance to the world religion of the future, then Christian faith finds itself in a serious dilemma. It is impossible to believe in a deity who left two-thirds of humanity in utter darkness while he patiently enlightened the elect remainder! The early Fathers of the Christian Church—most of them converted Greek philosophers—recognized this dilemma very clearly, and met it with their doctrine of the Eternal Word or Logos: "the light that lighteth every man that cometh into the world," and that in all times and places has been preparing men for further revelations yet to come. Jesus Christ was to them "the Word made Flesh," and his living Spirit, within the Church, was guiding it into truths before which all the wisdom of the ancients seemed pale and colorless; but many of the Fathers (Clement of Alexandria, for example) considered that the Eternal Word had been acting as "schoolmaster" among the Greeks, preparing them for Christ through Socrates

---

[1] Cf. Stanley Jones, *Christ at the Round Table.*

and Plato as the Hebrews were prepared through Moses and Isaiah. The conception of the Logos related Jesus to his predecessors and rivals as the conception of the Living Christ relates him to his successors.[1] If the same Greek theologians were living today, they would doubtless make a wider extension of their conception of the Logos; for they would find in Buddha and Confucius as worthy fore-runners of Christ as they found in Moses and Socrates; and modern secular culture would demand assimilation into the body of divine wisdom as imperatively as did Stoicism and Platonism in the first century.

It is from this point—from the conception of an Eternal Logos, revealed in various degrees in every great religious tradition—that Christian thought mounts to the thought of God. It would be a grave error to suppose that Christian thought, at its best, means anything narrow or bigoted by the doctrine of the deity of Christ. The Christ who is called divine, the Christ who "alone" can save, is not the historical character known as Jesus Christ, nor even the glorified Presence known as the Living Christ; he is the Eternal Logos, who embraces in the unity of one magnificent concept all the healing, enlightening, person-ality-building forces which have ever enriched the life of humanity, in any quarter of the globe. It is impossible to be saved outside of this Christ, because there is no saving influence that is not reckoned to be a part of the meaning of the word "Christ"! Whatever of benefit there may be in Buddhism or Communism, psychotherapy or settlement work, is meant to be included when the word "Christ" is used! When Christians say that *Jesus* Christ is divine, they

---

[1] The Hindus, the Moslems, and the Buddhists all have parallel con-ceptions, which could easily be identified or linked with the conception of the Logos. The belief in a continuing succession of divine messengers or divine incarnations is an almost universal human belief. It is only the identity of the Supreme Prophet or Unique Incarnation which sharply distinguishes one religion from another.

mean (if the Nicene pronouncement is to be taken as authoritative) that this Eternal Christ or Logos, the summary of all divine revelation in all times and places, was uniquely epitomized, for us, in the person of Jesus the Nazarene, so that when we come in contact, through the Church, with his Holy Spirit, we are to all intents and purposes in touch with the sum of all saving influences, and so in touch with God Himself, the mysterious Ultimate Source whence the Eternal Logos flows. God the Ultimate revealed in God the Logos, the sum of all saving influences everywhere; God the Logos made uniquely manifest in the divinely human life of Jesus; the life of Jesus continued and expanded in the Living Christ, whose Holy Spirit has the Church as his Living Body: this is the doctrine of the Trinity, as taught by the Greek fathers.

We have now before us the most momentous step in the argument of this book: from the human and social resources which nourish the higher life of man, to the superhuman Cosmic Mind which is presumably their ultimate source. But before we can mount the ladder of reason and faith which leads to this alluring haven of theological speculation and religious yearning, there is a formidable difficulty which must be fairly faced and overcome. The belief in God, we are told, is a mere "escape mechanism," the product of "wishful thinking." Man has found the fact of an indifferent universe too grim to face; and he has, therefore, invented gods. All the arguments by which he defends his belief in their existence are but "rationalizations," like the systematic delusions whereby the paranoiac maintains his belief that he is the most important person in the world. The gods are perhaps not wholly subjective delusions; they are built out of the stuff of experience; but the realities they symbolize are purely human and social realities at best. The Logos exists, in the shape of a vast diversity of cultural and religious heritages, each embodying certain "social values"; and the Living Christ indubitably exists in the same restricted sense; but at the point where all religious heritages seem to aspire to blend, in the conviction that all are revelations of the same God, there is no great Reality, but only a great Void. This is the creed of modern "humanism"; and since it rests squarely upon a particular analysis of religious psychology, it can be met only by a more adequate analysis of religious psychology, in which certain psychological fallacies are detected and corrected. It will be our task in Part III to attempt this analysis. Beginning with an impartial survey of religious experience, to enable us to isolate whatever Objective Factor it may contain, we shall then go on to examine the process by which religious faith draws metaphysical conclusions from religious experience; and we shall then be in a position to decide whether, in rising from the thought of the Logos to the thought of an ultimate Personal God, religious thought is moving toward illusion or toward Reality. In the last chapter, we shall look back over the whole course of our argument and draw some conclusions concerning the ultimate meaning and destiny of human personality.

Part III

The Ultimate Source and Goal of Personal Development

In which religious experience is analyzed, to see whether it rests upon illusion or upon Reality; and God is found to be the ultimate source and goal of personal development.

When I seek Thee, my God, I seek a happy life.

Too late loved I Thee, O Thou Beauty of ancient days, yet ever new! Too late I loved Thee!

When I shall with my whole self cleave to Thee, I shall nowhere have sorrow or labor; and my life shall wholly live, as wholly full of Thee.—St. Augustine, *Confessions*, Book X, 29, 38, 39.

The appeal to "religious experience" as the touchstone for the testing of religious dogmas has been characteristic of modern theology ever since Schleiermacher. The adoption of a thoroughly empirical point of view has been an indispensable means of acclimatizing Christian thought in a scientific age; and the gain in intellectual integrity has been so great that any radical departure from the empirical principle can henceforth only be regarded as a step backward. It is becoming plain, however, that the concept of "experience" needs clarification, to free it from a certain persistent ambiguity. To say that theology is the science or the philosophy of "religious experience" may mean one of two things, according to the stress laid upon the subjective or the objective element in the concept of experience. It may mean that theology is simply the study of religious experience as a peculiar group of mental phenomena; or it may mean that theology is the attempt to erect, on the basis of such a study, a verifiable theory concerning the nature of the Object of religious experience— God. In the former case theology becomes a branch of psychology, as Professor Leuba insists it ought to; and it is easy to draw the further deduction—as he does—that the deity in whom the religious man puts his trust has a

[1] Originally printed in the *Journal of Religion*, Vol. VII, pp. 540-560 (October, 1927) under the title, "The Objective Element in the Experience of God." With the argument of this and the succeeding chapter, compare the argument of Chapters III and IV in my earlier book, *Theism and the Modern Mood*. The two arguments run almost exactly parallel, but supplement one another at certain points.

"merely subjective existence" in his own mind.[1] In the latter case, theology becomes a branch of philosophy, aiming to interpret the nature of reality in the light of certain types of experience peculiarly rich in metaphysical insight, while corroborating and correcting its interpretations in the light of experience as a whole.

Now, to accept the former of these two positions means the death of religion; for if there is one thing certain about religion, it is that its very essence consists in a reaching out toward an objective Beyond of some sort, through alliance with which man hopes to achieve a happier destiny. Professor Leuba himself goes so far as to say that "the objective existence of personal divinities or equivalent psychic powers is an assumption necessary to religion."[2] However that may be, one thing is sure: that when the objective element in religious experience—be it a personal God or an impersonal law, or an abstract but objectively valid ideal—completely evaporates, and a man comes to feel himself trapped in an air-tight chamber of subjectivism, alone with his own mental states, then he ceases to be religious. Especially since the rise of the psychology of religion, multitudes of people have become convinced that religion *is* a purely subjective phenomenon, an operation man performs upon himself; and they have accordingly ceased to be religious.

It is the perception of this rather alarming situation that is mainly responsible for the present revival of interest in religious metaphysics and epistemology, all those thorny and "impractical" problems which religious pragmatism was just congratulating itself upon having banished into the limbo of a defunct scholasticism! They have come once more to the fore because it has been proved that they are very practical questions after all; for it is plain that when

---

[1] Leuba, *Psychological Study of Religion*, pp. 10ff, 245ff.
[2] *Ibid.*, p. 18.

religion is not solidly grounded in objective reality, its pragmatic benefits fail to materialize. The quest for reality in religion, for some way of escape from the black hole of subjectivism, for genuine knowledge of God, has become the characteristic tendency of contemporary religious thought. The present chapter aims to contribute to that quest by analyzing the objective element in private worship, which is admittedly the most subjective form of the religious experience, after which a more general survey of the objective element in religious experience will be briefly essayed. My contention is that while the exact nature of the divine—whether personal or impersonal, one or manifold—must remain a matter of hypothesis, the objective reality of the divine is as certain as that of a tree or a child. God is in a certain sense an empirical Fact, or rather a great multitude of facts which it is the function of philosophical theology to gather up under a hierarchy of concepts. Theism, pantheism, and other philosophical hypotheses concerning the nature of God must justify themselves by their ability to make *all* these facts intelligible.

I. THE OBJECTIVE ELEMENT IN PRIVATE WORSHIP

I choose to begin with an analysis of the objective element in private worship, because it is just here that the problem of subjectivism is most acute. When a man deliberately goes into his closet, closes the avenues of his senses to all ordinary objective sources of stimulation, and consciously practices the presence of God, he is apparently retreating into the circle of his own subjective thoughts and feelings; and the more one studies the psychology of private worship, whether in its mystical form or in the more ordinary form of prayer and meditation, the more clearly does the subjective element in the process stand forth. It is small wonder, then, that popular religious thought jumps to the conclusion that the objective element is missing altogether, and accordingly abandons both the belief in a personal God and the practice of worship. Wherever the knowledge of the psychology of religion (and more especially the psychology of prayer) makes its way, religious doubt springs up apace. So long as prayer is performed naïvely, unanalytically, trustfully, one can believe firmly in a real divine Respondent, it would seem, in spite of unanswered petitions; but let the high-school stripling or the college freshman hear it rumored that "prayer is nothing but autosuggestion; it's just kidding yourself along," and lo! the scales are fallen from his eyes and he prays no more. In fact he comes to regard all forms of worship, private or public, as intellectually disreputable; and the professor who leads in public worship, or, worse yet, is suspected of engaging in private devotions, loses caste in his eyes. This attitude is extremely widespread among college students today. It is widespread also among enlightened workingmen, enlightened literary men, enlightened society women—in short, wherever that blessed word "autosuggestion" has gone on its mission of emancipation.

It may be asked whether so obviously hasty and fallacious a conclusion deserves serious consideration. So much of the popular argument is purely verbal! "Autosuggestion" is a sinister-sounding word; it suggests "auto-intoxication," "auto-hypnosis," "auto-erotism," and other enormities which to name is to condemn. Since M. Coué popularized conscious autosuggestion it is no longer so evident that autosuggestion is a bad thing; and a good many people who gave up prayer when they heard it was unconscious autosuggestion are now doing the Coué rosary like good Catholics. Yet there is more than a verbal misunderstanding here; there is a serious difficulty: the difficulty of worshiping whole-heartedly when the object of worship appears to be a figment of one's own imagination, and the difficulty of seeing where there is any room left for a real object of worship when a complete account of the act of worship has apparently been given in purely psychological terms. To deal fully with this difficulty it would be necessary to work out a complete philosophical theory of knowledge which would aim to dispel the illusion of subjectivism which has afflicted modern epistemology since Galileo and Descartes;[1] but perhaps it may contribute to the laying of that ghost if I give a plain empirical description of the act of worship, and show that even here, where the activity of the self or subject is plainly visible, we have to do, not with an absolute, but with a relative subjectivity which shades off by degrees into something like complete objectivity. At no point in the process, so far as I am able to discern, is the self alone with itself, without an object on which to lean. Air-tight subjectivity is a pure abstraction.

I concentrate upon *private* worship, because here the impression of subjectivism is strongest. In public worship there is at least the objective stimulus of the house of worship, the other worshipers, and the clergyman who gives form and direction to the act of worship. In private worship man appears to "lean upon his own understanding." It may be asked why I do not concentrate still further upon prayer, which is the most problematic form of private worship; but I feel that the nature of prayer will become plain only when it is seen in a larger setting, together with other forms of private worship. I shall, however, cut away certain confusing complications by eliminating all mention of intercessory prayer, prayer for material

---

[1] Professor E. A. Burtt's *Metaphysical Foundations of Modern Physical Science* gives the clearest account of the genesis of this illusion (cf. Whitehead, *passim*).

benefits, etc., and confining my attention to what I may call the recuperative function of worship. By this I mean the ordinary, normal process whereby man periodically regains his sense of perspective and renews his strength by turning away from the immediate task and readjusting himself to the whole meaning of life. This is a process as natural and necessary as sleep or play—whose function, by the way, it closely resembles—yet it contains the essence of true worship and the key to the mystery of religion. Beginning with an effort at self-rejuvenation, it finds itself driven, in order to accomplish its purpose, to escape more and more completely from the self, until at last it issues in complete disenthrallment from the self and complete absorption in the divine object. I distinguish four stages in this expanding movement, marked by the predominance of four different types of mental mechanism, all of them familiar to the religious devotee, and frequently described in manuals of devotion.

1. *Simple autosuggestion* (typified by Coué's daily jingle, or by the "affirmations" of New Thought). I am inclined to doubt the statement that "prayer is just autosuggestion." I am even disposed to be critical of the remark of Dr. William Brown, the British neurologist, that "it would be truer to say that autosuggestion is a form of prayer than that prayer is a form of autosuggestion." Strictly speaking, autosuggestion is not even a *form* of prayer, though it may be an *element* in prayer. Prayer always has the form of a dialogue, while autosuggestion has the form of a monologue—addressed to yourself, no doubt, but to a self that never answers back, and takes its instructions meekly. Prayer entreats; autosuggestion commands. Prayer despairs of the self while the self remains in its present impoverished condition; autosuggestion trusts in the ability of the present empirical self to screw its courage up to the sticking-point and devise means

for its own discipline and reform. Autosuggestion (to use one of Professor Coe's favorite illustrations) is what the baffled swimmer uses when he tells himself that he *can*, he *will*, reach the shore; prayer, as it seems to me, is more analogous to reaching out for a plank or crying for help. We shall come to prayer quite a bit farther on in our graded scale, near the pole of objectivity; meanwhile there can be no doubt that autosuggestion is an important and useful form of worship, though it lies near the pole of subjectivity.

Let me explain what I mean by calling autosuggestion the most subjective form of worship. Imagine yourself a poor sinner, "standing in the need of prayer"; or, if that is too much of an effort for your self-complacency, imagine yourself tired out and bewildered, seeking for light and strength. If you yourself—your *present empirical self*, in all its narrowness, weariness, perplexity, and perhaps sinfulness—can deliver yourself from this *impasse*, that will be the very acme of subjectivity. Now autosuggestion comes very close to being self-deliverance. The subject diagnoses his own case, prescribes certain powerfully suggestive thoughts as remedies for his disease, and throws all the remaining energies of his tiring will into their energetic verbal repetition or mental fixation. By assuring himself that he is getting better and better he makes himself feel more cheerful and actually improves his health; by affirming that he is an aggressive, dynamic, masterful personality he raises his courage sufficiently to enable him to face a difficult interview; by repeating to himself "I can do all things through Christ who strengtheneth me" he very effectively strengthens and calms himself.

Here, it would seem, is a miracle indeed! The becalmed sailor is making his own way out of the doldrums by blowing on his own sail with a pair of bellows! It seems too good to be true; in fact, when you come to analyze the situation you soon see that it *is* too good to be true. An impoverished self cannot recreate itself out of its own immanent wisdom and energy, any more than a Ford can run on its reputation when its gasoline gives out. What it is actually doing, when it succeeds in re-energizing itself, is reaching out for aid into a beyond—namely, its own larger and better self, temporarily obscured by fatigue and mental concentration. The auto-suggestions which work the miracles are gifts of the larger self. They represent formulas arrived at in moments of greater wisdom and power than the present, or—still more objective—formulas arrived at by other persons wiser and stronger than one's self. Autosuggestion is subjective in that these formulas are wielded by the empirical self in its own defense; it does not recognize its own fundamental inadequacy, and proposes, by aid of auto-suggestion, to keep on working at the original enterprise without serious reconsideration of the total meaning of life; but there are objective elements even in this most subjective form of worship, without which it would get nowhere.

Since the effectiveness of worship, as we shall see, is in direct proportion to its degree of objectivity, simple auto-suggestion is the least effective of all forms of worship. It is like the workman spitting on his hands and gritting his teeth; it may enable him to keep on for awhile, but it cannot take the place of a good night's rest. Those who have experimented with autosuggestion will, I think, confess that it is hard to work yourself into the proper condition of suggestibility to receive your own suggestions. The thought persistently obtrudes itself that you are playing a trick upon yourself. A rebellious voice whispers, "I am *not* getting better; I feel worse than I did at this time yesterday afternoon." How much more reassuring is an objective medical diagnosis by a competent person other than yourself! How much more comforting, too, in time of melancholy is some objective ground of hope than all the Pollyanna maxims that you murmur to yourself!

2. *Recollection* (French *recueillement*, implying not merely an act of memory, but a "pulling one's self together"). Even simple autosuggestion, we saw, reaches out spasmodically into the larger and better self; but it does not recover that self in anything like its totality. Eventually, however, all the operations of the empirical self, even with the aid of autosuggestion, become subject to a law of diminishing returns. The harder you try and the more furiously you coach yourself, the more securely you stick in the mire just where you are. Then you are helpless indeed unless you know how to call more completely upon that reserve wisdom and reserve energy which you carry continually within yourself but which is not all available precisely at the cutting edge of effort. That type of worship which consists in calling the past to the aid of the present, and the total self to the aid of the partial self, may be denominated recollection, or *recueillement*, a term much used by French Catholic writers on the technique of the devotional life. It begins with relaxation; otherwise the barriers between the partial and total self remain fixed, and the healing inrush of memories and impulses does not take place. Its goal, often attained, is to see and feel the task of the moment as an incident in one's whole life-purpose, and so get a flood of new light upon it.

I well remember one experience of this sort. My head was pounding and buzzing with a thousand plans and problems after a busy day's work. I went out on a walk, but at first got no refreshment. Then, as I suddenly came to an opening in the trees by the shore of a little pond, something said to me, "Come! Come! there's no use going on in this fashion. You don't know what your life's all about. Stop, and think." I stopped short where I was and made my mind as nearly a blank as possible. I found it hard to relax and fragments of anxious thought concerning the work immediately at hand continued to hurtle through my consciousness, while the blood in my temples continued to pound furiously. Then gradually a sense of calm stole over me; I got a vivid sensation of the whole landscape—wood, and pond, and sky—molding itself into a certain harmonious sphericity, and clothing itself with a beauty unobserved a moment before; most important of all, there flowed back upon me a great stream of recollection. I remembered who I was, and what my main purpose in life was. I reaffirmed the insights and decisions of my best moments, and saw the day's work in relation to them —important in its way, but nothing to worry about. My larger self had come to the rescue of my empirical self, reorientating and reënergizing it. Here is a type of worship distinctly more objective and distinctly more effective than mere autosuggestion.

3. *Prayer* (imaginative thinking in dialogue form). In facing all the *recurrent* problems of life, such as the periodic narrowing of the sphere of existence through selective attention to the day's work, we need no deliverer but our own larger selves. If we have solved a problem once, we can do it again; that is, if we can bring the whole self to bear upon it. But there are new situations to be faced in life—really new. In such situations our larger self can always help us through bringing up somewhat analogous instances from past experience; but it cannot always achieve a complete deliverance. We therefore reach out more energetically than usual, toward a Beyond wider even than our own widest experience, and call out for help to something which is now clearly recognized to be

an Other than ourselves. This is prayer, in the strict sense of the word.

In her little book on *The Psychology of Prayer*, Anna Louise Strong made the fruitful suggestion that the psychology of ordinary dialogue prayer was essentially the psychology of thinking, since silent thinking is derived from audible discussion with a visible interlocutor. This suggestion about the conversational structure of all thinking has been confirmed by recent studies of the incipient shaping of words in the larynx during silent thought. In all really intense thought, we find ourselves imagining the presence of an interlocutor—sometimes an antagonist, more often a sympathetic listener—before whom we set forth our argument as a lawyer pleads his case before a judge. As the argument waxes hot we begin to pace the floor, to speak aloud, to make persuasive and appealing gestures. At intervals we pause for a verdict and assume the rôle of judge. The more clear-cut is our picture of the personality of the judge, the more clear and enlightening is the decision likely to be. Who has not had the experience of going out on a long walk to mull over a difficult problem, taking with him as an imaginary companion some person whose character and wisdom he reveres? Whoever has done this knows how very definite and even crushingly decisive are the judgments which may be handed down by such a well-known and revered personality, even *in absentia*.

Prayer to God differs from ordinary imaginative thinking only because of the character of the Interlocutor, who is believed to be in some sense really present and responsive, and whose person is endowed with superhuman majesty, wisdom, and goodness. In one respect prayer to God may sometimes be inferior to an imaginary conversation with a trusted friend, or with some well-known historical character like Jesus or Abraham Lincoln or Henry

Drummond:[1] the character of God being more nebulous and many-sided than the character of the friend or hero, the judgment rendered on the problem at issue is less clear cut. But this does not constitute a serious objection; for the problem which has driven us to prayer may be, and commonly is felt to be, of a difficulty surpassing the powers of merely human minds. Hence we prefer a slightly nebulous ideal companion to a clear-cut portrait of a human friend. Moreover, we do not take God all at once; the mind could not grasp so great a concept in its present bewildered condition. We project before us that image of God which most exactly corresponds with our own needs. If we are worried and fretful, we think of one who lives in perpetual calm, "For we know that Thy completeness flows around our incompleteness; round our restlessness Thy rest." If we are lonely, we pray to the "Friend that sticketh closer than a brother." If we are puzzled over life's mysteries, we favor Royce's conception of God, as the All-Knower whose knowledge spans and includes our ignorance. Professor Farnell, in his Gifford Lectures on the "Attributes of God," points out that most of the appellatives which have been applied to the gods— and out of the compounding of these appellatives the developed concept of God has arisen—are the "projections" or "sky reflections" of certain specific human needs. This is a restatement of Feuerbach's well-known contention that the gods are *Wünschwesen*, ideal forms projected upon the cosmic screen by man's "wishful thinking."

If this is a true account of the psychology of prayer— and I believe it is essentially true, though doubtless incomplete—does it not follow that prayer is a wholly subjective process, necessarily involving a sort of self-decep-

---

[1] After Drummond's death, one who had known him well confessed that he found himself visualizing Drummond's face whenever he tried to pray to God.

tion; so that no man of intellectual integrity can continue
to perform the act of prayer after once becoming initiated
into the mystery of its psychology? My answer would be,
most emphatically, No! If it would be foolish to give up
thinking, because all thinking deals in subjective concepts
and may lead one into error; it would be equally foolish
to give up that vivid picture-thinking, that ardent "wishful thinking," known as prayer, because it, too, deals in
subjective concepts and may lead one astray. Professor
Leuba finds the psychological origin of religion in that
capacity for conceiving "free ideas" which is one of the
things that distinguishes man from the animals. This capacity for framing concepts of the absent, the remote, the
abstract, and dealing with the concept in lieu of the original experiences from which it was derived, is a frightfully
dangerous capacity, it must be admitted. Man can fall into
errors of which animals are incapable; he can combine
"free ideas" incorrectly to form mythical monsters like
the gryphon; he can feed his soul on pleasant lies, and
live in a dream. Yet the same capacity which may thus
lead him astray may be a means of making effective adjustment to wider and deeper ranges of reality than any
of the lower animals is capable of cognizing at all. If
magic and superstition spring from the use of "free ideas,"
so do science and rational religion. It is true that prayer,
with its headlong ardor, is in greater danger of self-
deception than more sober forms of thinking; but it also
contains greater possibilities, for it wrestles with reality in
its total concreteness with most unusual vigor and persistence, crying out, "I will not let Thee go until Thou bless
me!"

I maintain that prayer, like thinking and like autosuggestion, may be used either honestly or dishonestly,
and may, therefore, lead either toward subjective delusion
or toward objective reality. A man may think himself into

a delusion of persecution; he may convince himself by autosuggestion that evil is non-existent and effort unnecessary; he may pray himself into a delusive trust in a divine Santa Claus. Or he may force himself by thinking to face his own shortcomings; he may use autosuggestion to keep before his mind "how the other half lives," and freshen his sense of duty to the under-privileged; he may pray himself into a deep, discerning sense of the tragedy, mystery, and potential beauty of life.

I say "pray himself"; but is that entirely correct? Is the act of prayer a purely reflexive act? Is the divine Other who answers prayer merely the wider self? Yes and no. There is no hard-and-fast line between the empirical self, the wider self, and the divine Other. As the wider self flows into and inundates the empirical self whenever the tidal gates are opened, so the whole individual self is capable at times of lifting the barriers that segregate it from the social organism of which it is a member, and becoming merged in a larger life, the life of the group, the nation, the race, the . . . where shall we stop? Prayer is one of the most effective means of self-transcendence. By its very structure it proclaims its social origin and social import. It presupposes the reality of other persons; it implies that the self is not a windowless, unventilated chamber of subjectivity, but an "event" (to borrow Whitehead's term) organically related to all other events, and capable of undergoing indefinite expansion in meaning as it enters actively into *rapport* with its fellows. Whether the society to which the self belongs includes superhuman, cosmic selves—gods in the strict traditional sense—is a question we are not yet ready to approach; but we can already affirm that the word "God" has a tremendous trans-subjective significance. It refers, at the very least, to the highest elements in that world of human fellowships, of social traditions and institutions, in which we are all enveloped as in a matrix. It means the "highest social values" of my group; the idealized spirit of my nation, of my race, of the humanity that is yet to be. It is the most broadly human word we possess; he who invokes God evokes all the heroes, saints, and prophets of every race and every creed. Not all at once, of course; in the initial stages of worship the worshiper's powers are so depleted that he can evoke but a poor, shabby image of God, strictly relative to his own needs. (Even this image he owes to the race; if we had to invent God in each new act of worship, we should make slow progress!) Pouring out his distress before this image, he finds himself enlarged and capable of framing a better image—also bequeathed him by the race. Thus, gradually climbing out of himself by the aid of an expanding God-concept, he can travel far without exhausting its historic connotations; and the more he leans upon the objective social significance of the thought of God, transmitted to him by other worshipers, the easier does prayer become, and the more effective in its work of release. No, man does not "pray himself" out of his misery; all that is best in humanity (and more than that, perchance) comes to his rescue, in the thought of God.

4. *Contemplation* ("effortless attention"). To illustrate the psychology of contemplation, which marks the pole of objectivity in worship, I will take a case of æsthetic experience, verging upon the religious; for as imaginative thinking is the closest secular parallel to prayer, so æsthetic rapture is the closest secular parallel to religious contemplation.

It happened in Sanders Theatre, Harvard, where I had gone, in a mood of great depression and with a bad cold in the head, to hear a symphony concert. I had paid a quarter, which entitled me to a seat in the tiny balcony located directly over the orchestra; one could look down into the yawning throats of the wind instruments. I do not know what else they played that night; but they played the *Tannhäuser* Overture as only the Boston Symphony Orchestra, with Karl Muck conducting, could play it. I had of course heard that music before; but I had never heard it played by an orchestra—and such an orchestra! Bit by bit I was drawn out of myself until my whole being was centered in that majestic music. When it came to the finale, I was caught up out of my body; my center of consciousness, as nearly as I could determine it later, was located somewhere in mid-air, about twenty feet in front of me, high above the orchestra. I *was* the *Tannhäuser* Overture. When I came to myself I was reënergized from head to foot. The descending chromatics of the strings were still thrilling through me like fire. My depression was gone. My cold was gone. I walked on air for several days. I had not only experienced mystic contemplation; I had experienced the ecstasy in which it sometimes culminates. This was, of course, primarily an æsthetic experience; but it had also a strongly religious element, for the *Tannhäuser* Overture is an epic of the religious quest of our Western civilization. The Pilgrim's Chorus represents medieval asceticism, with its stern repression of human instincts. The dance of Venus and Tannhäuser's love song represent the recrudescence of pagan "self-expression" and *joie de vivre* at the time of the Renaissance. The great finale, in which the Venus theme remains to give power and passion to the reannouncement of the pilgrim theme, represents Wagner's dream of the religion of the future, in which human instincts shall be neither repressed nor released in disorderly fashion, but organized and integrated. That life should be like the finale of the *Tannhäuser* Overture—how could one better define the ideal of the Kingdom of God!

I say that contemplation marks the pole of objectivity

in worship. In prayer, the worshiper is still conscious of himself and his needs; in contemplation, the subject is completely unselfed, and the object of worship fills the whole horizon. In the experience just cited, objectivity was guaranteed by the presence of an external sensory stimulus, the overture. In much religious contemplation there is a similar external stimulus—a sunset, an image of the Virgin, the face of a friend—and yet I am disposed to affirm that when the object of contemplation is a *mental* image, the objectivity and metaphysical significance of the experience may be equally great, and perhaps even greater. Imagination is not necessarily a pathway to delusion; unless we use imagination, we are condemned to suffer from the delusion that we live upon a flat earth, and the celestial spheres revolve about us. All attempts to live in the light of ultimate reality and see life *sub specie æternitatis* make use necessarily of imaginative, symbolic objects of contemplation. Even the naturalistic philosopher, were he to indulge in devotional exercises— as he ought to do—would be obliged to use symbolic mental imagery in order to remind himself of his situation in time and space: a brief moment of life, constituting an episode in the life of a nation born yesterday, of a race just emerged from animality, on a tiny planet whirling about a minor star that is drifting—whither? A Bergsonian vitalist, an absolute idealist, a Christian theist, would have other images of ultimate reality; granting the approximate truth of the image, it would be a most effective means of adjusting one's self to the real world to contemplate that image—even if one were obliged to "withdraw from the world" and close all the avenues of the senses in order to perform the act of contemplation with due efficiency.

By the "objectivity" of the experience of contemplation I do not mean scientific objectivity. Scientific objectivity is achieved by "eliminating the personal equation"; that is, by applying impersonal mathematical tests to the object, which enable one to deal with it conveniently and detachedly as one of a class. So long as one feels strong personal affection or concern for the object of investigation, one cannot treat it with full scientific objectivity; for science aims at mechanical control and manipulation of the things it studies, and we cannot merely manipulate what we love. Contemplative objectivity also eliminates the personal equation in a certain sense, but in quite a different way: by the enthusiastic and affectionate giving of the self to the object. The more deeply one loves and admires the object, the nearer one is to contemplative objectivity. The acme is reached when one gets so completely inside the object that one can, so to speak, look back upon one's self through the very eyes of the object. Both forms of objectivity represent high forms of knowledge; but science can aspire to an exactitude that contemplation never can attain, while contemplation explores the full concreteness of the object in a fashion that makes science look like mere surface knowledge. There is no incompatibility between these two kinds of cognition; the great entomologist, Fabre, exercised them both upon his beloved ants, with astonishing results; only they cannot go on simultaneously.[1]

Looking back, now, over the path we have been mounting, may we not say that our search for an objective element in private worship has been richly rewarded? Worship may be subjectively motivated, and it may seek selfish ends; but those ends are attained (being considerably

---

[1] In a remarkable address at the International Congress of Philosophy in 1926 (*Proceedings*, pp. 146-54) Professor Overstreet distinguished these two kinds of knowledge-getting as "the appropriative kind and the kind in which one 'identifies-oneself-with.'" Cf. also Wieman, *Religious Experience and Scientific Method.*

transformed in the process) only when the worshiper re-
linquishes his self-sufficiency and reaches out humbly for
aid into a genuine objective Beyond. Contemplation, the
most objective form of worship, is at the same time the
most effective; in it the ancient paradox is fulfilled, that
we find ourselves by losing ourselves. We are now certain that an object of religious experience really exists;
it remains only to determine its exact nature.

2. THE NATURE OF THE RELIGIOUS OBJECT: GOD AS FACT AND AS HYPOTHESIS

An empirical account of the nature of God must begin
by finding a criterion to distinguish the experience of God
from other experiences. It will not do simply to analyze
the object of contemplation; for not all contemplation is
religious; and we need a criterion to tell us which is religious and which is not. Now, considerable progress has
recently been made toward the establishment of such an
empirical criterion as we require. To put briefly what
seems to me to be the upshot of recent investigations: the
adjectives "divine," "holy," "sacred," are rightly applied
to anything which humbles him who beholds it and exalts
him who rightly adjusts himself to it. To the primitive
mind divine objects are charged, as it were, with a powerful current of electricity. Positively, this means that
they possess *mana*, or wonder-working power, which may
be transmitted to the needy individual with amazing results if he makes his approach reverently and cautiously,
according to the rules laid down by Those Who Know.
Negatively, these objects are *taboo*—must not be approached carelessly, on pain of death—which means that
wonder mixed with fear is the primary attitude of the
worshiper. This puts crudely and graphically a truth
which applies even to the most elevated forms of the ex-

perience of God: that the initial symptom of the presence of the divine is what Rudolf Otto calls the "creature-feeling," a sense of inferiority or unworthiness in the presence of a *mysterium tremendum*. But if the divine object's first effect upon the worshiper is to repel and abase him, it nevertheless continues to fascinate him; and when at last he yields himself completely to its power, in all reverence and humility, he finds life intensified and enlarged in all its dimensions. Whatever can do this for a man is, by definition, divine.

With this criterion in hand we are in a position to pick out the facts upon which any rational belief in God must rest. If we range rapidly over the history of religion, neglecting those concepts of the divine which are obviously superstitious, and concentrating our attention upon those which rest upon experiences that are still reproducible, it will appear that there are three main approaches to the experience of God: through nature, through society, and through the inner life. In each of these three regions are to be found realities which naturally evoke the creature-feeling in the candid beholder, and adjustment to which means enhancement of life.

1. *Nature worship must be considered in any well-balanced survey of the history of religion.* That the genesis of the god idea can be completely explained in terms of the worship of the group spirit by the individuals composing it is a theory which illustrates that "exaggeration of the social" which was pushed to such grotesque extremes in the generation just past. It is a truism to say that primitive man apprehended nature in terms of social categories; the truism still holds for civilized man; but it gives no legitimate excuse for eliminating the strong cosmic element in the traditional concept of the divine. One may indeed claim that this cosmic element rests upon delusion, while the social element points to a reality

worthy of worship; but from a purely empirical point of view must we not recognize in nature much that is truly divine? He who can look up at the stars without humility; who can gaze at the Alps or pass through a storm at sea without a religious thrill; who can sit before the crackling hearth on a wintry night and never feel the impulse to pour a libation to the kindly flames; who can walk in the open on a warm spring day without praising the sun for his life-giving rays—that man is incompetent to speak on the subject of religion. Is not the problem of living in tune with the mighty energies of nature which give health and power to him who rightly uses them and deal death to him who misuses them, a perpetual part of the religious problem? Is the problem solved when we have merely learned to exploit and manipulate nature, in scientific fashion? I suspect that the loving contemplation of nature, as practiced by a Wordsworth or a Tagore, does something for the worshiper and reveals something about nature that is beyond the ken of science. Was the primitive animist with his naïve personification of the powers of nature any farther from the truth than the modern positivist who thinks nature completely expressible in mathematical terms? "Great God! I'd rather be a pagan suckled in a creed outworn."

2. *I do not wish to minimize the great services rendered by Durkheim's "social theory" of religion.* It has cast a flood of light upon one great trend in the history of religion—for ethical religion, the most significant trend. Ancestor worship, tribal and national divinities, hero worship, emperor worship, and the modern "religion of social passion"—all fall naturally into this framework. Society is as inescapable as nature and as full of the divine. To the child, society means the family, and his parents are his first gods. From them all blessings flow, and in their will is his peace. Later his horizon expands

to include the nation and the race; and his life takes on serenity, dignity, and power in proportion as he devotes himself loyally to the welfare of some larger social whole. Wherever in the broad expanse of human history he meets with an individual who humbles and encourages him by his transcendent moral nobility; wherever he can discern a moral order in human affairs that claims him as its servant and promises a happier destiny for mankind, there he recognizes the divine. That he should go on to look for something fatherly and friendly in the cosmos is inevitable; it is the natural outgrowth of his effort to find support for his highest endeavors by allying himself with the widest and worthiest social environment conceivable.

3. *To many modern thinkers nature and society between them exhaust the dimensions of reality.* The individual is but a social unit, and what used to be called his "inner life" can be completely described in terms of visceral and laryngeal contractions. To the medieval mind the region accessible to introspection was a whole world in itself—"the Beyond that is within," as the mystics call it. All the infernal and celestial topography of the Divine Comedy refers allegorically to this inner region. It seems scarcely credible that a whole world of carefully described phenomena should be a pure fabrication; I am disposed to believe that *as we moderns are superior to our predecessors in our knowledge of things external, so we are still surpassed by Dante and St. Augustine in what concerns the contents of the soul of man.* Now here is a third region in which man has always experienced the divine, and where the experience is still to be met. Much that the mystics met along the path leading in toward the ground of the soul must be characterized as hallucinatory; yet it is an empirical fact that there are resources of energy, insight, and moral heroism within us which are beyond the reach of our ordinary selves, but which religious wor-

ship makes available by its vigorous "reaching down." Let James's essay on "The Energies of Men" suffice to substantiate this point.

It is empirically certain, then, that at least three divine objects exist: the God of nature, the God of society, and the God within, corresponding roughly to the Father, the Logos, and the Holy Spirit of the Christian Trinity. It is when we try to conceive the exact nature of these three types of deity, and their relation to one another, that we pass from the realm of fact to the realm of hypothesis.

Is deity one or many, personal or impersonal? We cannot answer these questions categorically; but this we can say: that certain hypotheses concerning the nature of the divine have already gone definitely into the discard; and the issues in the great controversy are becoming progressively clearer with advancing knowledge.

For primitive man, nature was a pantheon of quarreling gods, some dreadful like the god of lightning, some kindly like the glistening sun god. For modern man nature has become a unity; *all* her mighty energies are seen to be dangerous to the maladjusted and benevolent to the adjusted. The conception looms up—a mere hypothesis as yet—of one great universal cosmic energy, expressing itself in different shapes and at different levels of intensity. As social science has lagged behind natural science it is more difficult to see the laws that bind human history into a connected drama; and yet the thought of a divine moral order has haunted the mind of man, and some of the least credulous of our modern thinkers have believed in a "power not ourselves that makes for righteousness," dramatized by Mr. Wells as a growing God. Still vaguer are the laws that rule the world within; yet in spite of all these uncertainties, theistic religion has dared to venture upon a further hypothetical leap: it has identified the God of the heart with the God of society and history, and with the ruler of the cosmos; and it has conceived him in personal terms.

The difficulties of this colossal concept are obvious; but pantheism and humanism, its chief contemporary rivals, involve difficulties of their own. The problem of evil is more acute for pantheism than for theism; while the humanist buys his solution of the problem at the price of severing man from the cosmos. If the humanist is ready to admit that the inner life of the individual, apparently isolated, is really capable of merging with the larger life of humanity, why may not humanity, in turn, be capable of transcending its apparent isolation and allying itself with some larger cosmic life? Here we run beyond our empirical tether; but we cannot avoid taking sides and living as though one of these hypotheses were the true one. Faith can never completely give way to knowledge in these high regions; yet a theology that is thoroughly empirical in its starting-point and candid in its desire to do justice to rival hypotheses may yet lead us nearer to a genuine knowledge of God than we dare hope at present.

I take it that the modern man may best approach the question of Christian faith in God by first inquiring how the Christian feels when he "experiences God"—what types of experience tend to become conscious of themselves as experience of the divine—and what concept of God tends to arise spontaneously out of such experiences. The concept, thus formulated, may then be summoned to the bar of science and philosophy to defend itself.

1. THE PSYCHOLOGY OF CHRISTIAN THEISM

No one can feel his neighbor's feelings, or precisely think his neighbor's thoughts after him; so I had best draw my illustrations from my own experience.

One of the most impressive religious experiences I have ever had came to me, not in church, but—shades of my Puritan ancestors, avert your faces!—in a New York theater, where John Drinkwater's *Abraham Lincoln* was then playing. As scene succeeded scene, and the soul of Lincoln was more and more completely revealed—triumphing over his own misgivings, forsaking ease for the sake of the well-being of all, unflinching in his opposition to evil, but overcoming evil with compassion, giving his life at length as a ransom for many—I found myself at last looking upon the stage with the eyes of a worshiper, and I said to myself: *"This, this is God."* Nor

---

[1] Sections 1 and 2 of this chapter were originally printed in the *Journal of Religion* (Vol. III, pp. 598-615, November, 1923) under the title, "Reasons for Believing in God"; section 3, in the *Student World* (July, 1930) and also in the *New Humanist* (November, 1930).

was I a solitary worshiper. Consciously or unconsciously, each person there worshiped God that evening. I felt it in the applause, and in the still more significant silences; and the fellowship of adoration added greatly to the depth of it for all of us; for it helped us to feel that this was not merely *my* God but *our* God—yes, the God of all mankind.

Now what do I mean by saying I met God in Drinkwater's *Lincoln?* Well, what did I mean at the time? Let me scrutinize the workings of my mind. I think that Lincoln's divineness in my eyes consisted precisely in that "combination of ideality and final efficacity" which was the criterion of the divine for William James. I got a double impression of moral nobility in the highest degree, and of irresistible power. In the first place, Lincoln humbled me as the ideal always humbles the actual; his human figure, with its homely qualities and obvious limitations, became, as it were, translucent, and through it shone a pure and unwavering light, the light of the ideal, making me long unutterably to be like him—and unlike myself. But this was not all; he was for me the incarnation of irresistible might. This was, if possible, the stronger of the two impressions. "This is the spirit that is bound to win," I said to myself. I saw it triumphing before my eyes—winning the respect of the supercilious Seward and the cantankerous Stanton, turning a condemned youth into a hero and bidding fair to bind a nation into a unity based on justice and mutual forgiveness. I saw it hushing a miscellaneous New York audience into reverence. And then, the theater could not contain it. I looked out beyond the stage into the tangled world, and I saw that spirit, embodied in the messages of President Wilson, putting an end to a great war, and arousing fabulous hopes in the hearts of all the peoples—and chaos and despair rushing back upon the scene when that spirit which had governed us in war failed to get incorporated in the treaty of peace. I thought of the triumphs of many folk, ordinary and extraordinary, missionaries, reformers, plain people, in whom this spirit finds more or less imperfect embodiment, and I said to myself: "It's irresistible; it's almighty. No one can stop it. Nail it to a cross and it smiles at you and continues. Sooner or later, it is going to capture the last redoubt, and rule in the hearts of *all*."

If my enthusiasm had permitted me to stop at this point, I should simply have been affirming, as you see, that the God whom I glimpsed in Lincoln was *a tendency in human history, a growing social entity* if you will, of such a nature that it was bound to overcome all obstacles and become the organizing principle of human society and the object of each human individual's allegiance. Poetizing a bit, I should easily have arrived at the conception of an Invisible King or Captain of mankind, growing with the growth of mankind, yet always leading on. That such tendencies or social entities really exist and that they deserve our worship, I gladly admit. The religious traditions of the Australian clan as symbolized in the totem animal and the *churinga*, the Athenian πόλις, appealed to by Pericles in his "Funeral Oration," the "Soul of America" as Stanton Coit conceives of it, and the Church, the body of Christ, the mediator of divine grace to the needy individual—all these I regard as real entities worshipful in various degrees, which would, to be sure, vanish if their component members were annihilated, but which are still something more than aggregates of individuals.

But I did not stop at this point, just on the margin of metaphysics, where all good humanists draw the line. I pressed on—rashly, perhaps—and it began to rain metaphysics, thick and fast. "The spirit of Lincoln," I said in my haste, "*must* triumph. The nature of things is such—

human nature, of course, but nature in general too. The universe is built that way; that's why the universe is on his side." "Yes"—and here I took a terrific leap, from an impersonal moral order to an anthropomorphic deity—"there is at the heart of things a spirit like that of Lincoln, a personality like his." Thus did the primitive Christian reason concerning Christ; and thus, I admit it, I reasoned concerning Lincoln.

The religious experience is many-sided, and I do not rest my conception of God upon any one experience or any one type of experience, of course. I rest it in part, inevitably, upon the experiences of my Christian predecessors, as crystallized in the words and notions I was taught in childhood—words and notions that inevitably shape my own experience. To complete the picture of what God means to me, I must touch upon a few other types of experience of the divine with which I am familiar, not to be classified with the experience of the divine in a historic personality.

There is, first, the experience of the Holy Spirit, which has sometimes come upon me when worshiping in company with a number of like-minded individuals. This experience was really present as an overtone in the experience I have described, for I was distinctly conscious of intimate fellowship with the rest of the audience in the theater.

Then, there is the experience of ethical insight. Once, while crossing the path in front of Memorial Hall, Harvard, on my way to lunch, I met a negro workman, whose eyes met mine, quite accidentally, as we passed. In that instant I felt certain that the veil of flesh had dropped away from both of us, that I had seen into his soul, and he into mine. We smiled simultaneously, a smile of perfect mutual comprehension; then passed on without slackening our pace, for there was nothing to say; but I, at least, had been momentarily transported into a world of spiritual realities where the childishness of race prejudice was transparently evident. "This is the way things look to God," I said to myself; "how can He ever bear with our blindness!"

Then, finally, there is the more definitely mystical type of experience, in which no human values seem to be prominent, and the individual self finds itself merged in a sort of cosmic consciousness. For me, the sight of an extensive and harmonious landscape, preferably mountainous and far from the city, or the sight of the starry sky on a clear night most naturally leads to such experiences. Once, I remember, while lying on my back on a settee by the shore of a pond, listening to the swash of the waves and watching some birds flying far overhead, I fell to thinking about the vastness of the universe and my own littleness and transitoriness. Eventually I seemed to feel myself caught up out of myself into a larger consciousness, and found myself smiling down upon my poor little empirical self, far down below there upon the settee; and as the sensation passed, I said to myself: "How paltry are most of the things with which I occupy myself. How much more there is that *matters*, besides what matters to *me*!" And again I said: "This is how things look to God."

I may define the conception of God which seems to emerge spontaneously from such experiences as these by comparing it with the conception of God which Professor Royce defended in his earliest writings. It would agree emphatically with him that God must be conscious; if not omniscient, at least far more widely conscious than we are; for the conclusion we jump to in our moments of elevation is that there is some mind which always sees things as we see them at these moments. On the other hand, the religious consciousness seems to object strenuously to Royce's conception of a God lifted above time, taking no part in history except to survey it at a glance. The God of religion belongs in that "World of the Powers" in which Royce[1] could find no God; He is a Power among powers, the Power that is progressively victorious, not by compulsion, but through the gradual impartation of His purpose and outlook to the leaders of mankind.

2. THE LOGIC OF CHRISTIAN THEISM

But now comes the moment to abandon the mood of enthusiasm, and begin to examine critically these metaphysical conclusions which the religious consciousness so boldly and naïvely draws from its own experience. The question at once arises: Is not this whole process of springing nimbly from my own worshipful feelings to the conception of a superhuman spirit worthy of worship, simply a case of what is called the "pathetic" fallacy, the fallacy of *empathy* or *Einfühlung*, whereby man naïvely assumes that the object on which his attention is concentrated at moments of extreme emotion is itself a personal being, filled with an emotion which is the obverse of his own, whereby also he concludes in general that whatever matters to him and his tribe matters to the universe?[2] The history of religion certainly gives us ample cause to mistrust this primitive and naïve tendency. This it was which produced that multitude of gods and spirits with which the woods and streams and air were filled in the ancient world. Today we should most of us admit that when poets personify a river or a tree it is poetry and nothing more; and when Fechner speaks of an Earth-Soul, it is very bad metaphysics. We may be opposed to absolute materialism

---

[1] As, for example, in *The Religious Aspect of Philosophy* and *The Conception of God.*

[2] Cf. William James's description of how he personified the San Francisco earthquake, cited and discussed in G. F. Moore's *The Birth and Growth of Religion*, pp. 8-11.

in philosophy, and conceive of atoms and molecules as in some sense psychic; but we should never try to carry on a conversation with them and expect them to have anything significant to say to us.

I admit, therefore, that the god-idea sprang originally —at least in part—from a very dangerous emotional snare, which still threatens to entangle all who do not guard themselves against it. Now if, as many allege, the religious consciousness, after once forming its hasty conclusions, is thenceforth "impervious to experience," then the same condemnation which falls upon primitive animism falls upon modern theism; it is at best a "rationalization" of an essentially illogical position, reached through loose emotional reasoning. I do not think, however, that the history of religion justifies such a generalization. The god-idea has obviously gone through tremendous transformations since primitive times, and those transformations are the result not only of rationalization but of a sort of empirical process of trial-and-error, which has repeatedly brought the god-idea to the test of the *facts*, and so provided for its correction. The Hebrew prophets, for example, repeatedly used their idea of Jahveh as a means of historical prediction, quite as scientists use hypotheses as a basis for prediction. "Supposing Einstein's theory to be true, then you will observe certain curious phenomena at the next solar eclipse." "Supposing Jahveh to be a God of justice, then the Israelites will eventually perish as a nation if they persist in social injustice; supposing he rules all nations, then the Assyrians, too, will fall, if they persistently oppress other nations." When the prophets' predictions failed, as they frequently did, they were not always content to rationalize and explain the unaccountable exception by hook or crook, under the old hypothesis. They frequently *modified their idea of God*. When, for example, the undeserved sufferings of Israel created a problem for those who believed in a God who always requited measure for measure, many, to be sure, concluded that Israel must have sinned; others, with more insight, decided that God does not requite measure for measure, but permits the wicked to prosper and the good to suffer. Hard facts have had their share in the creation of the modern idea of God; and to cast such an idea aside would be to throw away a perfect treasure-house of hard-won truth.

The question remains, however, whether the truth of the idea of God is not a purely practical sort of truth, expressing the way the cosmos affects our interests, and not what the cosmos is in itself. Is not Santayana right in saying that the mythologies and theologies which man has constructed reveal the truth, not about the universe, but about man's moral nature?[1] I think he is so nearly right that I am not going to take the trouble to argue the matter. I think it is perfectly evident that religious discovery is mainly discovery of values, and that the religious consciousness deceives itself when it thinks to learn truths about the astronomical constitution of the universe, by mystic revelation, as Swedenborg did. The Hebrew prophets often confused meteorology and morals, even in their truest intuitions. The intuition that the Assyrians could not triumph was a good one; yet it is probable that it was expected that Jahveh would send down lightning from heaven upon them at the critical moment, whereas the real rock on which Assyrian militarism and all militarism splits is human nature. Yes, I grant it: Theological truth is primarily practical and relates in the first instance to the sphere of human values; as a representation of cosmic reality it is more or less symbolic, and much of it needs to be regarded as poetry rather than as literal truth.

[1] Cf. Santayana, *Reason in Religion*, Chapter I.

But does this mean that theology is wholly irrelevant to metaphysics, and that the movement of thought from the human to the cosmic is wholly illegitimate? Is the "moral order" which the prophet discovers a purely human and social entity, and does it reveal nothing about the nature of the universe? To make any such assertion seems to me very rash; it creates a wholly unreal and artificial chasm between man and nature. I grant that man's self-importance needs to be disciplined; he needs to be told over and over again that he is *not* the center of the universe, and that if things are "made for" anyone they certainly are not made for him, or him alone; he needs to be told that things as they appear to him and as they affect him are not things in themselves; but for all that, I do not see how any sane person can persuade himself that human history and human aspirations and human ethical insight reveal nothing about the nature of the cosmos.

There are two considerations that seem to me to establish the legitimacy of a certain type of inference from human to cosmic reality, and justify in a measure that swift leap by which the religious consciousness rises to the conception of a cosmic Personality.

The first is this: If we adopt Professor Leuba's distinction between "mechanical" and "anthropopathic" behavior,[1] there is no reason, *a priori*, why the success of mechanistic science should make us conclude that mechanical behavior alone is appropriate in dealing with the cosmos. It may be said that, when man and the higher animals are subtracted from the universe, all that remains is precisely that sphere of law and impersonal force where

---

[1] See the opening pages of his *Psychological Study of Religion*. Mechanical behavior would be illustrated by a sailor's conduct when he furls his sails at the onset of a storm; anthropopathic behavior, by his conduct when the storm threatens to wreck the ship, and he prays for deliverance.

anthropopathic conduct is futile. Now it is obvious that mechanistic science has had magnificent success in dealing with this "residual cosmos"—success which makes one look askance at the religious conduct which until recent times held sway in the same field. We do not dispute that lightning rods are better protection in a thunderstorm than sacrifice and prayer, and medical treatment is ordinarily better than exorcism in organic diseases. Still, if we use our daily experience as a guide, there is nothing more certain than this: that the same thing may often be dealt with *either* mechanically or anthropopathically, and that in such cases it is anthropopathic behavior which gets us in touch with the deeper and the more inclusive reality. I am unfortunately forced every day to deal with multitudes of my fellow men mechanically, as mere objects in my environment, responding in certain definite and predictable ways when properly approached. The street-car conductor is to me hardly more personal than the prepayment machine he manipulates. Yet that same conductor, if I take the pains to scrape an acquaintance with him, responds to me in a very different and far more significant way. I see no reason, *a priori*, for denying the possibility of tapping new depths of reality in the residual cosmos by means of anthropopathic behavior. Daily experience, on the contrary, would encourage me to make the experiment. In the environment which immediately surrounds me, I find certain objects which respond only to mechanical behavior; others which respond both to mechanical and to anthropopathic behavior. Why may not the residual cosmos, too, contain objects of both types?

This first consideration is merely preparatory, and is addressed only to those in whose minds there is an inhibition against even entertaining the hypothesis of a cosmic mind. Such people are not rare. They need to be made aware of the fact that they are unconscious dogmatists, resting upon *a priori* convictions with almost mystic tenacity. Leaning over backward to escape the fallacy of "reading in," they have fallen into the fallacy of "reading out."

The second consideration is this: All development takes place under the influence of external stimuli; the nature of the development—particularly in its later stages—reveals the nature of the stimuli; consequently, the nature of human development reveals the nature of the cosmic stimuli which called it forth.

The validity of the general principle I am laying down will be perfectly evident if we confine our attention at the start to individual development.[1] The human individual, from the moment when the egg is first fertilized by the sperm to the moment when, having made his own all that his social environment has to offer, he stands face to face with cosmic reality and dares to dream dreams of a better society than earth yet can offer, is constantly under the influence of external stimuli, which beat upon him incessantly from his immediate material environment, from his social environment, and from his cosmic environment. His growth is conditioned by his response. At first he reacts only to the grosser sensory stimuli, and his growth is mainly physical growth. Next he begins to react to stimuli which beat upon him from his immediate social environment, the family; next, to the widening worlds which open up to him as he explores the neighborhood, goes to school, and comes in contact with various social groups; finally, if the study of science or philosophy, or the presentation of religious ideas, makes a strong-enough appeal to him, he may come to live in a world coextensive with the known universe, and the cosmos itself, as he conceives it, may come to play such a rôle in his life that

---

[1] Let the reader reflect upon Professor Cooley's description of the development of the self in *Human Nature and the Social Order*.

he feels himself able to look down upon current ideas and ideals from a certain height, and so becomes a scientific or ethical or religious reformer. Reacting to these new stimuli, the individual grows—and this now means not merely physical, but mental, moral, and religious growth. All this illustrates what Professor Holt calls the "recession of the stimulus": the reaction of the organism to more and more distant and more and more spiritual stimuli.[1] What really changes, however, is not the stimulus but the response; the stimulus was there all the time, but the organism was not yet capable of responding to it. Hence I say that the later, wider, subtler responses of the organism reveal more of the nature of the stimulus than the earlier, grosser responses. A codfish reveals more of the stimuli which play upon a given region of the ocean than does an oyster; he has responded to more of them. An eight-year-old child reveals the kind of family in which he has been brought up more exactly than a two-year-old baby; and if you are trying to read the father's character from the son's, you will do well to pay attention to his half-inarticulate aspirations, for they are often more significant than his settled habits, which represent earlier and grosser reactions.

The significance of external stimuli in individual development, and the significance of the response—particularly at later stages—as a clue to the nature of the stimulus, is perfectly evident to all of us, *because we can stand outside the process of development and survey stimulus and response at a single glance.* It would not be so apparent to us, if we were condemned to stand inside the process, and the exciting stimulus were invisible to us. Such would be the plight of a consistent solipsist, who refused to admit the objectivity of his sense impressions,

---

[1] Cf. E. B. Holt, *The Freudian Wish and its Place in Ethics*, pp. 75-99.

and the external source of the ideas he got from other people. He would be conscious of a certain persistent widening of his horizon, and a constant enrichment of his store of meanings and ideals, but he would attribute it to his own vital urge, and if scientifically minded could easily connect each new sense impression and each new idea in a causal sequence with all that had preceded it, thus conclusively exploding the notion of an objective world and proving that he alone was the cause of all that went on in his mind. If, however, his imaginary other self should succeed in convincing him, by some *tour de force*, that an external world existed, our solipsist might still maintain that this external world was a realm of impersonal force and immutable law, so that it would be absurd to behave anthropopathically toward it. Meanings and ideals, commonly associated with personal selves, certainly appeared to spring up in the Ego as a result of contact with the external world; but might not such personal ideas spring up in the Ego as the result of contact with impersonal forces? Might they not be simply the way the external world affected the Ego, and would not the Ego be committing the "pathetic" fallacy, and reading in its own emotions, if it rashly entertained the hypothesis of the existence of personalities external to its own? To this argument it would be difficult to reply, unless the Ego were willing to admit the principle that personal ideas can only be awakened by contact with personalities; and he would probably object that this principle opened the way for the wildest mythologizing. Yet we ordinary common-sense mortals, looking on from the outside, should know all the time that the most significant part of our solipsist's development was due to contact with other minds, and his mental and moral development would seem to us to be a perfect clue to the precise nature of the social environment in which he had been brought up.

Now when we turn to the development of the human race, we are all of us precisely in the solipsist's predicament; we cannot survey at a glance the development of the race and the cosmic stimuli which called forth that development, because the cosmos is too vast and we know too little about it, and because we see it through the spectacles of the human understanding—through those "collective representations" which, as the French sociologists remind us, have come down to us from primitive times. And our bias[1] is the solipsist's bias: we are tempted to assume that human evolution, beginning with the evolution of life out of inorganic matter, and culminating in acts and aspirations like Lincoln's, which we instinctively call "divine," is a self-explanatory process, inwardly motivated, bursting up spontaneously like the *élan vital*. Any such view, with all due respect to most of the philosophy we have had since the epoch of Romanticism, is essentially absurd. It is like explaining the sprouting of grass in the springtime without taking the sun and the rain into consideration; it is like describing the development of personality in a child without taking his parents and playmates into the picture. Human history, taken by itself, is like one end of a telephone conversation; it irresistibly suggests the existence of an external stimulus to which it is the response.

As to the nature of those stimuli which have evoked the evolution of man, again I suggest that the later stages in the evolutionary process are the most significant. Just as physical stimuli may seem sufficient to explain the first stages in the growth of a baby, so an almost mechanical

---

[1] I think that this bias, to which the modern man is peculiarly liable, is just as dangerous as the animistic bias to which primitive man was subject—which may serve to explain my previous remark, that in leaning over backward to escape the fallacy of "reading in," one falls into the fallacy of "reading out."

theory of evolution may seem sufficient to account for the appearance of life upon the earth and the origin of species; but as we mount the path of human history, it becomes increasingly difficult to account for the strange new meanings and values and ideals and aspirations that meet us there, except on the hypothesis that they came into human history through contact with some external mind. This is the hypothesis which we know to be true, so far as the new meanings and ideals which enter the individual mind are concerned; and we should quite lose patience with a solipsist who disputed it. Why should we turn about and become solipsists when we transfer our attention from the relations between the individual and society to the relations between society and the cosmos? Why not adopt the hypothesis which is the most natural of all hypotheses: that man is growing up under the tutelage of a Person or Persons greatly superior to him in wisdom and in goodness—so much superior to him that it is not in the light of man's actual career and actual characteristics, but rather in the light of his intuitive presentiments and inchoate longings that the depth and richness of that superior type of personality can best be conceived. Individuals of transcendent genius seem to require some such hypothesis to explain them, for they have outgrown all that society had to teach them, and look up and out to something above and beyond society; much more is this the case if we think of the evolution of mankind as a whole. This is the hypothesis which saints and prophets in all ages have set forth, not as a hypothesis, but as an immediate certainty; my argument is that the quality of the ideas with which such people have enriched humanity makes their naïve hypothesis the most probable one.

It is only fair to point out that to admit validity of the argument here presented for the existence of personality in the extra-human cosmos would not be to commit one's self to the traditional type of theism, to belief in an Almighty Creator and Sustainer of the universe. Development takes place chiefly under the stimulus of the *immediate* environment; the nature of the development reveals the nature of the immediate environment more clearly than it reveals that of the more remote environment. The child's development reveals the character of his parents better than it reveals the character of his casual acquaintances. Hence all my argument tends to prove is that over the little stream of cosmic history, in which you and I are tiny eddies, there broods the influence of Personality greater than man's. Whether the scope and sway of that Personality are universal and uncontested or limited and provincial, whether we should think of it as a single, well-organized Central Mind or as a sort of Spiritual Commonwealth like Felix Adler's[1]—these are questions to which my argument does not permit me to return a categorical answer.

The question of monotheism versus polytheism, it seems to me, is still very much of an open question. "Man is not a monotheistic animal"; at any rate, he never immediately experiences the divine unity. The divine Personality comes to him most intimately and persuasively through the medium of human personalities, through Christ's personality to a most extraordinary degree, through other personalities in various degrees, through one's own personality at certain exalted moments. If the divine be one at its source in the external cosmos, it nevertheless must filter down to us by devious paths, first through the social atmosphere in which we all live and move and have our being, and then through the fog of individual experience in which each one of us is en-

[1] Cf. Felix Adler, *Ethical Philosophy of Life*, Book II, Chapter VI.

shrouded; and in so doing it is refracted into all the colors of the rainbow and takes on a thousand bizarre and subjective forms. How can we tell at what level the plurality of the divine-as-we-experience-it gives place to the unity of the divine-as-it-is-in-itself? By what right shall we brush aside the Catholic angelologies and gnostic theogonies which carry the principle of divine plurality out into the cosmic realm? The religious consciousness itself is in a strait betwixt two in this matter; it does not know whether it wants to believe in one God or in many —witness the Christian doctrine of the Trinity, which carries the principle of diversity into the very heart of the divine nature, while at the same time affirming the divine unity in the most emphatic terms.

At just one point, however, the verdict of the history of religions in favor of monotheism is clear and specific: A plurality of warring gods, differing in character and function, is no more tolerable in the long run than a plurality of moral standards. However diverse may be the *forms* in which the divine is made manifest, the *quality* of the divine must always be the same. We demand the same consistency, orderliness, and unity in the realm of the divine which we have come to discern in the physical universe and which we hope to create in human society. The great affirmation of Hebrew and Christian monotheism is that the moral law which rules the destiny of men and nations is as international, impartial, and invariable as the laws of Nature; and that in the working of the moral law there is to be discerned a divine Purpose— single, unswerving, indefatigable—whose goal is the creation of a world-wide commonwealth of justice, peace, and good-will among men. Singleness of character and quality, singleness of purpose, this is the kind of divine unity that it is practically important to affirm; and this kind of unity might be predicated either of a single divine personality or of a community of divine personalities. So far as I can see, it is a matter of indifference to the religious consciousness—unity of purpose once being granted —whether the God-head be single, triple, or multiple. Personally, I prefer to think of a single cosmic mind, whose influence comes to us in manifold forms, most impressively through the medium of human personalities and social groups; but I do not think the evidence for such a conception is decisive, and I do not see why speculation in this field should not be left absolutely free and flexible.[1]

If the question of the numerical structure of the divine Personality is largely an academic question, irrelevant to the religious problem, the same cannot be said of the question of the scope of the divine influence in the cosmos— or, to put the question in its familiar form, the relation of God to Nature. Whether God's influence is confined to our corner of the universe, whether behind Him there stands a Veiled Being, ready to overrule His holiest purposes as Ἀνάγκη overruled the will of the Olympian gods, or whether, on the other hand, Nature is malleable to His will and full of the evidence of His working, are questions of the utmost practical concern. To be forced to admit the former alternative, after arriving at a belief in the existence of a personal God, would be almost equivalent to losing God after finding Him.

It is just at this point that the teleological argument for the existence of God becomes significant. By itself, the evidence of the existence of "development and purpose" and trends toward harmony in the physical and biological realms is not sufficient to prove the existence of a Personal God such as the religious consciousness demands. The

---

[1] Among recent treatments of the conception of God, the one with which I find myself in heartiest agreement is that of Professor Montague, in the concluding chapter of his *Belief Unbound*.

best that Nature, animate and inanimate, reveals, is a series of incipient tendencies toward organization and harmony, which, could they once get fairly under way, might prove to be as significant as the tendency which issued in human evolution. Only a tendency come to fruition, or such partial fruition as we find in human evolution, can reveal such a God as we have been describing, or justify us in assuming His existence; and, perhaps on account of our astronomical situation, we are as yet acquainted with no other similarly advanced tendency. But this does not rob the teleological argument of its value. The initial stages of the process of evolution which eventuated in man were identical with the stages which the whole observable cosmos appears to be going through. Once grant that the existence of a Personal Stimulus must be assumed in order to account for human evolution, and the universal presence of rudimentary purposive trends in the cosmos will then appear to be a most cogent argument for the universal scope of the operation of that same Stimulus.

What, then, is the relation of God to Nature? Well, Nature is, in a sense, an abstraction, a blanket term covering everything that can be handled by mechanical conduct and mechanical concepts; that is, *everything, including ourselves*. If, however, the term "Nature" be restricted to mean *all that does not respond to anthropopathic behavior*, I think the evidence marshaled by Hobhouse in his *Development and Purpose* appears to justify the belief that Nature is increasingly coming under the divine control.[1] Those aspects of Nature which are clearly

[1] I hope it is clear that I do not identify God with any tendency toward harmony in Nature (as Hobhouse sometimes seems to) any more than I identify Him with any tendency toward righteousness in human history. These are signs of the working of God, the response that proves the stimulus; I do not worship them, but I worship the stimulus that called them forth. Thus God, as I conceive Him, transcends Nature. For the

purposive may be regarded as the furniture of the cosmic schoolroom, the medium through which God stings and stimulates the dormant personalities of His creatures. Those aspects of Nature which are clearly chaotic and resist all efforts at teleological interpretation may be regarded as the cosmic parallel to such human phenomena as unfinished work and unrequited love. As for the underlying laws and conditions of the cosmic process, they are at any rate such that harmony, life, and perhaps eventually personality spring up as naturally in every quarter of the universe as vegetation springs up in a plowed field, and over the whole creation the divine control visibly—if slowly and haltingly—advances. To affirm this is to affirm the essential part of the conviction which has traditionally expressed itself in the doctrine that God created and sustains the universe.

3. THE MEANING OF CHRISTIAN THEISM

Having indicated how Christian faith in God takes its rise in experience, and how it may be rationally defended, I wish in conclusion to develop its implications somewhat more fully, and define its meaning more precisely. From the point of view of practice and of theory alike, the fundamental fact which must never be overlooked, is that *Christian theism is meaningless apart from Christian ethics.* That is to say, faith in the Christian God grows naturally out of faith in the Christian way of life. The latter can conceivably be understood without the former, but the former cannot be fully interpreted without the latter.

Genuine Christian theism is the natural culmination of a series of adventures in faith beginning in the sheltered

---

general conditions of life, which seem to be under His control, I give Him thanks as devoutly as my Puritan ancestors; but I recognize that there is much to be changed in Nature, by Him as by us.

circle of the home, the church, and the neighborhood, stretching out through the hostile spheres of industrial, interracial, and international relations, and plunging boldly at last into the dark shadows of cosmic mystery where the ultimate secret of human destiny lies hidden.

Why does a man become a Christian in the first place? Not because of his acceptance of any formal line of argumentation, but because he has been impressed with the beauty and power of the Christian spirit, individually embodied in some parent, or friend, or pastor, and socially embodied in what we call the "atmosphere" of his family, or his community, or his church. Something within him responds; and he finds the first evidence of the power of the Christian spirit in the harmony, joy, and sense of exhaustless resources which it creates within his own personality.

Then, almost simultaneously, he begins to get evidence of the power of Christian love to create ideal social relationships. He experiences the vast reinforcement of energy and heightening of life's significance which comes from Christian fellowship; and relying upon these resources, he begins to try a few timid experiments in overcoming evil with good. In spite of many failures and rebuffs, he begins to believe that, wisely and skillfully practiced, Christian love and forgiveness have the power to melt the hardest heart; and it occurs to him that these principles must have some wider application to the great world that lies outside the sphere of the neighborhood.

If he really takes this notion seriously, he is in for a trial of faith far more severe than anything he has yet experienced; for in the economic and political sphere he will find it taken for granted, even by many calling themselves Christians, that a Bismarckian policy of "blood and iron" is the only one that can succeed. Driven in upon himself by opposition, ridicule, and failure, he will find himself reaching out for support to a larger fellowship than that of the local church—a fellowship which stretches back across the centuries and includes the great creative spirits who have faced loneliness and frustration unafraid, because they have believed that love is stronger than hate and stronger than death.

It is at this stage that fellowship with Christ and personal loyalty to Christ come to be something more than a form of words to the modern Christian. As he finds himself—somewhat to his embarrassment—marching with the little band of pioneers at whose head that colossal figure strides on, he feels his admiration and affection for his leader kindle; and he begins to realize that there are heights of faith that he has not yet scaled; for the leader's eyes are turned upward, and his faith is sustained by a fellowship that is more than human. Candidly, our modern Christian does not find it easy to share the faith of Jesus, for he lives in an age which regards the non-human cosmos as a mere reservoir of mechanical energies, to be scientifically studied and technically manipulated; yet he is never nearer to sharing it than when he shares, in any measure, in his leader's sufferings and disappointments. At such critical moments, when the brutishness of man and the indifference of the universe seem to bring all hope of a Kingdom of Love to the verge of absolute shipwreck, something rises within him to protest against the verdict; and he has a sense that he is not alone. "Man's extremity is God's opportunity." It is precisely when all human aid vanishes that there arises most compellingly the conviction that a spirit like Christ's is present, and potentially dominant, not only in the human but in the cosmic sphere as well.

"Wishful thinking"! Yes, that is just what it is. Genuine theistic faith is not the product of cool impersonal scientific analysis or calm disinterested philosophic contemplation of the world as it is, leading to a reasonable hypothesis concerning its ultimate Ground or First Cause. That kind of thinking by itself leads not to theism, but to pantheism. It springs from Greece, and not from Palestine. Genuine ethical theism of the Hebrew-Christian type springs from an active, ardent desire to make the world better than it is. Its God is not the God of things as they are, but the God of things as they ought to be, and may be. He stands over against nature and society, not like an artisan content with his finished and perfect work (as in eighteenth-century Deism) but like a teacher or a states-man, dealing with refractory material, but confident of his power to make it eventually into an ideal pattern. A kind of provisional dualism is thus inevitable in the Christian view of God's relation to the world. God cannot without reservations be described as the Creator of the world-as-it-is, or the instigator of "whatsoever-comes-to-pass." When Christian faith ascribes the creation of the world to God, it does so not by way of logical inference from natural phenomena, but by a daring exercise of wishful thinking, which finds in God the beginning of all things because in Him it finds the end toward which, it hopes, all things are being drawn.

Emotional, loose-knit, metaphorical thinking of this kind is severely frowned upon by many contemporary critics of traditional Christianity. In the name of scientific method—the one sure method of reaching reliable con-clusions in every sphere—we are urged to put away childish fancies, and view the facts of life, not as we would like them to be, but as they really are. If we are to have a theology, we are told, let it be a scientific theology, based upon a cautious, step-by-step process of inductive reason-ing from known facts to probable hypotheses, with no giddy speculations and no intuitive leaps of faith. That there are real possibilities in such a cautious method, and real dangers in wishful thinking, it would be futile to deny. God is not merely an object of faith; He is an object of human experience; and as such, He can be scientifically studied and analyzed. Such study and analysis ought to make it progressively more clear precisely what we mean when we say that we rely upon "God" as an "ally" and "moral resource" in time of need. Nevertheless, I think it should be made plain that, in matters of religion, scientific method can never be cool and impersonal, as it is in the sphere of physics and chemistry. The religious experimenter must throw himself, heart and soul, into the experiment; he must perhaps live a whole life on unproved assumptions, and appeal to posterity for the verification of his hypotheses. If he abandons his hopes whenever they run against adverse facts, and resigns himself to a drab and constricting view of reality because he fears to play the fool, he may be missing his chance to discover some pathway out of the morass of human misery which will not reveal itself to a less ardent and impetuous investigator.

It was the great service of the Hebrew prophets to mankind that they engaged in a mortal wrestling-bout with human destiny, and throwing themselves headlong into the encounter, refused to accept a negative verdict, or to desist from the struggle until their highest hopes were somehow vindicated. The faith in God which they bequeathed us is not a cool intellectual induction, but a hot emotional conviction, like faith in humanity, faith in democracy, or faith in the abolition of war. No self-respecting pacifist or democrat or humanitarian permits his faith to hang in the balance every time he opens the morning newspaper. He is convinced that what ought to be, can be; and though he is ready to modify his program, and even his central principles, in the light of cool reflection and scientific experimentation, his ultimate appeal is to a verification that lies far beyond the span of his own lifetime. If "humanists" and other humanitarians are "wishful thinkers" in this sense, why should they criticize theists for pushing the same process of thought a step further? Where does the danger of moral cowardice leave off, and the danger of childish credulity begin?

"But what, literally, does Christian theism mean?" our humanist friends will ask. "Is it merely a figurative way of expressing your belief in the ultimate triumph of Christian love in human affairs; or do you really believe in a personal God? When you speak of God in the masculine gender, when you refer to His power and goodness, when you call Him Father, or Teacher, or Friend, do you mean what you say, or are you using old terminology in some new and allegorical sense, dishonestly? Do you really believe in the anthropomorphic God in whom Jesus trusted —the God who marks the sparrow's fall, and numbers the hairs of our head? If you do, we marvel at your *naïveté*, and wonder how you happen to be living in the twentieth century. If you do not, we ask you precisely what you *do* mean, and why you persist in calling yourselves Christian theists." These are fair questions, and I propose to answer them as honestly as I can.

If I rightly understand the faith of modern Christian theists, it consists of a hierarchy of convictions, ranging from practical certainty through varying degrees of assurance, and shading off at the far end into overbeliefs and hopes. The foundation of this hierarchy of conviction is, as I have been insisting, the conviction that what we call Christian love—the spirit which is best expressed in the life, teachings, and death of Jesus of Nazareth—is the best and most powerful thing in the world. It is the *best* thing in the world, and *deserves* to prevail; this is bed rock, with all of us. We would rather perish with Christ, if it comes to the pinch, than triumph with his enemies;

and if the God of Mussolini is the reigning despot of this universe, we are bound to be rebels and revolutionaries. But we further believe, with an almost equal conviction, that love is not weak; it is the strongest thing on earth. It can easily be wounded and slain; but it conquers even in death. We are, therefore, led to affirm concerning Christian love what all ethical idealists implicitly affirm concerning their own most cherished ideals; that there is *something in the nature of things* which makes for its triumph.

What is that "something in the nature of things," and how does it "make for" the triumph of love? I think that the force of this affirmation is best conveyed by the assertion that love is the supreme moral value, and that, like all great values, it is not merely based upon human desire, but inheres in the stable structure of reality as a whole. There is a school of thought which looks upon the whole world of values and meanings as a realm of pure subjective fantasy, in which all is relative to the whim or the taste of the individual, and one man's preference is as good as another's: *de gustibus non disputandum*. Christian theists pretty universally reject this view. We recognize, of course, that a man's momentary desire is a factor in the determination of what is best for him to do at the moment; but we insist that there are other factors: the whole structure of his character, the whole structure of the social order, and the whole structure of the universe. A desire which brings a man into a state of division within himself, or a state of perpetual friction with his neighbors, or which dooms him to butt his head ineffectively against the general structure of reality, is a bad desire. The nature of things "makes for" the triumph of love, because love unifies personality, creates mutually satisfactory social relationships, and brings us into a state of harmonious dependence upon and effective partnership with the whole structure and process of the universe.

This last clause demands further elaboration. What do we mean by "harmonious dependence" and "effective partnership"? Here we come to an aspect of Christian love which we have hitherto been neglecting, in our emphasis upon its ethical bearings. Christian love, as described in the New Testament, is not merely a strenuous moral attitude of good will; it is at the same time a serene religious attitude of dependence and trust. Professor Moffatt has shown in his book on *Love in the New Testament*, that in the experience of love as found in primitive Christianity the religious attitude is primary and the moral attitude secondary. What this religious attitude of dependence means, in purely empirical terms, has been beautifully expressed by one who cannot possibly be accused of religious fanaticism or romanticism, Professor John Dewey:

Yet the last word is not with obligation nor with the future. Infinite relationships of man with his fellows and with nature already exist. . . . Even in the midst of conflict, struggle, and defeat a consciousness is possible of the enduring and comprehending whole. . . . There is a conceit fostered by perversion of religion which assimilates the universe to our personal desires; but there is also a conceit of carrying the load of the universe from which religion liberates us. Within the flickering inconsequential acts of separate selves dwells a sense of the whole which claims and dignifies them.[1]

All religious men, Christian or non-Christian, will testify that this is an exact description of what they experience in the act of worship; but the ultimate nature of that "whole" of which Professor Dewey speaks still remains to be defined. For theists, as distinct from pantheists, it is not the ALL; because they are seeking to *change* the world

---

[1] *Human Nature and Conduct*, pp. 330, 331. Published by Henry Holt & Company, New York.

in many of its aspects, and one does not rest for support upon that which one is seeking to dislodge. Nor is it a static, lifeless structure. We live in a growing, changing world, in which there is not only a stable structure, but a flowing process of which human history is an integral part. Looked at impersonally, through the eyes of physics and chemistry, our world seems to be the expression of grim, mechanical forces, indifferent to all our highest values; but this is an artificial and partial view. Looked at concretely, down the long funnel of human history and cosmic evolution, the world about us is seen to be at least organic and vital. Not only the individual but the race is supported and environed in a larger Life which is responsive to need, as the body is responsive to the needs of its members. In the act of worship, we consciously participate in this larger Life, and through it are brought into mystic fellowship with one another.

Shall we go a step further, and assert that this divine Life is purposive, intelligent, and personal? That *human* purpose, intelligence, and personality are organic parts of this Life is plain; and this means that mere vitalism is no more competent than mere mechanism to express its rich complexity; but if man's collective wisdom is the highest wisdom there is, it would seem a bit misleading to talk about the wisdom or personality of God. If God had no focalized consciousness apart from man, if He came to consciousness only in man, then one could not look to God for guidance, but only for energy. God would be like a great organism whose coördination was defective, or a great community lacking an administrative head. Now there is much in religious experience that makes the simile of an enfolding organism or great community seem appropriate when applied to God. The figure of the vine and the branches and the figure of the body and the members are classical in Christian literature. But I hold as an overbelief, in common with most Christian theists, the conviction that the divine organism has an intelligence of a higher-than-human order, and the divine community has a governing head. I am sustained in this conviction by the almost irresistible sense of guidance which comes to religious men whenever they make themselves most completely the organs of the divine Life—an impression confirmed when one glances over the great expanses of history and sees the effects of such lives upon the course of events.

If I am asked what such a subtle philosophical concept has in common with the loving Father or celestial King of Christian tradition, my reply is that the great religious geniuses have never been so naïvely anthropomorphic as is sometimes supposed. The Russian peasant who turned atheist and joined the Communists after his first ride in an airplane, because when he got above the clouds he looked all around and couldn't see God anywhere, is not representative of Christian thought at its best. The language of religion is the language of poetry, but there is a literal truth beneath its symbolism which theology must try to express in more technical terms. Modern theology does not feel itself bound to reproduce precisely either the language or the thought of primitive Christianity; but there is such profound religious insight embedded in the classic literature of our faith that one recurs, over and over again, to the very words in which it was expressed. God was not discovered yesterday; and although we may hope that closer analysis of religious experience, coupled with the general progress of science and philosophy, may progressively enrich our knowledge of his nature, the broad outlines of the truth were sketched long ago, in the Book of Psalms, in unforgettable phraseology:

"Lord, Thou hast been our dwelling-place in all generations."

"The Lord is my Shepherd! I shall not want."

The whole argument of this book has had to do, in a sense, with the destiny of human personality.

It became evident, early in our discussion, that the pattern of human life was susceptible of almost endless variation. Flexibility and malleability, we found, were among the most outstanding properties of human nature. Human destiny, it must now be evident, is not determined by one or two simple factors, but is spun out upon a vast web in which the warp is nothing less than the whole cosmic process, and the woof is woven by the responsive organism, selecting from its environment (at first instinctively, then more consciously and purposefully) that which it finds to be germane to its own development.

Amid the endless variety of possible human lives, our attention has been concentrated upon two main types. One is characterized by stagnation, regression, contractiveness; the other by progression and expansiveness. One type of individual is dominated by the law of least effort and the egocentric point of view; the other is dominated by the urge toward completeness and the tendency to widen his point of view by identifying himself with what lies beyond and above himself. The first type of individual is characterized by his proneness to fear, anger, or other contractive emotions. His inner life is full of jangling conflicts, from which he finds release only through flight from reality, or regression to a vegetative level of existence. Socially, he is a parasite; and the cosmic process has to resist him in order to maintain its onward course, as the organism has to resist disease germs in order to maintain its life and health. The second type of individual is the precise opposite of the first. His attitude toward his fellows and toward the universe is open, expansive, and friendly. If he has conflict in his inner life, it is only because he is moving toward a larger harmony, which requires that certain elements in his life be removed from a central to a subordinate position. Socially he tends to ally himself, more and more widely as time goes on, with all that makes for the ultimate unity of mankind; and the cosmic process finds in him a willing and intelligent co-worker.

These two contrasting ways of life correspond to what our fathers used to call The Path of Sin and The Way of Salvation. As was noted many centuries ago, the first is broader and easier than the second; but the second, though rough and difficult at first, becomes at length a path of light, "which shineth more and more unto the perfect day." One need not appeal to any doctrine of a future life to vindicate this judgment; the destiny of the villain and the saint (and us whose classification falls somewhere in between) is already manifest in that fragment of life's fabric which is woven before death clips the threads. The sinner imprisons himself in a hell of his own contriving. Walling himself off from all those divine agencies that make for life and health and enduring joy, he pines away within those walls; or if he ventures forth into the social arena, he creates domestic discord and civil strife, until society in self-protection has to immure him in some prison or asylum. The saint, exposing himself gladly to those vitalizing influences which the sinner refuses to admit, finds his blessedness in the inherent worthfulness of the good life itself, and makes his heaven on earth.

That is not to say that a calculus of pleasures and pains, on Benthamite lines, would always come out on the side of the angels. The pleasures of sin and the sufferings of the righteous are both very real; and they make it difficult

to persuade one who is traveling the broad road to destruction that he ought to change his course. Yet an all-
wise disinterested observer of the whole human scene,
capable of participating in all types of human experience,
would surely agree with John Stuart Mill's dictum, that
"it is better to be Socrates dissatisfied than a fool satisfied";
and he would agree with Plato's contention that, were a
man given the "ring of Gyges," permitting him to perform all manner of evil deeds invisibly and with impunity,
the way of righteousness would still be best. We are not
all-wise, and we are far from disinterested; yet there
come times to all of us when some testing experience enables us to get a broader conspectus than usual. At such
times, passing judgment upon ourselves, we affirm with
striking unanimity that the end of sin is remorse, and the
reward of righteousness is serenity.[1] The pleasures of sin
are hectic, passionate, and short-lived; by permitting one
side of our nature to run to gluttonous excess, they starve
the rest of it; while the satisfactions of the good life spring

---

[1] A friend of mine who for many years has been a reporter attached
to a metropolitan daily, writes as follows on this subject: "Tell me how a
person died and I can tell you how that person lived.

"Man can't die until he has evened his score with Nature. Man must
atone by his suffering on earth for all the suffering he has caused, for all
the hurt he has caused, and for all the meanness he has spread. And the
man who hurts love—better that he had never lived. . . .

"I have watched people die. Not one or two, but many. As a reporter
and an active one, I have been on the scene of countless tragedies. It is part
of my work. . . .

"I am convinced that if you have lived a decent, kind, sincere life
your death will be relatively painless. If you have been a mean, cruel,
relentless person, one who has hurt those who trusted you, your death will
include more suffering—physical, mental, and emotional—than you ever
knew you could endure. . . . I am forced to believe that emotional suffering purifies people. And I am also forced to believe that until you
have purified by suffering the suffering you have caused in other people,
you can't die."

This may be too neat and too precise a way of formulating the "law
of compensation"; but I am convinced that there is truth in it.

from the harmonious expression of our whole nature, in union with that which sustains and fulfills it: the Life of God.

I. THE UNITY OF HUMAN DESTINY

There is in all this no excuse for the strutting spiritual pride of the "unco guid," no justification for self-right-eous severity in judging the sinner. The freedom of the will may be (as I believe it is) a primary and irreducible datum of consciousness; but no man has ever saved him-self or lost himself by his own free-will alone. Freedom of choice is at best freedom to subject oneself to the right external influences. Without social aid and social initiative, no individual would ever become sensitive to the best in-fluences in the first place, or maintain himself unwaver-ingly in the presence of the best, once he had chosen it. The sustaining "grace of God" may be designed equally for all; but its availability is largely determined by the social environment in which we happen to grow up. No individual can be saved except through the mediation of some social group, which becomes to him a "channel of grace"; and he is not truly saved until he himself becomes a mediator of saving influence to the less privileged por-tions of society.[1] Ultimately all men stand or fall together. So long as any are lost none are fully saved, for we are members one of another. The saint sees this clearly; he is humble about the undeserved graces of which he has been the recipient, and conscious of his responsibility for the less fortunate. The sinner does not see it; and half of his misery roots in the delusion that he can achieve happiness

[1] Cf. Royce, *The Problem of Christianity*, Lecture on "The Realm of Grace"; and Rauschenbusch, *Theology for the Social Gospel*, chapter on "Individual and Social Salvation."

for himself by reaping profits from his neighbor's mis-
fortunes.

There is one ultimate destiny, then, toward which, by
virtue of the law of social solidarity, we are all moving
together. Either we are headed for a triumph of the principle of Life and Love, which human sin and weakness can
delay but not prevent; or we are headed for a cosmic
catastrophe which all the merits of the saints cannot for-
fend. The final consummation may be very remote; it
may be approached only as a limit that is never reached;
nevertheless, we all participate in it by hope or fear, and
it powerfully affects the whole complexion of life in the
here and now.

It is the fashion in this pragmatic age to decry all speculation about far futures and ultimate outcomes. "One life
at a time" is the favored rule. "What is good is good,
whether it fades and dies tomorrow or lasts forever." This
attitude represents a wholesome reaction against the exaggerated other-worldliness of our ancestors, who saw in
the present life nothing worthful in itself, but only a prep-
aration for the life to come. Yet it may fairly be asked
whether our present exaggerated *this-worldliness*—living
wholly in the here and now, without a single glance at
the far horizon, or the least curiosity concerning the final
outcome—is not more characteristic of beasts than of men;
and one cannot help suspecting that it is only a pose. It is
a fundamental condition of mental health that a man
should find some worthful enterprise in life, to which to
devote his energies; and the worthfulness of the enterprise depends in large measure upon its *permanence*. In
a game, it may be proper to exert terrific effort, just for
the sake of the fun and the exercise; but in real life, it is
necessary to believe that human activity has more lasting
results than the blowing of bubbles or the building of
sand-castles. It makes a tremendous difference whether,

in giving himself to the work of the artist or the states-
man or the educator, a man believes he is living in a world
where all precious things are fleeting and evanescent, or
in a world where (spite of death and change) nothing of
value is ever utterly and irredeemably lost. The same
great law of solidarity which unites the destiny of the saint
with that of the sinner, also unites the present with the
remote past and the remote future. All that has happened,
or shall happen, to any son of man concerns me, affects the
meaning of my present deed, and is part of my destiny.

I make no further apology, therefore, for closing this
professedly practical and empirical discussion upon a
speculative and metaphysical plane, and raising once more
the ancient question of the final destiny of human personality. It is my intention, however, to stay upon the empirical plane as long as possible; which means that the order
of topics must be, first "What Do We Know?" and then,
"What May We Believe?"

2. WHAT WE KNOW

It would seem, on the face of it, that the answer to the
first question is, simply, "Nothing at all!" Every human
personality at last goes out beyond our ken, through the
dark gateway of death, and its further destiny—whether
it be extinction or continued life—is shrouded in impene-
trable mystery. Death is "the bourne from which no trav-
eller returns." So to conceive the situation, however, is to
overlook the presence of a great body of facts, clearly
known and indubitable, which, if they do not settle the
problem of personal destiny, at least bear pretty directly
upon it.

Some of these facts seem to point, quite definitely, to
blank extinction as the final destiny toward which mankind is moving. The first of these is the great universal

fact of death itself, which inevitably awaits every human being, as it awaits every living thing. It would seem, indeed, that the higher and more delicate forms of life are the most subject to death. Monocellular organisms reproduce themselves by the simple device of splitting in two, and so enjoy a sort of immortality; but there is no such continuity of life for the higher organisms, of which the human body is typical. Here there is a clear gulf between the generations; germ-plasm alone is immortal; the old must die, and their carcasses must be removed from the scene, that the young may inherit the earth. And in their death, it would seem that most of the values which have been embodied in them must be dissipated. We can no longer conceive of the soul, as our remote ancestors did, in the guise of a ghostly "double," freely detachable from the body and capable of escaping from the mouth at death, as a mysterious vapor. We know that the soul is deeply implicated in the life of the body: a blow on the head, an attack of indigestion, a deficiency or excess of the secretion of the thyroid gland, all may produce profound alterations of personality. How is it conceivable, then, that there is anything in a human being which can survive the death of the body?

The fact of death is counterbalanced, to some extent, by the fact that, in two senses at least, personality does certainly survive. I am referring here to what are commonly called "biological immortality" and "social immortality." *Biological immortality* means, simply, that certain characteristic traits of the parents survive in their children. It does not apply to childless people; and even in the case of people who have children its consoling power is considerably weakened by the fact that the laws of heredity do not guarantee that children will resemble parents. But we are less concerned, after all, about the survival of germ-plasm than we are about the survival of ideals and purposes; and for this reason *social immortality*, or "immortality of influence," is for most of us a much more genuine source of comfort. I see no reason why anyone should despise the consolation and inspiration which resides in the fact that our lives are capable of leaving a lasting impress, for good or for ill, upon the lives of others and upon the whole social order. This was the only consolation which Pericles offered to the bereaved Athenians in his great "Funeral Oration"; and it seemed to satisfy them. It is a mark of mental maturity to be able to identify ourselves with great social ends—the continuation of a noble family tradition, or the upbuilding of a nation, or the enlightenment and salvation of mankind—and so to launch forth upon a long career in which our individual lives are only minor episodes. In so far as we thus forget ourselves in the service of larger ends, we become socially immortal; and whether our names are remembered or not, our lives are extended into the remote future and we can face death with equanimity. In so far as we identify ourselves with narrow and selfish ends, on the other hand, we condemn ourselves to an immortality of evil influence, and death becomes to us a final calamity, because it apparently destroys the only thing for which we care—our precious self!

But no sooner have we reached this point in our reflections, than a new array of "irreducible and stubborn facts" comes rushing in to beset us and to upset our equanimity. It is a fact that institutions die, as well as individuals. Families die, nations die, civilizations die. Oswald Spengler is probably mistaken in his theory that there is an exact "morphological" identity between all cultures and civilizations, past and present; but he is probably right in his general contention that our Western civilization, like its predecessors, is following a vast cycle of growth and dissolution.[1] It is a fact, moreover, that the whole long process of biological evolution upon this planet, of which human history is the climax, runs upon a margin so narrow that it seems certain to end, at last, in universal death. Life, as we know it, is possible only within a narrow range of temperature—so narrow that, when marked upon a scale ranging from absolute zero to the heat of the sun's surface, it makes one dizzy to think of it! We do not know, for a fact, that life exists anywhere else in all this vast, engulfing universe. Professor Eddington and Professor Jeans think the evidence is against it. If this is so, consider how brief and trivial an episode the whole story of "emergent evolution" becomes! Life is but a temporary effervescence, a "fungoid growth," appearing on a minor satellite of a third-rate star at a certain stage in its development, and then disappearing forever! If not a cosmic accident, it is at any rate a very minor cosmic incident! What then becomes of the comfort that resides in social and biological immortality? What inspiration can there be in pouring one's life-blood into a life-stream that is so certain to end in destruction?

If life, and consciousness, and all the ideal values which spring like flowers from that soil are on so precarious a footing in the universe, the only reasonable and noble attitude to assume is that of Promethean defiance.[2] Baffled and beaten by the world of facts, we must withdraw our allegiance from any object of worship beyond humanity, and devote ourselves, without great hope but without childish repining, to the worshipful contemplation of that realm of pure essence, that realm of ideal values which we have ourselves created. These beauties are fleeting,

---

[1] *The Decline of the West*, opening chapter.

[2] Classically expressed, of course, in Mr. Bertrand Russell's great essay on "The Free Man's Worship."

these goods are ephemeral, like ourselves; but that does not destroy their value, while they last; and we have a long time yet to create and contemplate them. If we have not immortality, we may at least have a quality of life which deserves to be immortal.[1] Let us cherish beauty and goodness all the more tenderly, since we know them to be passing incidents that have simply happened to occur in a universe which on the whole is either hostile or indifferent to all ideal values.

But before we accept so discouraging a verdict as final, there are certain other facts which deserve to be noted. Life may look very insignificant in the universe; values may appear to be strangers in a world of "omnipotent matter, rolling on its relentless way"; but there are many things that tend to give the opposite impression, and make us believe that both life and consciousness, and the things which are valuable to them, are more deeply rooted in the nature of the universe than they seem to be at first glance. Life may be a late comer on this planet, and it may not be discoverable elsewhere through the longest telescopes; but once it is here, how it thrives, and how boldly and bravely it comports itself! J. Arthur Thomson has a telling passage, in his *Introduction to Science*,[2] on the *insurgence* of life, as one observes it in the high Alps, near the snow-line.

Not only are there many beautiful flowers coming up at the thinned edge of the snow on most inhospitable ground, but there is a rich insect life and quite a number of birds, besides hundreds of things unseen. Very conspicuous are the large, white-bellied Alpine swifts, perhaps the most rapid of all birds in their flight, continually swirling about in the cold air, with

---

[1] See the chapter on "Ideal Immortality" in Mr. Santayana's *Reason in Religion*.

[2] Pages 185, 186. Published by Henry Holt & Company, Inc., New York. (1911.)

a note of victory in their cry, the very emblems of insurgent life. Shy marmots whistle among the rocks and strange flocks of white moths float up in the mist, rising like the souls of animals that have died far below. Everything is unpropitious, yet life is abundant; we feel what Bergson calls the *élan*, the spring, the impetus that is characteristic of livingness. We feel the *insurgent, indomitable, self-assertive character of living organisms*—something foreign to the purely physical.

Coupled with this quality of insurgence, there is what we may call the *resurgence* of life. Beaten to earth, overpowered by hostile forces, apparently pulverized and extinguished, it rises miraculously, time and again, to reassert itself. Faced with the necessity of radical change and readaptation, it undergoes metamorphosis, performs magic slights of legerdemain, and continues under a new name or a new form—the same, yet altogether different. The imagination of primitive man was captivated by the miraculous resurrection of vegetation in the springtime, and he attributed these strange phenomena to the activity of mighty deities. Children are still thrilled today by the magical metamorphosis of the caterpillar into the butterfly. Are we to say that modern biology has dissipated the wonder of these facts or destroyed their significance? Do they not suggest that life is more powerful, and more at home in the universe, than a purely naturalistic or mechanistic philosophy would make it appear?

The same qualities of insurgence and resurgence which characterize life at the biological level, characterize it, in a still higher sense, at the psychological, sociological, and religious levels. Human desire looks like a feeble thing when confronted with the inexorable forces which tend to thwart it; and we have seen in how many ways the quest of self-realization may go astray; yet thwarted desire seems to grow stronger in proportion to the strength of the opposing forces,[1] and the most depraved and disintegrated personalities may suddenly be regenerated, just at the moment when all hope is fled. On the sociological level, there is an analogous persistence of folkways and cultural values, which spring up afresh and reassert themselves, after every great social revolution, like vegetation after a frost. Civilizations and social systems die; but they never wholly die, as every historian knows. The persistence of Græco-Roman paganism in the culture of medieval Christendom and its great Renaissance in the fifteenth and sixteenth centuries present classical instances of this law. Finally, on that level of "emergent evolution" to which Professor Alexander and Professor Lloyd Morgan have dared to give the name of *deity*—a level to which humanity as a whole has not risen, but to which we may perhaps assign that little group of saints, prophets, and saviors whom other men have worshiped as "godlike"— here, too, the same law prevails.

Nothing is frailer to look upon than a prophet. He stands alone, "a reed shaken by the wind," with the whole social order arrayed against him, and only what he calls "God"—an invisible, intangible, hypothetical Something —on his side! Yet when such a man appears, the established order quakes to its core; and the authorities, quick to detect a threat against their vital interests, clap him in jail or hurry him off to the scaffold. They sense a certain mysterious *power* in him, and they are not mistaken; for though it is easy to capture and slay him, it is not so easy to kill the Spirit that resides in him. That Spirit has in it an insurgence and resurgence like that of life itself. Its

---

[1] Hadfield, *Psychology and Morals*, p. 62: "If an instinct is given expression, it is satisfied; if it is denied this expression, its impulses, instead of weakening, become stronger, until it forces satisfaction in direct ways (as when we give way to passion) or indirectly as a nervous disorder."

influence streams out, unimpeded by prison walls. It rises from the dead.

The Resurrection of Christ presents many difficult and almost insoluble problems to the modern mind: Confused and self-contradictory accounts of what happened . . . a body materialistic enough to leave an empty tomb and retain the marks of the crucifixion, yet immaterial enough to pass through closed doors and vanish without notice . . . final ascension of this body, through the clouds, in an upward direction, presumably headed for a non-existent, pre-Copernican heaven! Were we to attempt to grapple with these problems, we should be plunged into a sea of speculative difficulties. At present, our concern is with knowable facts. The knowable fact about the Resurrection of Christ is that his flaming spirit, undismayed by the final disaster which overtook his cause, somehow contrived to leap the gap of death and became incarnate in the discouraged hearts of his followers. It is most appropriate that the festival of the Resurrection should be celebrated at Easter time, coinciding in time as well as in mood with the ancient pagan festival of the resurrection of vegetation from the death of winter; for it marks the supreme expression, on the spiritual level, of that principle of the insurgence and resurgence of life which we first encountered on the biological level. It marks the assurance that death is as powerless against the "soul-force" of a personality like Christ's, as is the onslaught of winter against the swelling tide of spring.

"But," one may object, "all this is beside the point. These facts may have some bearing upon the destiny of life in general—the great stream of life in which you and I are little eddies—but they have no bearing upon the destiny of the human individual; and that is the real question at issue. When the word 'immortality' is used, it is *personal* immortality that is immediately thought of.

Now, when this is the issue at stake, it is vain to talk about Alpine flowers, and spring vegetation, and the renaissance of classical culture, and (hollowest of all!) the survival of a dead Christ's spirit in the hearts of his followers—who certainly would not have recovered from their discouragement if they had not supposed that their Leader really lived, in some less sophisticated sense than this! Be so good as to come to the point, then, for all your argument so far has had nothing to do with the case."

Nothing to do with the case? On the contrary, I protest, these facts have much to do with the case—much, every way! For if life in general is a cosmic accident, if there be no general life-stream, flowing broad and deep through the midst of the whole cosmic process, then the question of personal immortality cannot even be raised. In such a lifeless universe, there would be no medium in which a surviving personality could exist. If it somehow escaped the death of the body, it would stifle as in a vacuum! But if, on the other hand, we are to trust the facts that seem to point to the existence of a vast stream of Spiritual Life, surrounding and supporting us on every side, and springing from the very heart of the universe, then the question of personal immortality becomes significant; for then, if personality survives, it has, so to speak, a medium in which to float, an atmosphere in which to live and move, a "heaven" to which it can "go." Ever since Copernicus and Galileo abolished that transcendent heaven in the skies, to which the imagination of our medieval ancestors looked so confidently and so yearningly, the belief in personal immortality has been in a most parlous plight. To believe that the soul survives, but to doubt that heaven exists—what an anomaly! How cold have the cosmic spaces looked to the little shivering ghost preparing to leave its bodily habitation and find itself a new home!

The existence of heaven must, therefore, first be argued, before the question of personal immortality can be broached; and this is what I have been trying to do—in terms which may, no doubt, have veiled my intent.

But to come at last to the point which is, after all, climactic for us human individuals—are there any facts which bear, negatively or positively, upon the question whether personal identity, memory, consciousness, and activity can persist beyond bodily death?

There is first of all to be considered that fascinating and impressive body of data embodied in the *Proceedings* of the Society for Psychical Research; for many believe that these data contain the definite and affirmative answer to the question at issue. Many others, to be sure, are inclined to rule this whole body of evidence out of court, on the ground that it is utterly fantastic in character, and vitiated by repeated exposure of deliberate fraud, on the part of the most celebrated mediums. For my own part, having examined certain of the volumes of the *Proceedings* with much interest and some care, I find myself unable to disregard their findings entirely and unable also to share the conviction of Sir Oliver Lodge, that they contain the conclusive proof of immortality.[1]

On the one hand, I am impressed with the convergent mass of testimony which goes to show that a living person may, under certain exceptional conditions (such as the trance state of the medium, or supreme emotional stress), make contact with the minds of living persons, and even perceive events at a distance, without the use of the usual means of communication. I know, of course, that the pos-

---

[1] The reader will find a convenient and relatively unbiased summary of these findings in *The Newer Spiritualism*, by Podmore. Note especially the Introduction, and pp. 255-276. A briefer summing up of the evidence, with conclusions similar to my own, will be found in John Haynes Holmes's *Is Death the End?* Chapter V.

sibility of telepathy would be roundly denied, in almost derisive terms, by a great number (perhaps a majority) of contemporary scientists; but I cannot escape the conviction that the modern scientific mind is herein guilty of a most unscientific type of dogmatism. It reminds one of those theological dogmatists who refused to look through Galileo's telescope at the satellites of Jupiter, because they already knew there could be no such things; and who, when they were at length persuaded to look, were readier to believe that some demon was deceiving their senses than to give up their preconceived ideas. The phenomena of telepathy are indeed somewhat hard to reconcile with a certain type of materialism which has wide currency in scientific circles; but the true scientific rule is not to force the facts to conform to one's preconceived theories, but to alter one's theories to fit the facts. I am convinced that telepathy is a fact, for which a fuller explanation must be discovered. In a world where radio and television have become commonplace, the explanation of telepathy need not take one into the realm of the occult.

On the other hand, I am far from convinced that the *Proceedings* of the "S. P. R." contain anything which points indubitably to the hypothesis of "survival." If I did not believe in telepathy, I might indeed be forced to adopt "survival" as the best alternative hypothesis. There are some astounding and mystifying passages in the *Proceedings*—notably those having to do with the alleged attempts of the late Mr. F. W. H. Myers (former president of the S. P. R.) to prove his continued existence. Here one encounters an elaborate system of "cross-correspondences" or messages given simultaneously through several independent mediums, which upon examination are proved to contain cross-references to certain passages in classical literature with which Mr. Myers had been acquainted.[1] The triviality and disconnectedness of even the best of these purported messages is a constant source of perplexity and irritation to the reader; yet if no simpler hypothesis offered itself, the conjecture might be risked that those were really the first imperfect, stammering attempts at establishing trans-mortem communication—distorted by the mind of the medium, as the first radio messages were distorted by "static." But there is, as a matter of fact, a simpler hypothesis, the hypothesis of *telepathy from the living*; and this hypothesis is powerfully supported by the fact that, among all the well-authenticated accounts of ghostly apparitions collected by the S. P. R. in its famous "census of hallucinations," the vast majority involve the appearance of a man's "ghost" either at the moment of his death or at some emotional crisis in his life which did *not* result in his death![2] Once grant the hypothesis that the mind of the medium may telepathically draw upon the thoughts of the sitters, and of other persons at a distance, and it is thenceforth almost impossible to prove that alleged "messages" could only have come from such-and-such an individual on "the other side." I am forced to conclude, then, that while the patient and impartial investigations of the Society for Psychical Research have contributed greatly to what might be called "supernormal psychology," they have not settled the question of immortality in the affirmative.

Can it not, then, be settled in the negative? Do not all the facts of physiology and psychology point to the conclusion that personality, if it is not *identical with* bodily behavior (as one school of psychology claims), is at any rate so *dependent upon* the physical organism that it can-

---

[1] See Podmore, *The Newer Spiritualism*, pp. 255-267, on "The Lethe Incident."

[2] See Gurney, *Phantasms of the Living*.

not possibly survive its dissolution? There are many who think so; and their views must be considered.

The *identity* of thought and personality with bodily behavior is a view which cannot be maintained without falling into absurdity; for it implies that all human opinions (*including this one*) are neither "true" nor "false," but simply more or less powerful muscular tensions.[1] Intelligent adherents of the behaviorist school are no longer maintaining that there is "no such thing" as mind, consciousness, or attention, but only that these concepts represent aspects of reality which psychology, for its own scientific purposes and from its own specialized point of view, can safely ignore. Even such critical behaviorists, however, are inclined to emphasize the close, deterministic dependence of personality upon the functioning of the physical organism; and the problem then recurs whether consciousness, admitting its existence, can possibly survive the death of an organism on whose normal functioning it is so slavishly dependent.

William James long ago suggested, in his famous Ingersoll Lecture, that this difficulty is not so insuperable as it looks. To say that consciousness is "dependent on" or "a function of" the organism need not mean that the organism *produces* it, as an incandescent arc produces light. It may mean only that the organism *transmits* personality, as the glass bulb transmits the light produced by the arc. If the organism is enfeebled, consciousness is obscured, as the light is obscured when the bulb is thickly covered with

---

[1] A student of mine recently wrote a very able paper in which, starting from the proposition that the behavioristic psychology is the only true psychology, he argued his way logically and in all seriousness to the conclusion that all judgments concerning truth and falsity, right and wrong, are out of place in a behavioristic world, since no one can help having precisely those attitudes which he has been "conditioned" to have. Such a conclusion constitutes a *reductio ad absurdum* of the premise on which it is based.

dust and dirt; but personality, like the electric arc, may be glowing as brightly as ever behind the obscuring medium of transmission. Henri Bergson, adopting a similar "transmissive" or "interactionist" theory of mind and body, argues that consciousness "overflows" the brain on every side, and uses it as its "organ of attention" to reality.[1] From this point of view, the brain and the whole physical organism are but tools in the hands of personality, which is something quite other than its tools. When the tools grow dull, personality suffers; but it might quite conceivably discard them altogether and get a new set! Whether or not the interactionist theory commends itself as highly probable, it at least prevents one from settling the question of immortality prematurely in the negative; for it does justice to all the known facts of physiology and psychology as well as any rival theory can claim to do.

But if personality is not the product of the organism, of what *is* it the product? If it is, to a degree, independent of the organism, on what could it depend, and whereby could it be sustained if its bodily taproot should be severed? To ask these questions is to be brought face to face with a very important consideration, which has been commonly overlooked in discussions of immortality: *Personality is not the product of the individual organism alone, but of a process of interaction between a group of organisms—a process into which the whole cosmic environment ultimately enters as a supreme determining factor. Personality, as it grows, becomes less and less dependent upon its physical taproot, and more and more dependent upon social and cosmic sustenance.* The truth of this will appear if we pause for a moment to retrace the life history of a human individual.

The story begins obscurely, within the dark enclosure

---

[1] See his *Mind-Energy*, Chapters I and II.

of the maternal womb. Utterly dependent upon the mother, both for physical sustenance and for those first glimmerings of character and personality which are laid down before birth, in the form of reflex arcs, the embryo seems so much a part of the parent organism which surrounds and protects it that one considering these phenomena for the first time might be pardoned for supposing that the severing of the connection between the two would inevitably prove fatal to the tiny parasite. Yet in the months preceding birth, the embryo has been developing new organs of nutrition, which at length make its passage into the outer world, and the cutting of the umbilical cord, mere episodes (crucial and dangerous, to be sure, but not ordinarily fatal) in its ongoing development.

The infant delivered from the womb is still enclosed in a matrix—not so closely confining and not so tangible as the womb, but just as real. Cast out from that matrix and exposed to the inhospitable elements, he would perish immediately. I refer, of course, to the *home*. It is in the intimate fellowship of the home that the child forms his first habits and attitudes, and, through learning to talk, enters into his heritage as a human being. Language, or the use of symbols, is a most momentous factor in the development of personality. By its means, the stored-up wisdom of the past and the significance of the remotest cosmic phenomena begin to filter into the narrow environment of the home, and stimulate the deeper capacities of the child. Helplessly dependent at first upon the family group for nourishment, protection, and guidance, he begins, toward the end of childhood, to develop the ability to fend for himself, and so is made ready at length to step out into the larger matrix of organized society.

Leaving home is as great a crisis as being born. It has to be led up to, by stages. First brief excursions to school or church, under strict supervision; then longer excursions, to college or shop; until at last the dependent nestling is ready to try his own wings and fly off to seek his fortune. Many never surmount this crisis, and pass their lives in childish dependence. But it would be a mistake to regard the normal self-reliant man as a wholly *independent* being. He, too, lives in and is sustained by an environing matrix; the organized life of his nation or his tribe, beyond which there stretches out the more loosely organized life of humanity as a whole, and over which there arches the vast environing matrix of the cosmic order, dominating all human affairs as the blue vault of heaven dominates the earth.

If one should inquire precisely *where*, at what point in the "space-time continuum," the personality of a full-grown, well-educated individual is located, the question would be hard to answer. He is anchored, plainly enough, to the place and time in which his body walks and gesticulates; but as his personality develops, it tugs at the anchor. Is it truer to say of the scholar, writing in his study, that he is located then and there in his swivel-chair in front of his desk; or that he is living in those distant times and places from which his knowledge and inspiration are derived, and in those distant times and places to which he means to travel through his books and the influence of his pupils? Is it truer to say that he lives upon beefsteak and potatoes, or that he lives (as Plato would say) upon eternal ideas? When he was a child, he was not so hard to locate; for he was not yet accustomed to abstract thinking, and never strayed far from his body; but now that he has become a man, and has acquired the use of those seven-leagued boots which we call concepts and meanings, he traverses the universe every day, in all four dimensions, and returns to his body only once in a while, at meal time or at nightfall. The body may be his "taproot"; but as one beholds his multifarious activities in remote times and places, one wonders whether he is not, like the banyan tree, capable of dropping new roots into the soil of society, history, and the cosmos, which could perfectly well sustain his life if the original taproot were cut![1] Sometimes, indeed, it seems as though he—the real *he*—were located at a great height above the physiological plane where his body lives, and were ruling not only his own but many other bodies, by the sheer force of his thought.

The contemplation of such a fully developed personality may well suggest the question whether death may not be, for him at least, simply another of those transitions from a narrower to a wider matrix of life, of which birth is the first; whether the severing of his connection with his bodily organism may not turn out to be something as natural and as trivial as the cutting of an umbilical cord.

3. WHAT WE MAY BELIEVE

The raising of such a question as this warns us that we have now arrived at the frontier which separates the realm

---

[1] Cf. the following suggestive passage from Hadfield's essay on "Mind and Brain" in Streeter's symposium, *Immortality* (pp. 65, 66): "The tulip springs from a bulb, and in its early stages derives all its sustenance from the store of food in the bulb. But when its leaves are well established, and it has exhausted its store of nourishment, it begins to breathe in strength and force from the sunlight and air around, without which it would fade and wither and fail to produce the perfect flower. . . . The mind rises from the body and its sensations, but only in the sense that the dragon-fly springs from the grub which lives in the mud of the stagnant pool; its origin is humble but its life in the sunlight is a whirl of colored brilliance and wanton liberty. . . . Consciousness has a similar freedom and autonomy; it originated in physical sensations of the body, but has taken wing, breathes the air of the ethical blue, and is nourished by spiritual food. Thus the mind has now as little in common with the sensations of the body from which it sprang, as this fiery, dazzling creature has with the slime-covered grub." By permission of The Macmillan Company, publishers.

of fact from the realm of philosophic speculation and religious faith. The evidence is in; and it is not conclusive, either *pro* or *con*. It does not compel us to accept a lifeless universe, but neither does it compel us to believe in the final victory of life over death; it does not compel us to grant that death ends all for the individual, but neither does it compel us to follow that more hopeful line of speculation which has just been suggested. The question of immortality remains an unsettled question; and since it vitally affects the conduct of life, we are compelled to take up some sort of attitude toward it, and make some venture of faith in regard to it—positive or negative. Which shall it be?

Guarding the gateway that leads to a positive faith in man's immortal destiny there stands a barking Cerberus, whose fierce and overbearing mien has discouraged many, in our skeptical generation, from even daring to peer through; and the warning that he barks forth from all his seven mouths, with echoing reverberations, is "WISH-FUL THINKING!" It is surprising how men's faces blanch at the sound, and how hastily they back away from the gate! To oversophisticated minds—and there was never a generation prouder than ours of its sophistication—the one accusation which infallibly intimidates, whenever it is made, is the accusation that we are believing what we believe because it is pleasant to us to believe it. Rather than admit that we are guilty of such childishness as to believe what is to our advantage, we are ready to assume that anything which is to our disadvantage must infallibly be so—a judgment which is just as emotional, and just as likely to be wrong, as its opposite.

Now I am not disposed to shrink back before the barking of this Cerberus. More than once, in the last two chapters, I have gone out of my way to snap my fingers at him;[1] and I am proposing shortly to walk calmly by and enter in at the gate which he guards. But since so many are stuck fast at this point of difficulty, and since the warning against wishful thinking is peculiarly impressive when applied to faith in immortality, I think it only fair to pause for a moment to consider the real extent of the danger.

The danger is not imaginary. There is indeed grave risk of self-deception involved in all religious faith and hope. Baffled and rebuffed by the hard facts of life, men have a natural but often disastrous tendency to take refuge in a world of dreams, where desire flies swiftly to its goal without the need of toilsome effort, and all the frustrated longings of the soul find perfect fruition. The negro slave, condemned to live a life of dreary and incessant toil, comforts his soul with spiritual songs, in which heaven is depicted, with a pathos fit to stir the hardest heart, as a state precisely opposite to that which he must endure on earth. Heaven *is* the land of heart's desire; that is why we find it so easy to describe what it must be like; and that is why the picture of heaven varies so bewilderingly, as climate and cultural environment and a thousand other accidental influences alter man's desires. No one can read Rupert Brooke's satiric description of the fishes' heaven without beginning to wonder whether our human heaven, too, is not "such stuff as dreams are made of":

HEAVEN

Fish say, they have their Stream and Pond,
But is there anything Beyond?
This life cannot be All, they swear,

---

[1] I have, for example, referred to prayer as a form of "wishful thinking"; and I have admitted that faith in the Christian God springs from a kind of "wishful thinking," very remote from cold logic. Both these admissions, for reasons now to be stated, leave my intellectual self-respect quite unimpaired.

For how unpleasant if it were! . . .
We darkly know, by Faith we cry,
The future is not Wholly Dry . . .
But somewhere beyond Space and Time
Is wetter water, slimier slime!
And there (they trust) there swimmeth One
Who swam ere rivers were begun,
Immense, of fishy form and mind,
Squamous, omnipotent and kind;
And under that Almighty Fin,
The littlest fish may enter in.
Oh! never fly conceals a hook,
Fish say, in the Eternal Brook,
But more than mundane weeds are there,
And mud, celestially fair;
Fat caterpillars drift around,
And Paradisal grubs are found;
Unfading moths, immortal flies,
And the worm that never dies.
And in that Heaven of all their wish,
There shall be no more land, say fish.[1]

It would be impossible to state the indictment against "wishful thinking" more forcefully than Rupert Brooke has here stated it, or apply it more convincingly to the case at issue. What follows, then? Is it not proved that heaven is a pure chimera, born of childish desire and hope, as hell is born of childish fear and remorse?

If religious faith and hope at their best were really so childish as this, there would be no more to be said. But have we done them justice? Is it fair to represent religious men as mere followers of the pleasure-principle: "This life cannot be all, they swear, for *how unpleasant if it were!*" Is it not, on the contrary, a cardinal principle of all "high religion" that desire must be disciplined and

---

[1] *Collected Poems of Rupert Brooke*; p. 127. Copyright, 1915, by Dodd, Mead and Company, Inc. Quoted by permission.

brought into conformity with reality? If, therefore, it be true—as it is, in part—that religious faith and hope are guided by wishful thinking, this need not mean that they are guided by the animal fear of destruction, nor by infantile "visions of sugar-plums." When a mature religious individual finds himself faced with the necessity of making a venture of faith, for lack of conclusive evidence, he does not close his eyes dreamily and say, "What do I wish were true?" He opens his eyes, takes a broad survey of the situation, and then, in the light of all his best-founded convictions, he inquires, "What *ought* I to wish?" —a vastly different question. It is a form of wishful thinking; but the deepest wish, that dominates all the rest, is a wish addressed to the Ultimate Source of all Good: "Thy will be done, whatever may happen to me." As Dr. Richard E. Cabot puts it, "You want to be fair to your own elmental cravings as well as to the claims of other people"; and hence you do not simply stifle your own wishes; but you put them all "conditionally," with full willingness to modify them if the welfare of your fellows and the welfare of the universe so requires.[1]

All men have moments of emotional elevation, which determine their convictions for long periods of time. I am conscious that my own faith in immortality has been largely determined by one such moment; and I owe the reader an account of it, if only that he may have the opportunity of judging whether it has introduced an unconscious emotional bias into this whole discussion. The question I wish him to bear in mind, as he reads, is whether or not the faith in immortality which spontaneously arose

---

[1] *What Men Live By*, pp. 302-308. Published by Houghton Mifflin Company, Boston. Mature religion has never been more magnificently described than in this book, especially in the concluding Part IV, devoted to "Worship."

in me on that occasion is to be discounted, as a case of wishful thinking.

I was walking one summer evening alone along the beach, on an island off the coast of Maine. A waning sunset had tinted the sea and the sky with gentle pinkish hues, and the whole scene quietly beckoned to the soul, to come out and range through larger spaces. I was absorbed and lifted up by the beauty round about me; but my thoughts could not rest in that beauty. War had recently been declared; and I could not but contrast the serenity of that scene with the sickening carnage which I knew was going on, across the ocean. For the hundredth time since the declaration of war, I began again to grapple with the tragic destiny of mankind, and to try to see myself in relation to it. As a follower of Tolstoy, I saw nothing but futility in war, and nothing but self-deception in a "war to end war." I wanted to live; but I knew I had no right to live when men as good as I were dying by the million, unless in some way, more effective than the way they were taking, I could serve the end for which they died: a world of peace and justice. For that matter, if I could see some good emerging from my sacrifice, I would gladly die . . . or so I thought . . . but precisely what should I do? How could I live or die most characteristically, as the world's dire need and my own peculiar abilities (and disabilities) might require? I looked back over a thousand years of senseless strife, and tried to peer into the distant future, to see the lines along which peace and justice might best be furthered. . . .

Just at this juncture, I stubbed my toe against an unexpected obstacle—the dark was beginning to gather—and looking down, saw that I had stumbled over a large dead fish, in a most unpleasant state of odoriferous decay. The thought darted through my mind, "That's death. And that's what *you* are coming to." Quick as a flash, came the rejoinder: "Am I the sort of thing that *can* come to that?" And with that question, there boiled up within me a great tide of conviction. "No," I said to myself, "the real *me*, the self that has been thinking these thoughts and praying these prayers and making these resolutions, is *not* the sort of thing that can come to that! Whatever may happen to my bodily *me*, I know henceforth that my *real* self is something other than that, which lives on other than earthly food, and finds its true habitat in the life of God. I do not know what He intends to do with me when I die. If He likes, He may melt me down and coin me again. I am not now in a mood to set much store by my precious self. But of one thing I am sure, that when I die God will have to dispose of something besides a stinking carcass like *that*!" No one, I suppose, believes continuously in immortality; but from that day to this, the conviction that it is indeed a sober fact has recurred again and again, at moments of similar emotional exaltation.

Now, was this "wishful thinking," in the bad sense? Was my revulsion at the sight of that dead fish an expression of brute terror, which generated the hope that nothing so unpleasant as death could possibly happen to me? Perhaps so, unconsciously; but so far as self-observation can report the truth, I swear that this was not the case. My emotion, as I remember it, was closer to amusement than to fear. I had already surmounted fear, and self-pity, and excessive concern about my own fate, in order to arrive at the emotional elevation on which I stood. I was emotionally ready, as the old theological test-question ran, to be "damned for the glory of God." And when, standing on that height, I was suddenly forced to look down at the phenomenon of bodily death, it looked so irrelevant, so unexpectedly trivial, that I was tempted to laugh in exultation. My mood was very like the mood of Ishmael, in *Moby Dick*,[1] when, faced with the dangers of a whaling voyage, he became suddenly conscious of the greatness of his own soul:

Yes, there is death in this business of whaling—a speech-lessly quick chaotic bundling of men into Eternity. But what then? Methinks we have hugely mistaken this matter of Life and Death. Methinks that what they call my shadow here on earth is my true substance. Methinks that in looking at things spiritual, we are too much like oysters observing the sun through the water, and thinking that thick water the thinnest of air. Methinks my body is but the lees of my better being. In fact take my body who will, take it I say, it is not me. And therefore three cheers for Nantucket; and come a stove boat and stove body when they will, for stave my soul, Jove Himself cannot.

I believe, in all sincerity, that the insights which come at such moments of heightened feeling give so true an outlook upon the meaning of life and its ultimate destiny that they equal in significance all the bald facts which nearsighted and uninspired research can heap up in the other pan of the balance. In that belief, I make bold to risk a few concluding conjectures concerning the nature of the life that lies beyond death. These are but over-beliefs of mine; but since they spring as consequences and corollaries from the total body of my religious convic-tions, they may help to give a final perspective upon the whole trend of my thought, and help the reader to esti-mate it at its true worth—whatever that may be.

On the one hand, I am confident that the new life will be in some respects really new and different—as different as the life of the child is from that of the embryo, or the life of the man is from that of the child. It will be carried on in a larger matrix, and it will no longer be anchored to an individual organism; for death surely means the

---

[1] Herman Melville, *Moby Dick*, Modern Library Edition, p. 36 (1926).

abandonment of one important set of relations. I do not believe that the soul will be wholly absorbed into the life of God, so as to lose its individuality; for I see in the whole evolutionary process a marked trend toward the conservation of individuality. The fish spawns millions of eggs, most of which go to waste; but human individuals are produced more sparingly, and regarded, as it were, more reverently by the cosmic process which produces them. Individuality will survive, then, but under conditions so changed that it may be hard to recognize the fact of survival. Perhaps it may be the destiny of all individuals to become after death the animating principle, or *part* of the animating principle, of some social organism —as Christ has become the indwelling life of the Christian Church. Perhaps we may not immediately enter upon the final state for which we are destined, but pass through many deaths and many rebirths, each time passing (if we continue to live normally) from a narrower to a wider matrix of life, and finding the organic rootage of our being in vaster and vaster ranges of the universe, till we are at last—if there be any *last*—made part of the life of God, retaining our unique individuality but surrendering our separateness.[1] Here, in union with God and one another, would be found the goal of that long quest of self-realization which began upon earth. Perhaps even in heaven it would be found to be a flying goal.

If the new life is thus different from the old, its beginning must partake of the character of a fresh start. Now, all new departures and fresh starts involve a sort of Judgment Day—as Barrie's *Dear Brutus* reminds us. The danger of contractive behavior and infantile regression is always present; and some who have done well in this life

---

[1] Cf. Royce's Ingersoll Lecture, "The Conception of Immortality," which ends with the memorable phrase, "I wait until this mortal shall put on— Individuality!"

may shrink back before the opportunities and responsibilities of the new life, like youths unwilling to face the responsibilities of manhood. This act, like all sin, will be its own condemnation. Others, on the contrary, who have made a sorry mess of this life, may be brought to themselves in their new environment, and experience conversion. It is possible that the brain, as Bergson suggests, is a sort of screen, keeping the main flood of our memories from sweeping out into consciousness, and selecting only the few that are germane to the deed that is next in order. As the whole history of one's life sometimes rushes before the mind at some moment of great danger,[1] so it may be at death, when the brain-screen is removed. Nothing could be more favorable for repentance than such complete and sudden self-knowledge! Moreover, it is possible that we may be in more intimate touch with other personalities, once we are stripped of the organic envelopes which so effectually separate us from one another; and this new appreciation of the worth of other souls may also help to induce repentance. But, there as here, every possibility for larger life is also a possibility of evil, and hell continues to dog the footsteps of the angels.

This is to say that *continuity* as well as changed conditions must be predicated of the new life. Although the special conditions of life may be altered, the fundamental laws of life will remain the same. If one lived upon a remote island, whose inhabitants were all compelled, at a certain point in their life history, to set sail upon the pathless sea and never come back—and this is a true parable of our human situation—it would be a safe rule, under these conditions, to assume that North and South

---

[1] A student in one of my theological classes told me that he experienced this when on the point of drowning in the River Somme, during a battle —as a result of which he repented of his past misdeeds, and decided to enter the ministry!

were still North and South, on sea as on land, and that the stars overhead still kept their relative positions unaltered. So, it is safe to assume, in any future life, God will still be God, and His laws the same laws.

Most of the traditional accounts of the future life—especially in our Protestant eschatology—sin against this elementary canon of reason. In the next world, contrary to all that we know of this, the good man attains to "immediate sanctification," and becomes a white-robed saint as soon as he has drawn his last breath; while the sinner, robbed of all future chance of repentance, goes immediately to hell, where he writhes endlessly and meaninglessly throughout all eternity. Neither the saint nor the sinner really goes on living, according to this view; he merely subsists in an eternal state of suspended animation, passively enjoying or passively enduring the bliss or the torment which is allotted to him. Far superior to this is the Catholic view—not as interpreted by orthodox theologians, but as one might freely imbibe it from a reading of Dante—according to which there is moral effort and social intercourse in the next life as in this, and perfect solidarity between the church militant on earth, the church suffering in purgatory, and the church triumphant in heaven. Even hell, in spite of the forbidding inscription over its entrance, is a place through which the poet himself can pass, as a part of his spiritual discipline, escaping thence by a secret passage, as if to prove that there is no absolutely hopeless condition. Somewhat along these lines, it is possible to conceive of a future life which continues the moral discipline and moral progress of this, on a grander scale. Whether its activities continue to be confined to this earth, or whether they overleap the interplanetary spaces, they take place in the same universe that surrounds us; and they are sustained by the same God, who continues always to be the "light of the minds that seek him, and the strength of the hearts that find him."

I believe it is the destiny of all mankind to be gathered at last, together with all other sentient creatures, into one great fellowship, whose unity is the life of God. There are many, indeed, who look like poor candidates for such a destiny, and whose presence would mar the harmony of such a fellowship. When one considers their case, and reflects upon the difficulty with which human nature is transformed, one is often attracted by the theory of "conditional immortality," to which Matthew Arnold[1] gave expression in a noble sonnet:

IMMORTALITY

Foil'd by our fellow-men, depress'd, outworn,
   We leave the brutal world to take its way,
   And *Patience! in another life*, we say,
The world shall be thrust down, and we up-borne!

And will not, then, the immortal armies scorn
   The world's poor routed leavings? or will they,
   Who fail'd under the heat of this life's day,
Support the fervours of the heavenly morn?

No, no! the energy of life may be
   Kept on after the grave, but not begun!
   And he who flagg'd not in the earthly strife,

From strength to strength advancing—only he,
   His soul well-knit, and all his battles won,
   Mounts, and that hardly, to eternal life.

From a sternly moralistic and rigidly individualistic point of view, this is very satisfactory; but I believe that

---

[1] "Sonnet on Immortality," in *Sonnets of the 19th Century*, ed. by Wm. Sharp, p. 7. From Arnold's *Poetical Works*. (1905 edition, p. 183.) By permission of The Macmillan Company, publishers.

mercy is more deeply embedded than justice in the nature of our world, and I know that no one can be either saved or lost by himself alone. If the life of God is, as Matthew Arnold suggests, a high region into which we must mount by our own unaided efforts, without any help from above, then few, indeed, will they be that attain unto it. But the life of God is not thus aloof from the life of man. It streams down through a million channels of grace, to seek and to save that which is lost. Through all the agencies that make for the enlargement and redemption of personality—through the home, the school, the clinic, the court-room, and the church—God's life is continually seeking our life. Whenever a human child is born, God is born in him, and seeks through him to find self-realization. Whenever he goes astray, God goes with him, and suffers his pangs of remorse. The life of God is not merely to be found in the spiritual *élite*, at the highest moments in their existence; it penetrates obscurely but mightily to the very roots of all creation. It is through God's self-identification with man, that we have faith in man's eventual self-identification with God.

Faith in immortality is the last and boldest corollary of faith in God. It sets the capstone in the arch of the whole religious system. Perhaps the whole arch is built of nothing more substantial than dreams! But if it is indeed, as I believe, honestly built and solidly braced, then one should not hesitate to give its structure the completion it demands.

Index